GENUINE TEXAS HANDBOOK

ROUNDED UP BY ROSEMARY KENT

WRITERS

Rosemary Kent
Christopher Power
Kibbe Smith

PHOTOGRAPHER

Robin Holland

ILLUSTRATOR

Michael Trossman

WORKMAN PUBLISHING, NEW YORK

Dedication

The *Genuine Texas Handbook* is dedicated to
the memory of my Daddy, L.F. "Doc" Kent (1908-1980) — a genuine Texan —
and to the one I love best:
my husband and honorary Texan Henry Meltzer.

Cover and book design: Paul Hanson
Cover illustration: Nancy Stahl
Photograph of Willie Nelson
on back cover: © Bonnie Shiftman

Library of Congress in Publication Data

Kent, Rosemary.
The genuine Texas handbook.

1. Texas — Anecdotes, facetiae, satire, etc.
I. Title.
F386.6.K46   976.4   81-40503
ISBN 0-89480-192-9 (pbk.) AACR2

Workman Publishing Company, Inc.
1 West 39 Street
New York, New York 10018

Manufactured in the United States of America.

First Printing October 1981

10   9   8   7   6   5   4   3   2   1

Acknowledgments

Many hands, hired and otherwise, went into rounding up *The Genuine Texas Handbook*. Therefore, these printed acknowledgments can never fully express the enormous gratitude I feel on completion of this project. What follows is a list of people I would like to thank first — my sidekicks at Workman Publishing — whose creative encouragement, editorial advice, and sense of humor I will always appreciate. Deepest thanks go to: Louise Gikow, Paul Hanson, Jim Harrison, Jan Hersh, Sally Kovalchick, Gail MacColl, Julienne McNeer, Cheryl Moch, Christopher Power, Richard Rew, Jennifer Rogers, Kibbe Smith, Geoffrey Stevens, Ludvik Tomazic, Eve Wallace, and Peter Workman. In terms of further gratitude I thank Betty Anne Clarke, my literary agent, both professional advisor and supportive friend.

Plenty of Texans, in and out of the Lone Star state, also helped create the Texas book — as did a whole slew of Yankees! I would like to sincerely thank each one of the following for their time, support, and information: the staff at the Texas and Southwestern Cattle Raisers Association, almost every Chamber of Commerce office in Texas, Don Clark and Dick Roberts of the Texas State Department of Highways and Public Transportation, John Callas and Hal Foster of Callas & Foster, Dr. G.T. King of Texas A & M University's Department of Animal Science, and Phil Livingston of *The Paint Horse Journal*. Also: Joe Armstrong, Julie Anne Booty, Pamela Zauderer Bryan, Stephen Castlebury, Michael Davis, Rebecca Dean, Kenneth Ellis, Chris Eddy, Bill and Katy Ferguson, Peter Heyne, Carmen Hill, Beverly and Tommy Jacomini, David Johnson, Richard Keahey, Virginia Simmons Kent, Barry and CeCe Kieselstein-Cord, Dr. Murray List, Don Loerwald, John Merrill, Toni Moreno, Sharon Parkey, Becky Crouch Patterson, Christina Patoski, Jay Pilevsky, Steve Proffitt, Lanie Sauder, Mary Jane Shackelford, Jeff Sharlach, Alice and Vernon Smith, Liz Smith, Jancy Stephenson, Brooke Stollenwerck, Carol Taylor, Katerin Tolleson, Michael Trossman, Linda Weisser, A.G. Wilhelm, Mason Wiley, John Lan Williams, Jr., and Charles Wilson.

Additional thanks to the following merchants and suppliers for their help and cooperation: Leo Camarillo, Cottonwood Cafe, El Coyote Restaurant, Gerri Gibney of Cadillac Motors, Charles Kauffman of Kauffman & Sons Saddles, LaCrasia Creations, M.L. Leddy & Sons, Sam Lewis, Al Martinez and Robin Steakley of To Boot, Rolando Reyes of The Common Ground, Ryon's, Sarajane Sacks of Cutter Bill, Alison Stooker of Ford Motor Co., Tex Tan, and The Wooden Star.

Special thanks to all the nonprofessional models who posed so professionally in front of Robin Holland's camera: Gigi Benson, Marcy Bramas, Kay Evans, Cha Cha Foxhall, Don Gettinger, Jim Hurley, Sallie Jackson, Cha Cha Kent-Meltzer, Wayne Kirn, Nicole Kluberdanz, Sally Kovalchick, Gail MacColl, Henry Meltzer, Sarah Newell, Gaspar Martin, Wendy Palitz, Kalim Pearson, Paul Phaneuf, Pat Robbins, Jennifer Rogers, Bert Snyder, Jennifer Smith, Robin Steakley, Geoffrey Stevens, Joanne Strauss, Liz Thurber, Michael Trossman, and Elizabeth Workman.

Rosemary Kent

Photo credits

Contents

MEMBER
TEXAS & SOUTHWESTERN
CATTLE RAISERS
ASSOCIATION

Chapter 3

CATTLE & SADDLE

Chapter 4

STRIKING IT RICH

(713) 464-02

Chapter 5

POWER & MONEY

Chapter 6

TEXAS SIGHTS

Chapter 7

KICKER CULTURE

Chapter 8

DUDIN' UP

Chapter 9
LOVE & LARD

Chapter 10
HOOTIN' & HOLLERIN'

Chapter 1

LONE STAR FEVER

10 THINGS TEXANS WOULD RATHER FORGET

In the midst of all the celebrated optimism, Texans have had their share of depressing moments. Although Texans say they'd rather forget them, they can't for one moment.

1. Windfall profits tax.

2. Firing of Bum Philips from Houston Oilers.

3. Removal of "No Bopping" sign at Garner State Park.

4. Enforcement of 55 mph speed limit.

5. Closing of Chicken Ranch in La Grange.

6. Ralph Lauren Western wear.

7. Film version of *The Alamo*.

8. November 22, 1963.

9. 1978 Cotton Bowl game (Notre Dame 38, UT 10).

10. Alaska's admission to the U.S.

TOO MUCH AIN'T ENOUGH

The Texas State of Mind

Texas has an area of 267,339 square miles. That means the Lone Star state possesses 7 percent of the country's land mass, and is larger than any country in Western Europe. It's 801 miles from the northwest tip of the Panhandle to the mouth of the Rio Grande; at its widest point, 773 miles between the state's eastern and western borders. (Beaumont is closer to Chicago than it is to El Paso).

Dimensions like these give a person certain ideas. For something to be worthwhile to a Texan, it has to come in extra-large sizes. Things like oil fields, cattle empires, presidents. Talk is liberally sprinkled with the adjective *big*, both for personal matters — the Big Spread, the big bankroll, big plans — and about sources of civic pride — Big Tex, Big Bend, Big Oil (the last may sound ugly to many Northerners, but it's music to a Texan's ears).

This bigness can be tricky linguistically. What Texans call big, others would label "mind-boggling," "excessive," or "unbe-lievable." It's not that Texans are modest, or dislike polysyllabic adjectives. It's just that there's no easy way to describe the state habit of excessive, hog-wild behavior. If you have some thoughts on politics, you don't send a letter to the editor, you buy the paper (and throw in a chain of radio stations). If you really dislike someone, you scheme all your life to ruin him (murder is a viable option) and you never, *never* forget a slight. For your wedding anniversary, you don't just take your wife on that weekend trip to New York. You wait till you're on the plane, then announce a spontaneous European vacation (you can buy clothes over there). Too much really ain't enough.

And it never will be. Not in the land where small is plumb stingy and less is exactly that. Talking small and medium just means that you're a Yankee inside — you've probably had charitable thoughts about the fifty-five-mile-an-hour speed limit and the cancellation of the B-1 bomber. To be Texan, think big. It's the only way.

A GALLOPING GLANCE AT THE BIG EVENTS

Texas History Time Line

Right from the beginning, folks have been moving to Texas — the Spanish, the French, the Mexicans. In search of gold and paradise, they found only cows and crabgrass. Later, of course, someone found oil, but by that time six flags had flown over Texas and the well of legends had started to blow in. To know a little of the history is to understand a lot of the hoopla: the ups and downs, the windfalls and windstorms that make for a spirited citizenry as well as some self-congratulatory hot air.

SIX FLAGS OVER TEXAS

SPAIN 1519-1685/1690-1821. After several disastrous expeditions (starvation, fever, mutiny), the Spanish settled down and gave Texas touristy mission churches, the patio, and the horse.

FRANCE 1685-1690. La Salle claimed Louisiana for France and then, as an afterthought, sailed to Matagorda Bay to take over Texas, thus establishing the state's taste for nonchalant power plays. La Salle was murdered, and his claim didn't stick.

MEXICO 1821-1836. The period that provided the state with Tex-Mex and several chapters in every Texas history book: Davy Crockett, Colonel Travis, Santa Ana, and the Bowie knife. Now they say there's more oil south of the Rio Grande than there is north (which isn't neighborly at all).

REPUBLIC OF TEXAS 1836-1845. As everyone knows, the Republic was just a ruse. The Lone Star state had been meaning to annex the rest of the U.S. all along. Which it did, in 1846.

CONFEDERATE STATES OF AMERICA 1861-1865. Texas seceded and joined the Confederacy out of sheer animal spirits. They fought *their* last Civil War battle a month after Appomattox.

UNITED STATES 1846-1861/1865-present day. The end of the Civil War ushered in a boom that's still going strong. The only thing that hurt — Alaskan statehood.

Alonzo Alvarez de Pineda explores and charts Texas. Jamestown wasn't even a glimmer in the eye of Captain John Smith.

Mission San Antonio de Valero founded, won fame later when it became the Alamo. Remember?

Mexico wins independence from Spain; Texas becomes part of Mexico.

Sam Houston defeats Antonio Lôpez de Santa Ana; J. K. and A. C. Allen, brothers from New York City, buy Houston.

| 1519 | 1528 | 1718 | 1812 | 1821 | 1835 | 1836 | 1839 |

Cabeza de Vaca shipwrecked near present-day Galveston. Coronado and Fray Juan de Padilla are there, too. Three Spaniards sightseeing.

First cattle brand recorded in Texas. The "AR" brand of the Alamo Regiment Compañia del Alamo de Bexar of the Spanish Army. No longer remembered.

Texas Rangers are formed as one of the toughest arms of the law in U.S.

Texas adopts the Lone Star flag. Never out of sight since.

Captain Richard King founds the King Ranch. Still in the family.

John Herdon becomes Texas's first certified millionaire when he admits to U.S. Census-taker that his Brazoria County plantation is worth $1.6 million. No brag, just fact.

Texans ignore events at Appomattox Courthouse and keep shooting. They finally join the Confederacy in defeat a month late.

Judge Roy Bean appointed justice of the peace for Pecos County.

| 1853 | 1854 | 1860 | 1861 | 1865 | 1879 | 1882 | 1883 |

The first Texas longhorns reach New York City slaughter-houses.

Texas votes for secession (44,300 for; 13,000 against); Texas secedes from the Union.

Barbed wire first used in Texas; the good neighbor policy begins.

First Texas Rodeo; University of Texas opens its corral to Longhorns.

Dr. Pepper invented by a Waco druggist. Burp.

Neiman-Marcus Co.

Elm and Murphy Streets, Dallas

Bluebonnet adopted as the state flower by request of the Society of Colonial Dames in Texas; Lucas No. 1 comes in at Spindletop oil field near Beaumont.

Neiman-Marcus opens its fashionable doors in Dallas.

Big Bend Park established.

| 1885 | 1894 | 1901 | 1903 | 1907 | 1908 | 1914 | 1917 |

Oil is discovered by accident (crew was drilling for water) in Corsicana, Texas.

John Long Sinclair writes "Eyes of Texas" in "B" Hall dorm at UT.

LBJ born near Stonewall.

World's first indoor rodeo held at Cowtown Coliseum in Fort Worth; Humble Oil founded.

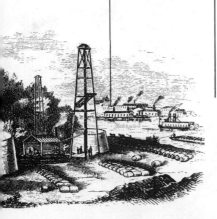

LBJ wins his first elected office—**U.S.** representative from Tenth District, big with ghost town voters.

Southwestern Bell Telephone introduces direct long distance dialing for Texas bigmouths.

"Texas, Our Texas" adopted by Legislature as official state song.

Texas's last legal hanging—in Waco.

1923   1924   1929   1934   1937   1942   1955   1960

"Ma" Ferguson elected first woman governor of Texas.

First margarita made in El Paso.

Dallas Cowboys organized as professional football team.

Texas Rangers kill Bonnie and Clyde.

Texas chosen by NASA for Apollo moon mission control; Hurricane Carla hits the Gulf Coast of Texas and Dan Rather becomes a star.

HemisFair, first world's fair in Southwest, opens in San Antonio.

Urban Cowboy has world premiere in Houston—Gilley's hasn't been the same since.

LBJ sworn in as thirty-sixth president of the U.S.

| 1961 | 1962 | 1963 | 1965 | 1968 | 1977 | 1980 | 1981 |

Diet Dr. Pepper introduced.

Texas Legislature adopts chili as state dish.

Houston becomes the nation's fourth largest city. Dallas and San Antonio not far behind.

Lady Bird Johnson launches Beautify America program after learning that Texas leads nation in highway eyesores.

LONE STAR LEGENDS
Trail-Blazers, Hell-Raisers, & Star-Gazers

The Texans listed below are not all well-known, but name recognition is not the point of being a Lone Star Legend. Whether you're a president of the United States, a trigger-happy Ranger, or a Christian businesswoman, to be a Lone Star Legend requires you to pursue your field of endeavor with a model combination of country-bred manners, supreme self-confidence, and perpetual excess.

ERASTUS "DEAF" SMITH
(1789–1837)
b. NEW YORK

The endearing hero of the Texas Revolution. Humble and hard of hearing, Smith was adept at slipping into Mexican costume and through Mexican lines. His spying helped defeat Santa Ana at San Jacinto. Smith got a county, a stone-ground flour, and a brand of peanut butter named after him.

STEPHEN F. AUSTIN
(1793–1836)
b. VIRGINIA

The man who founded Texas once said, "There is no degradation in prudence and well-tempered moderation." Prudence? Moderation? In Texas? Austin opposed independence until Santa Ana clapped him in jail, curing him of a cautious nature that no Texan has suffered from since.

SAM HOUSTON
(1793–1863)
b. VIRGINIA

President of the Republic, governor and senator of the state. Sam defeated Mexicans repeatedly, drank heavily, and disagreed with everybody. A typical Sam Houston quote: "Texas could exist without the United States, but the United States cannot, except at very great hazard, exist without Texas."

JAMES BOWIE
(1796–1836)
b. KENTUCKY

The murderous Bowie knife was legendary enough, but then he went and died at the Alamo, surrounded by carved-up Mexicans. A little-known fact: Houston actually ordered Bowie to abandon the Alamo, not defend it.

WILLIAM TRAVIS
(1809–1836)
b. SOUTH CAROLINA

A revolutionary from the start, Travis dashed off to the Alamo, where he reluctantly had to share command with Jim Bowie. Lone Star Legends have big egos, but everything ended happily. They were both killed and became heroes.

EMILY MORGAN
(1820–?)
b. NEW YORK

Emily belonged to a Texan, Colonel Morgan, when Santa Ana captured her after the Alamo. Ensconced in his red silk tent, the mulatto slave girl proved much more interesting to the Mexican dictator than ensuing military developments, such as Sam Houston's attack at San Jacinto. Morgan's role in Santa Ana's defeat is ignored by Texans, but her charms are listed in "The Yellow Rose of Texas."

JUDGE ROY BEAN
(1825–1903)
b. KENTUCKY

An illiterate ex-cattle rustler, Bean was installed as a judge by the Texas Rangers in 1882 in the West Texas town of Vinegaroon. Bean renamed the town Langtry, after the English actress Lillie Langtry, with whom he was obsessed (a less romantic version of the tale has the town named after a local railroad official), opened a saloon called the Jersey Lilly, and started handing down verdicts that kept everyone west of the Pecos in stitches. (He once fined a corpse forty dollars for carrying a gun.)

CYNTHIA PARKER
(1827–1864)
b. ILLINOIS

This is one story the Texas Rangers have been trying to live down. Carried off by Comanches in 1837, Cynthia forgot all her English, married the warrior Nocona, and lived as a squaw. In 1860 a troop of Rangers found her and bore her back to the white man's world. She died of despair a few years later.

CHARLES GOODNIGHT
(1836–1929)
b. ILLINOIS

Almost completely responsible for key elements of the Cowboy Mystique. Not only did he blaze the Goodnight-Loving Trail (complete with desert and Indians and thirsty dogies), he also rode with the Texas Rangers, owned the million-acre JA Ranch, invented the chuck wagon, and initiated the rancher's favorite game of crossbreeding herds.

LEANDER H. McNELLY
(1844–1877)
b. Virginia

The toughest, meanest Texas Ranger of them all. In the middle of a raid into Las Cuevas, Mexico, to retrieve stolen cattle, the U.S. secretary of war sent McNelly a cable telling him to retreat. McNelly sent back a telegram telling him to go to hell.

BELLE STARR
(1848–1889)
b. MISSOURI

Though billed as a Dixie Belle gone bad, Starr was just a simple farm girl who had this thing for men who went around shooting people. Her livery stable in Dallas was a hideout for bad ol' boys like Jesse James and Cole Younger. Belle was regularly hauled into court (horse thievery), married at least four times (twice to Indians), and was shot once (in the back, with everlasting effect). Within a month after her death she was a penny-dreadful heroine, *Belle Starr, the Bandit Queen: Or, The Female Jesse James.*

SAM BASS
(1851–1878)
b. INDIANA

Texans loved this affable young outlaw because he only robbed railroads and banks (universally hated) and treated anyone he met to a drink (always paid for in gold pieces). On his way to case a bank in Round Rock, Bass was shot in the chest by Ranger Dick Wade, who ran out of a barbershop with lather on his face to do the deed. After that, everyone began singing ballads about Sam.

JAMES S. HOGG
(1851–1906)
b. CHEROKEE COUNTY

Texas's most beloved governor. No one likes to admit it, but ol' Jim was practically a Socialist (thank God he isn't governor today) —although he did give Texas the Railroad Commission and Texaco (he helped found it).

SAMUEL TALIAFERRO RAYBURN
(1882–1961)
b. TENNESSEE

Inaugurated the era of Texan Prominence in National Politics, which reached its peak under Mr. Sam's protégé, LBJ. As a congressman and speaker of the House, Sam brokered the New Deal for FDR, held  Ike at bay, and said tremendously kind and understanding things about the oil depletion allowance ("I never considered it a loophole").

MARY LOUISE CECILIA "TEXAS" GUINAN
(1884–1933)
b. WACO

An original member of that peculiar species, the Transplanted Texan. As a New York City speakeasy hostess and nightclub singer (her famous line: "Hello, suckers!"), she marketed a special blend of New York sleaze and Texas sass. She had a very elaborate funeral.

WALTER PRESCOTT WEBB
(1888–1963)
b. PANOLA COUNTY

A historian of statewide and national stature, chronicler of the West and the Texas Rangers. Said Tom Lea, another Texas writer: "I think *The Great Plains* is one of the great books. It's so like Walter, so dry, so clean, just scrubbed well. No horseshit on his heel at all."

J. FRANK DOBIE
(1888–1964)
b. LIVE OAK COUNTY

The best known of Texas writers. "Pancho" Dobie is known for such classics as *Vaquero of the Brush County, The Longhorns, Tales of the Mustang,* and *Apache Gold and Yaqui Silver*.

WILBERT LEE "PAPPY" O'DANIEL
(1890–1969)
b. OHIO

In 1930 Pappy formed a hillbilly band, the Light Crust Doughboys, to advertise a flour company on the radio. His popularity as a band manager and radio announcer grew, and Pappy became governor and then senator, proving that for Texans, devotion to C&W is the same as love for the people, respect for the state constitution, and all-around political horse sense.

SHERIFF T. J. "MR. JIM" FLOURNOY
(1906–   )
b. LA GRANGE

Before Mr. Jim had to close down the beloved Chicken Ranch, he courteously used his six-foot frame, Colt .45, and sheriff's badge to remove anyone who started cussin' and fussin' at Miss Edna's establishment. When it was over, he told Larry King: "Them girls are clean, they got regular inspections, and didn't allow no rough stuff."

OVETA CULP HOBBY
(1905–   )
b. KILLEEN

The Clare Boothe Luce of Texas (though arguably more important). First secretary of HEW, wife of governor Will Hobby, organizer of the WACs and first woman colonel in the U.S. Army, former editor and publisher of the *Houston Post*. Oveta has always worn that sweet country-girl smile—in her Army uniform, beneath a Bergdorf Goodman hat—but it belies a formidable dollars-and-cents shrewdness (she was one of the first Houstonians to get into the television game).

STANLEY MARCUS
(1905–   )
b. DALLAS

The most tasteful man in Texas. Son of the founder of Neiman-Marcus, former chairman of the board of Neiman-Marcus Co., Stanley toured his stores like a general on inspection, using the middle finger of his right hand to check for dust in all places.

JOHN WAYNE
(1906–1980)
b. IOWA

John Wayne (born Marion Michael Morrison) never lived in Texas, but he might as well have. Every night on TV after the evening news, Wayne ritually embodies Texas for thousands of insomniac Americans: Davy Crockett, Red Adair, and a host of ranchers, cowpokes, and outlaws. The Duke will never die.

LYNDON BAINES JOHNSON
(1908–1973)
b. STONEWALL

He made a great discovery: Hill Country ranching and the Imperial Presidency are pretty much the same thing—both call for loyal hands, crafty horse trading, and big Lincoln convertibles. LBJ left his mark on everything—his luggage, Hubert Humphrey's shins, civil rights, and the Ho Chi Minh Trail. A quote: "I'm a powerful S.O.B., you know that?"

HONDO CROUCH
(1915–1976)
b. HONDO

The owner of Luckenbach, a puny Hill Country hamlet and focal point of Hondo's life as a prankster, goat rancher, and professional Texas folk hero. He once met an old friend, John Connally, then governor, who asked, "Hondo! What are you doing these days?" Hondo's reply: "Oh, still herding goats in the hills. What are *you* doing now?"

BETTE NESMITH GRAHAM
(1924–1980)
b. DALLAS

The famed grass-roots businesswoman, Bette used her kitchen mixer to whip up a recipe for Liquid Paper, a product that turned out to be an invaluable aid to typists, the basis for her own corporation, and a powerful religious experience: "I was listening for God to guide me, and it seemed to me as if He were guiding me this way."

DARRELL ROYAL
(1924–   )
b. OKLAHOMA

The former coach of the UT Longhorns. About football, he once said: "It's an in-the-trench battle. It's meat on meat, flesh on flesh, and stink on stink. And that's the only way you can play it. Maybe you'd better scratch out that stink on stink. Somebody might not like that." LBJ loved Darrell.

SISSY TARLTON FARENTHOLD
(1926–   )
b. CORPUS CHRISTI

Leader of the reformist "Dirty Thirty" in the Texas Legislature, first chairperson of the National Women's Political Caucus. Texans are perversely proud of Sissy, whose successes proved that when a Texas girl goes bad, she goes bad in a big way. (Going East to Smith College was the first step.) Former president of Wells College.

EDWARD H. WHITE II
(1930–   )
b. SAN ANTONIO

A stargazer, literally—the first American to walk in space (June 3, 1965). He wouldn't get back into the spacecraft when they told him to.

LARRY HAGMAN
(1931–   )
b. WEATHERFORD

His portrayal of J.R. proved that a Texan bad-ass could rival both Alan Alda and the Muppets in the ratings. *Time* noted approvingly: "The chief joy of life is watching him play an overstuffed Iago in a Stetson hat with such obvious zest and charm."

BILL MOYERS
(1934–   )
b. OKLAHOMA

LBJ's Baptist Boy Wonder. Formerly LBJ's press secetary, Billy Don now wrestles with senators, Yankee writers, existentialist professors, etc., on TV—and is still not led into temptation. Once said of his boss: "Hyperbole was to LBJ what oxygen is to life."

LARRY MAHAN
(1943–   )
b. OREGON

The uncrowned King of Rodeo, now in semi-retirement (he won six All-Around titles for earnings of $506,000). Like other Texans who specialize in professional Kicker Culture, Larry made sure all those bucking-bull rides translated into corporate diversification: rodeo schools, rodeo apparel, a rodeo singing group—and a little real estate.

EARL CAMPBELL
(1955–   )
b. TYLER

The Earl of Houston is 225 fast-moving pounds of Just Folks. After his first year with the Oilers (more yards gained than any other rookie), Earl bought a nice house for Mama; he married Reuna, his Tyler childhood sweetheart.

FUSSIN' & FEUDIN'

The Spirit of Rivalry

Stayin' mad can be serious business in the Lone Star state. For all the emphasis Texans put on being nice and friendly, a lot of large-scale feudin' goes on. It seems that there has to be a Number One in every imaginable area, causing much debate — who's the top heart surgeon, what's the car to drive, which is really *the* girl's camp to send your daughter to? Most of these rivalries are close-fought contests — so it's up to you to decide, with the help of the following, just who or what currently holds first place in its division.

DR. COOLEY   VS.   DR. DEBAKEY

DR. COOLEY — Surgeon-in-chief of the Texas Heart Institute. Former UT basketball star. From an old Houston family. Keeps C&W tapes in his antique-filled offices, has done very well in real estate sideline. Lives in River Oaks, has a 400-acre Brazos River cattle ranch, goes to parties constantly. Wears scrub suits furnished by St. Luke's or Texas Children's hospitals. Patches hearts with Dacron, is considered an able stitcher.

DR. DEBAKEY — Chancellor of Baylor College of Medicine. Operates — in more ways than one — at Methodist Hospital wearing royal blue scrubs with his initials embroidered on breast pocket and white leather boots with three-inch platform heels. Prolific contributor to medical journals, chaired LBJ's Commission on Heart Disease, Cancer and Stroke, was awarded Medal of Freedom. Famous patients: the Shah of Iran, Duke of Windsor, Sam Giancana.

BLUEBONNETS   VS.   AZALEAS

BLUEBONNETS — State flower. Against the law to pick those planted and maintained by Texas Highway Department. Named for head coverings worn by early Texas pioneer women. Also known as wolf flower, buffalo clover. Scientific name: *Lupinus subcarnosus*. Proliferates in farm and ranching areas. Annual Bluebonnet Trails are held last two weeks of April. Exceptional viewing spots: Brenham, Ennis, Chappell Hill, Mason, and Highland Lakes.

AZALEAS — Evergreen shrub with masses of hot pink and white blossoms. Stay-at-home foliage perfect for residential areas. Annual Azalea Trail pilgrimages (late March) are driving or walking tours complete with lovely young Texas ladies wearing antebellum costumes and big smiles standing around among bushes. Best places for peering: Beaumont, Newton (a prolific growth of wild ones on a canyonlike trail), Jasper, Tyler, Houston's Bayou Bend, and Turtle Creek in Dallas.

COWBOY HAT ▓ VS. ☞ GIMME CAP

For years synonymous with being Texan. The acknowledged crown king. Has sat on heads belonging to LBJ, Deng Xiao Ping, Khrushchev. The international symbol of freewheeling, high-rolling, hard-loving American manhood.

That's what you said when you saw one at a feed store or filling station, where they were handing them out for free. Billed cap is cotton with a nylon mesh panel, bears company logos, cattle brands, monograms, or sassy slogans.

NEIMAN-MARCUS ▓ VS. ☞ SAKOWITZ

Main store is in downtown Dallas. Is sometimes called Needless-Markup. First store in nation to have weekly fashion shows. Famous for outrageous "his and her" Christmas gifts (submarines; airplanes; complete arks with pairs of live animals) and gala in-store Fortnight, an annual social event in Dallas. Store catalogs are called Neiman-Roebucks. Will fly a special salesperson along with couture clothes, furs, and jewels to an interested customer. Bought by West Coast chain Carter-Hale several years ago, N-M has eleven stores outside of Texas.

Main store is in downtown Houston. Last privately held store in America still operated by the family that founded it. Clientele includes old-guard Houston families, Dallas jet-setters, visitors to the Texas Medical Center, and wealthy Mexicans (including the president of Mexico's daughter) who fly up for the day to shop. Its Sky Terrace is known for huge shrimp salads and a wishing-well fountain that benefits Texas Children's Hospital. Headed currently by fourth generation Robert T. Sakowitz; has a total of ten retail outlets including one each in Dallas and Scottsdale, Arizona.

JOANNE HERRING ▓ VS. ☞ LYNN WYATT

Fifth-generation Texan. Widow of Robert Herring; he was chairman of Houston Natural Gas Corporation. Former Houston TV talk show hostess, has a solid reputation for nabbing visiting heads of state for visits to Texas. Pakistan and Morocco have appointed her honorary consul from Texas — she runs these consulates between giving dinner parties in her twenty-three-room River Oaks mansion. Once shot partridges with Generalissimo Franco of Spain. Regularly trampolines in her backyard. Known for her amusing toasts and ability to loosen up guests. Never lets you forget she's a Texan.

Née Sakowitz, the only daughter of prominent Houston specialty store clan. Married to the extremely rich and controversial Oscar Wyatt, Jr. Truly a Texas-American Princess. Lives next door (but doesn't belong) to the River Oaks Country Club. The "Ambassadress of Texas Chic." Was given her own plane to decorate by Oscar. Entertains lavishly at Allington, their Houston home, and at Mauresque, their Cap Ferrat villa, formerly owned by Somerset Maugham. A chum of Princess Grace of Monaco. Gave an engagement dinner at Maxim's for Princess Caroline. Favorite charity: American Hospital in Paris.

HOOK'EM HORNS   📷 VS. 👈   GIG'EM AGGIES

Introduced to UT at a Friday night pep rally in 1955 in Gregory Gym by the head yell leader prior to a Texas Christian University game. Simulates the horns of a steer. Longhorn fans are forever "showing their horns" and yelling "Hook'em." Key places where horns *must* show: UT games prior to kickoff— Longhorns stand and "lock horns" with other fans; whenever "The Eyes of Texas" is played; and on Texas highways when passing a car with a UT sticker on rear window. Honk and hook.

Aggies are not sure when or where their famous hand sign originated. Some speculate that it has to do with a long-standing rivalry with TCU, whose mascot is the horned toad. The pronged poles used to catch these lizards are called giggers. Another speculation is that Aggies are constantly thumbing rides out of College Station. Aggies and Waggies (girls at A&M) make this gesture and yell "Gig'em" at football games in Kyle Stadium and at ex-student gatherings. "Once an Aggie always an Aggie" is the school motto.

CADILLAC   📷 VS. 👈   PICKUP

Remains the symbol of making it and having it. When you and the missus fly over to Monaco in August, you have the Fleetwood shipped over so you can drive it around the narrow Riviera roads. The late Jim "Silver Dollar" West owned forty-one Cadillacs at one time. Iran hostage William Boyer, Jr., was presented a yellow (for rose and ribbon) Caddy by Houston neighbors glad to have him back home.

Also known as the Cowboy Cadillac. Has many practical uses: office (glove compartments make excellent file cabinets), hunting and fishing lodge (the all-important gun racks hold rifles and poles), feed store (back can hold year's supply of hay and Blue Seal), tack room (bridles and bits should line truck floor neatly) and courtin' car (maintain your privacy behind iridescent screens of stampeding stallions).

CAMP MYSTIC   📷 VS. 👈   CAMP WALDEMAR

Older. On 650 acres on the South Fork of the Guadalupe. Campers are allowed to carve their names and initials on the stone cabin walls so they can show something to their husbands and children in years to come. The chosen camp for daughters of well-known Texas politicians. The children of LBJ, John Connally, and governors Dan Moody and Price Daniel were sent here. Best campers: M girls.

Plusher. On 1,200 acres on the Guadalupe River's north fork. Designed by an architect who renovated early Spanish missions. Little Texas princess training —white-coated black waiters serve soufflés family-style in the expansive dining room. Cabins, called Kampongs, have Mexican tile floors; some have fireplaces. The camp ring is turned into an elaborate cocktail ring and worn until replaced by an engagement ring. Seen in abundance at the UT Pi Phi house. Best campers called Ideal Girls.

HOUSTON VS. DALLAS

The outstanding rivalry in Texas. No one is sure when or how these two supercities got into this seemingly endless tangle of one-upmanship (example: Houston builds a twenty-story building, Dallas builds one higher). To add to the conflict, each city has developed character traits that annoy its rival. Dallas to a Houstonian is too planned, regimented, careful, and uptight; Houston to a Dallasite is too sprawling, brash, immature, and lacking in culture. New residents to either city are expected to develop instant and fierce loyalty to their hometowns, thereby perpetuating the rivalry. For some tips on people and places to adulate within your chosen city, consult the following chart.

	HOUSTON	DALLAS
ALSO KNOWN AS	International capital of the fast buck; the City of the Future; Baghdad on the Bayou	Seventeen parking lots in search of a city; Big D; Manhattan of the West
SOCIETY COLUMNIST	Betty Ewing in the *Chronicle*	Julia Sweeney in the *Times Herald*
HANGOUTS	Avalon Drug Store (for pecan pancakes and River Oaks gossip); Ouisie's ("Classy Home Cooking"); The Galleria; River Oaks Center	8-0 Bar; Quadrangle; S&S Tearoom; Highland Park Village; Lambert Landscape Company
GROCERY/ GOURMET STORES	Jamail's; Nielsen's; Fiesta Giant Mart; Antone's	Marty's; The Fresh Approach; Di Palma
RESTAURANTS	Tony's; San Jacinto Inn; The Hofbrau; Cadillac Bar; River Oaks Country Club	Mansion at Turtle Creek; Calluaud's; Old Warsaw; Zodiac Room; Highland Park Cafeteria
ANNUAL EVENTS	Pin Oaks Charity Horse Show; Theta Antique Show; Museum of Fine Arts Ball; River Oaks Garden Club Azalea Trail; Houston Livestock Show and Rodeo	State Fair; OU Weekend; Crystal Charity Ball; Junior League Follies Dance; Fortnight; Cattle Baron's Ball; Delta Charity Antique Show
CLUBS	River Oaks Country Club; Bayou Club; Houston Country Club; Houston Polo Club	Dallas Country Club; Brook Hollow Country Club; Preston Trails
SPECIALTY STORES	Tootsie's; Isabel Gerhart; Norton Ditto	Lou Lattimore; Marie Leavell; Harold's
CITY CELEBRITIES	Alan Shepard; Debra Paget; Gene Tierney; Baron and Baroness Enrico (Ricki and Sandra) di Portanova; Ron Stone; Gerald Hines	Bob Strauss; Roger Horchow; Roger Staubach; H. Ross Perot; anyone with last name (or cousin to a) Marcus, Hunt, Murchison
HAIRDRESSER	Lyndon Johnson (no kin to LBJ)	Grady Hall

SOME FEUDS THAT GOT OUT OF HAND

When football wars and surgical vendettas are not absorbing their attentions, veteran Texas feud followers start looking for a public falling-out to divert them, the kind in which a lot more than a man's reputation gets hurt.

They've never had to wait very long. There were blood feuds right at the beginning of Texas history (back then, whole tribes were entangled—Cheyennes, Comanches, Kiowas), and later on settlers got into squabbles that make the Montague-Capulet difficulties look about as ferocious as a Harvard-Yale Game. Nowadays there are still enough unbalanced millionaires, overheated extramarital affairs, and oil lease disputes to keep a passel of lurid updates on the news— as long as Texas feuds get out of hand, they'll never go out of style.

SMALL-TIME RANCHERS
vs.
BIG-TIME RANCHERS

A little flare-up that shows just how much Texans love good grazing. When barbed wire was first introduced to Texas, the big ranchers, in a burst of enthusiasm, fenced in everything—public land, roads, watering holes, their own property, other people's property. In 1883, the small ranchers, surrounded by dying cattle and with no place to go, started cutting the fences at night. The result: three deaths, twenty million dollars' worth of damage, and a statute that even today makes it illegal to travel in Texas with a wire cutter concealed on one's person.

THE SUTTONS
vs.
THE TAYLORS

This feud continued the War Between the States on a slightly reduced scale.

The Taylor boys of DeWitt County were of Virginia descent, had lots of friends, and firmly believed that Appomattox was a Yankee hoax. In 1867 Sheriff Billy Sutton, who worked with the occupying Union Army, shot Buck Taylor in the belly because he didn't like the pedigree of the horse Buck had sold him. The Taylor clan got paranoid and started thinking that the carpetbaggers were out to get them. They were absolutely right. By 1876, after nine years of ambushes, lynchings, and just plain murder, Sutton and other law officers had finished off almost all the male Taylors (not without losing some of their own). Sutton himself was killed in 1875. The feud sputtered on for twenty more years. Total dead: thirty.

BONNIE & CLYDE
vs.
THE TEXAS RANGERS

Two pint-sized crooks against every Texas Ranger in the state. In 1934, two Dallas lowlifes, Clyde Barrow and

Bonnie Parker, swept repeatedly through East Texas and Louisiana, robbing banks and acquiring folk-hero status in the Depression-plagued South. Frustrated at every turn, the Rangers called in one of their old captains, Frank Hamer, to hunt down the Barrow gang — which he did, after months of relentless pursuit. The final shootout is legendary. Afterward, the Rangers found that Clyde had kept on hand in his Ford: a supply of three BARs, two sawed-off shotguns, nine Colt automatics, and 3,000 rounds of ammunition. Texans love their weaponry.

MOSSLER
vs.
MOSSLER

In 1964, Jacques Mossler, the well-known Texas millionaire, was found in his Florida home with a crushed skull and thirty-nine stab wounds. He was dead. Hours later in Houston, the Rangers arrested Melvin Lane Powers, the nephew of the fortyish, extremely blond Candace (Candy) Mossler, Jacques's widow. Everyone suspected that Melvin and Candy had plotted the murder because Melvin was his aunt's lover (which constitutes incest). All was zestfully dragged out during the trial. Fortunately for Candy and Melvin, the defense counsel, Percy Foreman, the dean of Texas criminal law, so enthralled the jurors with his five-hour closing argument that they eventually acquitted the pair (Foreman was, after all, an ordained Baptist deacon).

ROBINSON
vs.
HILL

A prime specimen of Texas Gothic. Houston socialite Joan Robinson Hill died mysteriously in 1969 of an un-

analyzed virus and her daddy, Ash, suspected Joan's husband John — a moody, philandering plastic surgeon — of doing something unethical. Ash used his leverage (i.e., money) to get Joan's body exhumed for a new autopsy. No evidence of foul play was found, but Hill was indicted for murder anyway. He got off on a mistrial. Then, in 1972, John Hill was murdered by a hooded stranger. The stranger and the people who hired him were arrested. Before their trials, they allegedly claimed that Ash financed the hit contract. They are now either dead or in prison; Ash remains in his River Oaks mansion, surrounded by clippings of his dead daughter's equestrian achievements.

T. CULLEN DAVIS
vs.
THE STATE OF TEXAS

T. Cullen Davis is a living, completely free tribute to the oily skills of Racehorse Haynes, Percy Foreman's acknowledged successor. Cullen, a Fort Worth multimillionaire, was separated  from his fun-loving wife Priscilla. In 1976 a bewigged gunman broke into Priscilla's mansion (once Cullen's), wounded Priscilla, and killed her lover and daughter. Cullen was brought to trial; Racehorse got him off. Two years later Cullen was back in court, this time for conspiring to murder the judge who had presided over the earlier trial (to trap Davis, the judge posed as a catsup-covered corpse in the trunk of a car). Racehorse muddied the waters enough to obtain a mistrial. At the new trial Cullen was acquitted completely; he claimed he hadn't been conspiring, just working for the FBI. The jurors were patriotically moved. Cullen threw a big party.

LAWS OF THE LAND

Everyone knows that those who live amongst the armadillo carry on differently from people who live in the rest of the world. You can spot a Texan a mile away, partly by the way he or she dresses, but especially by the way he or she acts. Every Texan is raised and lives by these laws of the land.

1. ACT FRIENDLY. Texans are always excited to see other people. Even if the IRS agent arrives on your doorstep to inform you that your last five returns will be audited, you invite him in for a glass of iced tea. By the time he leaves he's found out you both have so much in common that, shoot, he may just audit your last *two* returns.

2. USE FIRST NAMES. Texans do this with *everyone*. A typical Texan would probably greet the Prince of Wales with, "Howdy, Chuck!" That way Prince Charles will know not to feel uncomfortable just because he's in line for the throne of Great Britain.

3. SPEAK FREELY. Texans will tell anyone anything. And the more personal the subject matter, the better. No divorce is too messy, no problem child too tempestuous to be the focus of a Texan's conversation with a complete stranger.

4. KNOW WHAT NOT TO SAY. The corollary to the above rule. It was probably all that forthrightness that got you into the psychological mess you're in now, but *never* let on that you have a therapist. That's a sign of weakness, and as a Texan you don't want to manifest any chinks in the armor, no matter how tiny. You're *always* happy.

5. DRIVE FAST. Texans live by their own common sense laws. They always drive faster than the speed limit and don't think of it as speeding. You wouldn't even consider poking along at the "dastardly double nickle," because it's just another mistake they made in Washington.

6. BE ROWDY. Above all, Texans have a good time. Even at the dreariest events, Texans love to hoot and holler. After you leave the party you want to make sure everyone's saying, "That Jim Bob! He sure is a cutter."

THE OUTLAW

Sadly, there are some Texans everyone would just as soon forget about. These are the ones who continue to boast about their Texas birthright but refuse to act according to the Laws of the Land. Most Texas outlaws:

1. Question Big Oil and the value of football.

2. Love New York City.

3. Subscribe to the *Texas Observer*.

4. Go out of state to college and never come back.

5. Drink Heineken.

6. Know their way around a Chinese restaurant menu.

7. Enjoy sissy European sports such as cricket and soccer.

8. Have never hunted.

9. Think Ingmar Bergman is a great film director.

10. Favor vacation spots such as Maine and Palm Beach.

11. See a shrink and admit it.

THE MAVERICK BREED

What it Means to be Born Texan

When you are born Texan, you are a marked individual. Texans, like their cattle, bear a brand that sets them apart from the rest of the herd. This Texas tattoo supercedes all other forms of identification. Even if you work as a stockbroker and live in New York City, if you were born in the Lone Star State you are a Texan before all else.

Texans, like members of any royal family, are born with a complete set of behavioral traits: it is in their genes to know how to look and act at all times. The Texas face naturally creases into a smile; Texas arms were made for grand gestures. A Texan never casually strolls into a party. He or she *sweeps* into the room, usually howling with laughter from the latest Aggie joke.

When you come from Texas, you have the right to use lots of cute, slangy expressions like, "I was so drunk last night a dog wouldn't piss on me." It also means you have at least a nodding acquaintance with country ways. It is hard for anyone to imagine a Texan who can't ride a horse. But even if you don't know the front end from the back, there's enough Texas horse sense in you to keep you from revealing your ignorance.

Possibly the best thing about being born Texan, though, is that it allows you to play cowboy or cowgirl with automatic authenticity by virtue of your birthright. Even if you're a completely citified Texan, you can sashay through New York City's Lone Star Cafe in cowboy hat and boots and they'll all just *know* you're the real McCoy.

TEXOCRACY

Any one of the following will qualify you as a genuine Texan. If you are a dyed-in-the-wool outlander, wing it by claiming one or more in your background.

• Ancestors who arrived in Texas before 1845.
• Spanish land grant in family deed box.
• Cattle brand registered in Texas prior to 1900.
• Relative who rode on the Chisholm Trail.
• Kinship to one of the four men who founded Humble Oil (Weiss, Sterling, Cullian, or Strake).
• Ancestors among the 300 that Stephen F. Austin brought to Texas from Kentucky.

Texas Type No. 1
TEX

Casts a three-foot shadow.

Resistol, precreased, authentically styled in black felt

smiling; Daddy just promised to take him white-tailed deer hunting

bandana tied around neck, outlaw-style

"Texas Sheriff" badge on gold-toned star

blue & white checked gingham shirt, smile pockets, pearl snaps

floral embossed cowhide belt with white buck-stitching, name hand-tooled in back

posters of Larry Mahan; Earl Campbell

cap pistol

Tex Tan's bucking bronco brass oval buckle

football

stuffed armadillo (Texas Teddy bear)

Lotto game, south-of-the-border version of bingo — gives Tex a chance to learn Spanish early

Wrangler jeans worn tucked inside boots

miniature saddlebags filled with Texas-size jelly beans

Justin's suede roughout boots with pointy toes, underslung walking heel

TEXANA

Daddy's little princess.

dark blue felt with white
cord brim, neck cord tied under chin,
Dale Evans-style

bandana tied around
neck

smiling; Mama just told her
she'll get a paint horse on next birthday

Stage West's floral calico
shirt with smile pockets,
piped yoke, pearl snaps

denim vest
with fringe,
slash pockets

embossed cowhide belt,
name hand-stamped on back

silver-toned tongue buckle and keepers

posters of Sue Pirtle;
Jaclyn Smith

Barbie doll in
cowgirl outfit

matching denim
full-circle skirt
with fringe

baton

makeup kit

cap pistol

piñata filled with
jalapeño lollipops,
Mexican toys

Tex Tan's hand-tooled
leather saddlebag

white calfskin boots with
deep scallops,
multicolored stitching,
walking heel

tack box contents:
neat's foot oil, curry combs and
brushes, jar of Swat, can of
Flys-off, hoof pick,
bot comb

UT—THE BIG CORRAL

Burnt orange fever is contracted early by a lot of Texans — especially if one or more parent attended the University of Texas at Austin. Established in 1876 by a state constitutional mandate, UT opened its doors to students in 1883. Originally 40 acres square, it now occupies more than 300, with 110 red-tiled Spanish Colonial-style buildings. A replica of the Santa Riata #1 oil well on the southeast edge of campus reminds its 50,000 students how rich the school actually is.

The only Southwestern member of the Association of American Universities, UT ranks fourteenth in the nation in academic quality, and has an outstanding Latin American Studies and American Studies program, a top French Department, and a law school that turns out candidates for Houston's Big Four law firms. UT graduates more petroleum engineers than any other institution in the world. The almost five million volumes in its library include one of the five Gutenberg Bibles in the country.

But getting an education is only part of the UT experience. Most students spend their four years in the following noble pursuits.

MAKING CONTACTS: UT is *the* place in Texas to make social, political, and business connections, and for landing the right husband or wife. Make further contacts at the Tejas Club, the *Daily Texan* office, Hardin House, the Scottish Rite Dorm, and the Student Union.

PARTYING: You can go to fraternity and sorority parties, lake house parties, Eeyore's Birthday Party, Bored Martyr meetings, Distinguished Alumni Awards parties, Round-Up Weekend, plus Scholz's Beer Garten, where a party has been going on nightly since this legendary Austin institution opened in 1866.

SHOPPING: Students spend lots of money in the stores on Guadalupe Street, which borders the campus and is known as The Drag. Shop at Rooster Andrews, the University Co-Op (save the rebate slips!), Clyde Campbell, The Cadeau, and Mrs. Brittain's.

FOOTBALL: Longhorn games are the biggest, boldest, and flashiest. The cutest cheerleaders cheer. The Texas Cowboys, a UT men's service organization made up of rich frat boys, fire Smokey the cannon. The Silver Spurs, an organization of supersmart UT boys, parade Bevo, the mascot steer, around the stadium. The Longhorn Band, in ranch suits and cowboy hats, marches at half time, spelling out *Texas* in body script formation while fiercely playing "Texas Fight." And, of course, the brawny Horns demolish the opposition, the 308-foot UT Tower glows burnt orange, and all Austinites know that the Longhorns have won yet another. Hook 'em!

BECOMING A TEXAS-EX. When you graduate from UT, you automatically join a gigantic Longhorn herd that ranges across Texas and the world. Walter Cronkite, Fess Parker, Farrah Fawcett, John Connally (and five other former Texas governors), Earl Campbell, Lady Bird Johnson, and Dr. Denton Cooley are all UT alumni.

WHERE ELSE TO GO

Hard as it is to believe, at least for a Longhorn, not *every* Texan wants (or can) go to UT. Here are the alternatives.

BAYLOR UNIVERSITY. *Waco*. Mascot: "Robbie" the bear. Colors: green and gold. Private institution affiliated with Baptist church. Founded 1886. Baptists welcome; playboys (and *Playboy*) not. No fraternities or sororities. Religion department excels. Outstanding premed school.

RICE UNIVERSITY. *Houston*. Mascot: "Sammy" the owl. Colors: blue and gray. Privately supported school. Founded in 1912 by William Marsh Rice, who was later murdered by his butler. Thinks of itself as Harvard of the South. Bumper stickers in the West University area claim, "I Must Be Smart I Go to Rice." Slide rule center of Texas.

SOUTHERN METHODIST UNIVERSITY. *Dallas*. Mascot: "Peruna" the mustang. Colors: red and blue. Affiliated with United Methodist Church but is nonsectarian. Founded in 1915 in University Park. Headquarters for Tex-Preps and trendiest-dressed coeds. Extremely active Greek system. Noted for its theater program and business school. Bob Hope Theater and the Algur Meadows Museum (fine collection of Renaissance art) on campus.

TEXAS A&M UNIVERSITY. *College Station*. Mascot: "Reveille," a collie dog. Colors: maroon and white. Begun in 1876, A&M was a Texas land-grant college. Fastest-growing major college in Texas. Called the West Point of the South, it's the home of future military generals, veterinarians, engineers, farmers. No such thing as an ex-Aggie. Famous for "War Hymn," shaved heads, dashing band uniforms, standing during all of each and every football game. "When the team scores, we score" is their motto.

UNIVERSITY OF ARKANSAS. *Fayetteville, Ark*. Mascot: "Big Red" the razorback. Colors: red and white. Established in 1871 as a land grant college. Strong Greek chapters. Good agriculture and architecture departments. Top football team and fanatic fans. Razorbacks have a unique, ear splittin' yell. "*Oooooo, pig, s-o-o-i-e, Razorbacks!*"

UNIVERSITY OF OKLAHOMA. *Norman, Okla*. Mascot: the Sooner Schooner, a covered wagon drawn by two ponies. Colors: crimson and cream. Started in 1890, this state-controlled institution offers pilot training on its own flying field. Top engineering, art, and environmental design departments. Too dry; too dusty. Pretty campus, though.

TEXAS CHRISTIAN UNIVERSITY. *Fort Worth*. Mascot: the horned frog. Colors: purple and white. Privately controlled institution with connections to Christian Church. Started in 1873 and moved to Fort Worth in 1910. Has the Brite Divinity School and a fine ranch management training program.

TEXAS TECH UNIVERSITY. *Lubbock*. Mascot: "The Red Raider" masked rider on "Happy 7-2" horse. Colors: red and black. Founded in 1923 on the high plains of West Texas. Small city environment. State supported. Strong medical technology, engineering, and science departments.

UNIVERSITY OF HOUSTON. *Houston*. Mascot: "Shasta 5" the cougar. Colors: red and white. Founded in 1927 by Houston oilman Hugh Roy Cullen. Now a state-assisted university. Third largest campus in the state. A "suitcase" school—80 percent of the students live at home.

Texas Type No. 2

THE UT FRATERNITY BROTHER

Has his eye on family business.

hair cut short, washed daily; barber: Agnes in East Austin

Canoe after-shave

smiling; just been tapped for Texas Cowboys

white cotton undershirt with orange Longhorn on front purchased at Rooster Andrews on The Drag

pink oxford cloth button-down shirt from Clyde Campbell's, starched so much the pockets won't open, monogrammed pocket flap

books: The Government and Politics of Texas; Fundamentals of Financial Accounting; Economics

hand-tooled leather belt with white braid

solid brass buckle with UT motifs — longhorn, Hook'em Horns, tower and university seal — bought from the Ex-Student's Association

UT class ring

Ace bandage (sprained wrist two weeks ago playing football against the SAEs)

pocket contents: check from Daddy; keys to pale blue Monte Carlo, graduation gift from Mama & Daddy; rebates from the Co-op; tickets to OU game; confirmed Dallas motel room reservation

on left wrist — diver's watch (grandparents' present when he graduated from St. Mark's); stamp from Silver Dollar North (Thursday is 50 cents-a-pitcher night)

Levi's, freshly dry-cleaned at Jack Brown's

Tony Lama boots, dark brown leather with multicolored stitching, polished nightly by new pledges

THE UT SORORITY SISTER

Has her eye on him.

streaked blond hair; very shiny, washed and blown dry daily, puts lemon juice on it when sunbathing on sorority house roof; pulled back in a bouncy ponytail and tied with grosgrain ribbon hand-painted with her name — from The Grandmother's Shop

diamond stud earrings; small 14-karat gold shell stud on right ear

perfectly made up at all times, morning, noon, and night

sorority drop hanging from 14-karat gold chain; 14-karat gold add-a-bead necklace

smiling; just been tapped for Bored Martyrs; perfect teeth

frat brother's pin buried in embroidery (hopes to replace it with engagement ring soon)

tan from swimming at Barton Springs, boating on Lake Travis

stamp from Silver Dollar North

Camp Waldemar ring

14-karat gold dinner ring, Christmas gift from Mama & Daddy bought from Sakowitz's Robert Wander

two 14-karat gold bangles, one with her name monogrammed in script

gold-&-silver Rolex

"La Bolsa" canvas bag with cutout leather monogram, mail-ordered from King Ranch's Running W Saddle Shop

contents: keys to pale blue moped, graduation gift from Mama and Daddy; check from Daddy; matchbook from Bean's Restaurant and Bar; rebate slips from Co-op; Jack's Party Pictures of her with boyfriend taken at last week's waterskiing party on Lake Austin; credit cards: Scarborough's, Joske's, Frost's, Neiman's, Sakowitz; picture of dress that would be perfect to wear to OU weekend torn out of Texas Monthly

hand-embroidered Oaxaca dress — a bit long, hasn't been hemmed yet — bought at Marti's during Border Town Binge

Bass leather strap sandals; toenails and fingernails painted hot pink

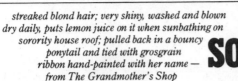

THE SHAPE OF THE STATE
A Collector's Guide

Loyalty to the shape of the Lone Star state is all-important. It is not enough to be able to pledge allegiance to it; a Texan must also show fierce state pride by wearing or in other ways showing off the familiar configuration. Aesthetically pleasing, the shape of Texas is well-balanced and distinctly recognizable. Fortunately, it can be found in many, often portable, forms. Texas-shaped bath mats, cutting boards, candlesticks, stationery, and cookware are available and in great demand. You can and should put the state on your earlobes, on your tie, and all around your home. To help you get into the shape of Texas things, here are some of the more outstanding versions.

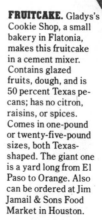

FRUITCAKE. Gladys's Cookie Shop, a small bakery in Flatonia, makes this fruitcake in a cement mixer. Contains glazed fruits, dough, and is 50 percent Texas pecans; has no citron, raisins, or spices. Comes in one-pound or twenty-five-pound sizes, both Texas-shaped. The giant one is a yard long from El Paso to Orange. Also can be ordered at Jim Jamail & Sons Food Market in Houston.

BATH SOAP. Makes Houston or Dallas dirt disappear right away. A Sakowitz exclusive, this chunky cake is French-milled and has a subtle sandalwood fragrance. Lather up, buckaroos.

CHRISTMAS ORNA- MENT. Hang Texas! . . . right on the Christmas tree with this red, white, and blue ornament made of baker's clay. Features the beloved bluebonnet and the Lone Star. From The Wooden Star, Houston.

PAPERWEIGHT. See clear through Texas. An acrylic paperweight personalized with your name, oil well derrick, or the Great Seal of Texas. Also available plain if you don't want anyone knowing your business. Very weighty. From the Hinsdale Collection catalog.

SWIMMING POOL. Dive into Texas with a really big splash. Have Charles Wise of the Wise Pool Company in Conroe put the map of Texas in your backyard. Pool is 734 square feet and has a 30,687-gallon capacity. Features a white cantilever deck, flag blue tiling, and a red tile Lone Star marking your hometown. Swimmers can enter the pool on steps in the Panhandle area.

ICE CUBES. The Ice of Texas℠—the Lone Star state's official ice tray—makes state-shaped "cubes." Margaritas on the rocks, iced tea have much more meaning with these chillers. Available everywhere from Scheplers to Sakowitz. For a real Texas meltdown.

POTPOURRI. The sweet smell of Texas. A mixture of dried wild flowers—including petals from the sacred bluebonnet—and spices packed in a clear plastic Texas-shaped box and tied with a bandana ribbon. From James Allen, Inc., of Houston. Perfect for perfuming the den after an indoor barbecue.

BAKING PAN. This takes the cake—or brownies, jalapeño corn bread, or whatever. Heavy cast-aluminum pan is sold at the Heritage Village Gift Shop in Woodville. Make your hometown your first bite.

EYEGLASSES. The better to see Texas with, my dear. Jim Knudsen of Knudsen Optical in Houston designed these gold-rimmed specs with tricolor (red, white, and blue) lenses. These eyes of Texas will certainly be upon you all the livelong day.

KEY RING. Keep the keys to the Big Spread, the El Dorado, the pickup, and the safe deposit box at River Oaks Bank and Trust all together on this stately brass key organizer. Has a protective screw-type closure and "Texas" boldly embossed across it. From The Wooden Star in Houston.

AIR FRESHENER. Wipe out any traces of the polecat that slept overnight in your pickup by hanging Crawford International's mint freshener from your rearview mirror. Comes with its own rawhide tie. Can be bought in all Texas convenience stores.

STATIONERY. Write on, Texas. This thick pad comes in yellow and can be personally imprinted with "Tall Tales from _____" across northern border. To order at Sakowitz. Makes fine invites to your next party at Green Pastures or for thanking Lady Bird for inviting you to the LBJ Ranch.

BASKET. A tisket, a tasket, this sturdy basket holds plenty of tortilla chips. Has a strong hardwood bottom. From The Wooden Star, Houston.

BELT. The "Big Tex" belt. A hand-hammered brass map of Texas buckle on a beige corded belt with brass tip. One size fits all. Warning: use care when bending over—the Panhandle can hurt. A real waist-full belt from the Lew Magram catalog.

COOKIE CUTTER. Sugar cookies will never be same. This tin cookie cutter made especially for Austin's Bon Appétit cookware store is also perfect for decorating a pie crust or cutting tortilla dough. Start nibbling along the Rio Grande border.

A TEXAS SAMPLER

All Texas treats don't come in the shape of the state—but they are no less Texan for that. To get a real taste, touch, and feel of the kinds of things no Texan worth his or her mineral rights can live without, here's a selection of some of the best "only from Texas" items.

TEXAS BS REPELLENT.

Cools down all those long-winded Texans who give you a big line of bull. Instructions suggest that you "aim atomizer . . . and spray for one second." For use around tall tales, political bombast, and exaggerated claims. In gift shops in Texas airports or at Magic Clown, Story Village Shopping Center, Irving 75062.

CITRUS FRUITS. For over fifty years, Pittman & Davis has been shipping plump, red grapefruit and navel oranges grown in South Texas's Rio Grande Valley. Individual fruits are tissue-wrapped in "Best Wishes from Texas" paper. Gift baskets packed in colorful, reusable Mexican baskets. Shipping season: mid-November to mid-March.

Mail-order catalog. Pittman & Davis, Inc., Harlingen 78550.

RUNNING SHORTS. A brief way to show your Lone Star pride. These running shorts, featuring the state flag motif, will turn heads on the jogging trail. In red, white, and blue nylon with elasticized band and an oversized star placed strategically on the right side. From JR Enterprises, 4904 White Elm, Austin 78749.

WILLOW FURNITURE.

Second-growth Texas willow is shaped into bentwood furniture and furnishings. Designed by Stephen Stefanou, these rustic, handmade chairs, chaise lounges, headboards, tables, porch swings, loveseats, and baskets look as good on a Turtle Creek terrace as they do on a Pasadena patio. Available through decorators or Christopher Designs, Inc., 1901 South Great S.W. Parkway, Grand Prairie 75051.

PASSPORT. To get you into and around the Lone Star state with tongue in cheek. This official-looking document is for natives and foreigners alike. Includes "visas" for all Texas cities. Sold in gift shops and airports across the state.

JALAPEÑO JELLY. For those who like it hot, Sam Lewis spices things up with his jalapeño jelly. Absolutely delicious on roasted meat. Lewis also makes jalapeño-stuffed olives and sacks of jalapeño lollypops for kids of all ages. Price list on request from Sam Lewis & Associates, 420 North Van Buren, San Angelo 76901.

LBJ RECORDING. Surely the world's only recording of an American president singing with his favorite dog. On "Dogs Have Always Been My Friends," Lyndon B. Johnson sings a duet with his beloved Yuki, an Austin mongrel rescued by daughter Luci. The ten-minute-long, 33⅓ rpm record, made in 1972, features Yuki's a capella howlings, LBJ talking about his Hill Country boyhood, and Lady Bird's giggles. A doggone good piece of LBJ memorabilia, from Awani Press, P.O. Box 881, Fredericksburg 78624.

COW PATTIE. For those of you who think you have everything. A genuine Texas meadow muffin in a glass case. For tabletop or desk. Dried, deodorized, and gold-finished. From Ryon's, P.O. Box 4280, Fort Worth 76106.

BARBED WIRE CHRISTMAS WREATH. A different holiday twist. Genuine barbed wire is coiled in a wreath. Decorated with Texas wild flowers, pine cones, feathers, and ribbons. Approximately eighteen inches in diameter, each is handmade in Texas. From Cutter Bill, 5818 L.B.J. Freeway, Dallas 75240.

Chapter 2
BEAUTY & BRAWN

SURVIVAL OF THE CUTEST & THE FITTEST

Beauty and brawn dominate the Lone Star landscape of looks. It's Darwin's theory of evolution with a Texas twist. Big, bullish, masculine men and pretty, sweet, ultrafeminine women are the primary body types. Those who weren't born with the right looks must quickly learn to compensate for this lack (with a talent for drinking everyone else under the table, for instance); those who refuse to adapt never quite get along in the state—they often move away.

If you're male, you want to be a good ol' boy, the kind of guy who drinks a lot, talks loud, loves sports, always has a toothpick hanging out of his mouth, and knows how to handle his women. You also should be tall, i.e., over six feet (cowboy boots can be a help here). There is enormous pressure to laugh hard and often. Good ol' boys love to roar at each other's jokes, even if they aren't particularly amusing. Roaring makes you look confident in that bull-in-a-china-shop sort of way.

If you're a woman, the burden is on looking and acting "nice." You just aren't supposed to be loud and aggressive and intelligent. Popularity is important and you're always up for a good time—within limits. You do not want the Dallas Cowboys defensive squad knocking on your door.

There is some speculation that so many good-looking people live in Texas because they are bred selectively, just like cattle; every bullish man is looking for that prize heifer that will help him generate a quality herd. Thus, the survival of the cutest and the fittest is assured. This system of unnatural selection has also led to what some might see as an unwarranted emphasis on the public—and competitive—display of cherished Texas traits. The chosen exhibition arena for men is football. For women, it is the beauty pageant.

FOOTBALL MANIA
Kickoffs, Halftimes, &
the Importance of Scoring

No purer passion hath any Texan than his or her love for the game of football. To most fans there simply is not a finer form of entertainment. What could be more fun than watching clusters of hulking males crash into each other on a playing field?

Football is cherished by socialites because it gives them a regularly scheduled event at which they can see and be seen. For businessmen the game provides the perfect backdrop for deal-making—all that cheering and enthusiasm encourages the cautious client to "go the distance." And teenagers find the game a great cover for forbidden activities. If pushed, some high-minded fans will go so far as to boast that it is the cultural value of the game that draws them to the stadium week after week—you know, the beauty of geometrical patterns in motion on the field.

To all Texans, football—high school, college, and professional—is a way of life. Some people believe the main reason there is a public school system is to give

Texans more football teams to root for. There are high school teams so popular that they must play some of their games in professional-sized stadiums to accommodate the crowds. It is that serious.

Many people believe football is an autumn/winter sport. These people do not live in Texas. Under the Lone Star, football demands a year-round commitment. Even when it's well over 100 degrees, Texans across the state pile into kilnlike stadiums to watch their heroes run and kick and otherwise sweat out the summer exhibition games.

It is not enough just to love the game; you have to participate. Luckily, there is a role in this mania for everyone.

OFFICIAL PARTICIPANTS

PLAYERS. Gridiron gods. If you are a Texas male in good health between the ages of thirteen and thirty-five, it is your civic duty to play football. Any Texan will tell you that playing the game prepares the young male for everything that will happen to him in his life. He'll learn teamwork, a key to future oil and real estate deals; he'll know how to use football terminology, crucial to successful political campaigns; and he'll be guaranteed of getting a girl—if mounted on the shoulders of a linebacker, even the most unfortunate-looking face can find true love.

COACHES. Surrogate fathers supreme. Spiritual guides to their teams. Revered in the community, trusted with their players' darkest secrets. Love their "men" so much they will reportedly reward them with a visit to a bordello after an exceptional performance.

CHEERLEADERS. Second in importance only to the players. Their presence on the field proves there is a place for women in football—cheering the men. Being a cheerleader allows women to let

THE BIG GAME

On the second Saturday in October, the Texas-Oklahoma rivalry reaches its climax in a football game in the Cotton Bowl, a Longhorns vs. Sooners confrontation that is the centerpiece of an event known as OU Weekend—a cross between New Year's Eve in Times Square, Mardi Gras in New Orleans, and the Battle of Bull Run squeezed into three days of football, intense drinking, fistfights, and arrests. A Southwestern tribal ritual more like a bloodletting than a friendly athletic contest, the territorial rivalry between these two angry teams has gone on for over eighty years.

No other game played by UT ever approaches the intensity of this one. "I coached twenty games against OU and I don't remember any other game that raised my temperature like those did," admits retired Longhorns coach Darrell Royal, who is from Hollis, Oklahoma. Part of the fierceness of this longstanding rivalry is due to the fact that many of the players on both sides grew up in Texas. OU, considered by Texans to be the all-time master robber of home-grown Lone Star football talent, has lured so many Texas blue-chippers across the Red River that the school is otherwise referred to in Texas as "the best team of Texans money can buy." In any given year, as many as eighteen of the twenty-two players on the field may be Texans. Although many people care *a lot* about the outcome of this duel-to-the-death game, the frenzied events surrounding it are almost as important as who wins. Attending an OU Weekend confirms a UT coed's popularity. Getting a fellow to shell out for a motel room, booze, tickets to the game, and gas to get from Austin to Dallas and back is considered a major social triumph.

loose with wild, near-the-threshold-of-pain screams. It also allows them to assert themselves in leadership positions — helping others get in touch with their mania. (At Texas A&M, the all-*male* cheerleading squad must — everytime Aggie scores — run into the stands and kiss their waiting girlfriends.)

ORGANIZED FANATICS

DRILL TEAMS. All-female kicking, marching, and parading groups. The sole purpose of the drill team is to entertain during halftime. Football fans like constant motion on the field.

MARCHING BANDS. For fans with a musical bent. They provide the backup music and beat for the drill team's high kicks.

PEP SQUADS. For all the girls and boys who couldn't make the cheerleading team. These youths express zealotry in its most extreme form. They organize pep rallies, sell ribbons and pennants, make posters, and pay homage to the team by egging and rolling (with toilet paper) the players' homes the night before a big game. The players always feel honored.

FREE-FORM FANATICS

FANS IN GENERAL. Before leaving the house you must tie crepe paper streamers from your car's antenna. This won't help you find your car in the parking lot, but you'll fit in. Team colors are worn at all times. This custom reaches severe heights of folly during the bowl season. Female UT fans have been seen in rabbit-fur coats dyed in Longhorn burnt orange and white. Entire families with Mustang Mania have been known to attend games in matching red-and-blue outfits.

THE COMMUNITY. Banks light their buildings to match the hometown team's colors. Attorneys cancel court dates to attend pep rallies. Stores display huge game schedules along with merchandise in their windows. Newspapermen may work for little or nothing on weekends just for the pleasure of writing about football. Small-town restaurants close on Friday nights because everyone is at the game.

PREACHERS. They beef up their Sunday morning sermons with football imagery and get a more attentive audience. "May the Lord carry you to victory through the goalposts of life."

ARTISTS. They bring culture to the game through their work. One Cowboy fan/painter was inspired by the game — and a wealthy patron — to create an oil portrait of the benefactor with a football where his head should have been. The work now hangs in his box at Texas Stadium.

THE KILGORE RANGERETTES & THE DRILL TEAM EXPERIENCE

In 1940 Gussie Nell Davis had a vision. She saw pretty, wholesome young girls all in a row who could kick in unison as high as their cowboy-hatted heads. But this was not a dream of some cheap chorus line; the girls would be smiling, innocent Texas beauties who would feel it their privilege and duty to entertain the masses during football game halftimes. No jiggly come-ons, no peekaboo outfits, just plain ol' star-spangled banner fun.

Thus, the Kilgore College Rangerettes and the Texas institution of drill teams were born. And over the forty-plus years since that vision, the Kilgore Rangerettes have become an institution. In 1977 they were honored as a "living art form" by the Contemporary Arts Museum, Houston.

Becoming a member of this East Texas junior college drill team is no easy trick. Each year, as many as a hundred fifty girls try out for roughly thirty slots on the line. If you can't kick as high as your head when the tryouts begin, forget it. You're out of the running.

Once a girl has made the grade, she must practice nine hours a week, keep up a good grade average, and stay single (married women have no business wearing short skirts on a football field). Rangerettes must also maintain a wholesome appearance at all times, even out of uniform. The team's mystique is taken so seriously that their red, white, and blue Texas-style uniforms are copyrighted (the Rangerettes are proud to have started the drill team tradition, but they don't want anyone copying their look).

Their renown is not limited to the borders of the Lone Star state. Over the years the Rangerettes have been seen in countless magazines, on national television, and in several movies, appearing with Burt Reynolds in *Semi-Tough*. Their stardom spans the globe, penetrating even the Iron Curtain (they toured Rumania in 1977). The ambassadresses of high kicks have also performed in such varied and unlikely locales as Hong Kong, Korea, and Macao.

Texas Type No. 3

THE CHEER LEADER

Smarter than she looks.

long, dark, straight hair — held back on each side with white poodle barrettes

smiling; she's been named queen for the homecoming dance

cute

retainer in mouth

hot pink lipstick and enough makeup so she'll be seen by quarterback during game

two gold chains, a necklace with her name in script

white satin blouse with huge balloon sleeves, pussycat bow

sleeveless, button-front weskit in maroon corduroy

circular maroon corduroy skirt lined with white satin

maroon corduroy panties, which she shows off a lot by doing more cartwheels than any other cheerleader; her Mama made this outfit from Butterick pattern

"We're Number One" sign

three huge white mums surrounded by gold plastic footballs and lots of streamers

Quarterback's senior ring with ¼-inch of Johnson & Johnson tape wrapped around it

tan from her last trip with quarterback to Galveston's Stewart Beach

skinned knee from one overenergetic cartwheel too many; Band-Aid applied during halftime

white-and-maroon Bass saddle oxfords

white cotton socks, pulled straight up

white-and-maroon pompon

maroon megaphone with "Bobcats" lettered in white

THE QUARTER BACK

Knows how to score.

cute

smiling; threw winning touchdown and spotted Fred Akers's recruiters in the stands

stick of Gator-aid gum in mouth

helmet in hand in anticipation of victory kisses from cheerleaders

team number and his last name printed on back of jersey with rubberized maroon paint

Rawlings R5 football; team will sign it later in field house

in back pocket: good luck charm— packet of Trojans

pulled hamstring muscle from throwing winning pass

athletic tape all over body (two rolls); hip pad, kidney pad, shoulder pads, knee pads

mouthpiece snapped on side of helmet so it's not lost when knocked out

white nylon jersey and pants

white cotton-and-Orlon socks with maroon band at top cover

mild case of athlete's foot

Puma white leather lace-ups with cleats — younger brother will soon double-lace them as postgame prank

THE DALLAS COWBOYS
Landry's Gentry

A MILLIONAIRE'S BALL CLUB

The organizing of the Dallas Cowboys in 1960 was the gridiron manifestation of a rivalry between two millionaire Dallas clans, the Murchisons and the Hunts. Clint Murchison, Jr. (total worth: $800 million) thought that Dallas needed an NFL team, because the AFL Texans—that piddly thing belonging to Lamar Hunt (total family worth: excess of $1 billion)—wasn't good enough for the town. The controversy that ensued split Dallas society, drastically reduced attendance for both teams, and gave Dallas sportswriters a chance for a lot of good copy. After the smoke had cleared—and Lamar's Texans had become the Kansas City Chiefs—everyone felt grateful to Clint

Roger
"The Dodger"
Staubach.

for giving them a helluva good time, and then settled back to enjoy what they thought would be a nice, mediocre football team. No one suspected that Clint would implement a winning three-step formula: (1) Think of football as a business (not a write-off). (2) Spend money on your business. (3) When all else fails, spend more money. (When he heard that the Cowboys had lost $1 million during their first season, Murchison shrugged and said, "At that rate, the team'll last a thousand years.")

Nothing works like simplicity. Murchison has spent lavishly on publicity, coaches, computers, and a stadium. The Cowboys have missed only one play-off since 1965.

THE MACHINE BEHIND THE MACHINE

In the early years Murchison made two key investments: a computer company called Optimum Systems, and an equally outstanding piece of equipment named Tom Landry.

Optimum Systems, acquired by Murchison in 1965, provides all the computers vital to the Cowboys' deep-background scouting and rating system. An Indian computer analyst, Salaam Qureishi, programmed this then-unique plan by narrowing down the characteristics of a professional football player to a formidable eight rating points, which the team's scouts use to grade practically every college player in the country. It's Mission Control, the FBI, and genetic engineering all rolled into one.

Then there's Tom Landry. The Cowboys' one and only coach has combined omniscience and infallibility to inspire a great deal of respect — and not a little fear. His long shots have been awesome.

The strength of Landry's patience is matched only by his frozen face muscles. Standing on the sidelines in tie and snap-brim, Landry registers the impact of penalties, touchdowns, and Super Bowl plays with the same noncommittal, impassive stare. (One Cowboy fan to another: "Sure he's got emotions — look, look, he just smiled!") When asked for a statement after the '72 Super Bowl victory, Tom replied: "I don't think I'm really conscious of my feelings yet."

BUILDING CHARACTER

Another Landry quote: "Gentlemen, nothing funny ever happens on a football field."

The last person on the Dallas squad to forget this was quarterback Don Meredith, who sang hillbilly songs going into the huddle ("I didn't know God made honky-tonk angels.") Dandy Don started bobbling the ball in the play-offs, and it became obvious that broad comedy was not part of the winning game plan. Landry finally found his ideal quarterback in Roger Staubach, a hulking embodiment of wholesomeness who didn't choke. (He won fourteen of his career victories in the last two minutes of game time.) Like Landry, Staubach was a member of the Fellowship of Christian Athletes and a company man. When he won a Touchdown Club award, Staubach's acceptance speech was reserved: "I don't know what to say. I'm waiting for Coach Landry to send somebody in with a statement." (He was probably only half kidding.) Staubach's retirement press conference was televised live on three Dallas channels.

THE DALLAS COWBOY CHEERLEADERS

Since they first appeared in patriotic seminudity in 1972, the Dallas Cowboy Cheerleaders (*not* the Cowgirls) have rallied the fans and given the males in the crowd an excuse for dreaming about pompons and pigtails long after graduation. That's the fun part. For the rest, Dallas Cowboy Cheerleaders must:

• practice up to five hours a day, five times a week in season.
• attend all rehearsals (if you skip two, you're off the squad).
• accept a salary of $15 a game (no games on the road).
• have a winning personality (and a good body).

Dallas Cowboy Cheerleaders must *not*:
• appear as Cheerleaders where alcohol is served.
• attend parties as a Cheerleader.
• wear jewelry while in costume.
• ever, *ever* date a Cowboy.
• gain weight.

A spot on the nation's number one cheerleading team may also mean regular trips to the orthodontist, lots of yogurt, and frequent shuttles between Dallas and, say, El Paso, where an off-duty Cheerleader is likely to work as a dental assistant. And laurel-resting is out. Every year the thirty-six Cheerleaders compete against all comers for their spots on the team. If dieting doesn't keep weight down, anxiety will.

PURTY GALS

The Yellow Roses of Texas

There are over two thousand beauty pageants annually in the state of Texas. That averages out to more than five contests for every day of the year. It's a wonder Texans can find time for rodeos and barbecues!

There are contests for six-year-olds and under, fifteen- to nineteen-year-olds, seventeen- to twenty-five-year-olds, preteens, post-teens, little misses, and every other possible permutation of female age groupings. They take place in high school auditoriums, arenas, and hotel banquet rooms across the state. Some are play-off level events that count toward those Super Bowls of the pageant world, Miss America and Miss Universe, while others are more like carnival sideshows. All are important to Texas women. This is where they learn how to turn their raw good looks into a self-effacing, perpetually-smiling ideal of glamour.

Texas beauty contests are the human equivalents of cattle auctions. Texans feel as though they're down on the farm when they're watching these spectacles. They admire the dolled-up heifers with their carefully sprayed, shiny hair. They feel spiritually enriched as contestants moo about the importance of clean living. They consider all views, full frontal, profile, rear. Which is really the quality pair of legs?

The pageantry of these contests also gives Texans a focus for their separatist fixation. Every beauty queen is a Lone Star Lady Di, commanding the awe and respect befitting royalty. Since Texans think of their state as an independent province, it is only natural that titled Texas beauties should reign supreme.

MISS TEXAS

The major leagues. The winner here goes on to the World Series—i.e., the Miss America Pageant. Seventy entrants train for the contest as seriously as Sugar Ray Leonard does for his next bout. Some girls actually lift weights (apparently Miss Texas missed becoming Miss America in 1981 because she naively admitted to this activity), and take speech lessons to soften their drawl. For titled pageant contestants only. (July, Fort Worth)

MISS COW CHIP QUEEN

More a test of olfactory fortitude than beauty. In conjunction with the Cow Creek Championship Chamber Chili Cookoff, about twenty young women get gussied up in untraditional beauty pageant outfits (one recent entrant wore a Carmen Miranda-style fruit headdress). Skill and imagination come into play when each contestant parades in front of the judges dragging a burlap bag filled with dried cow patties. The girl with the most unusual presentation of beauty and the bag becomes Miss Cow Chip Queen. No other talent is necessary. Along with the title, she receives a cow chip. (May, Waxahachie)

GOLDEN GIRL OF THE WEST

Only local high school girls may enter this Western-style event. Contestants are presented in authentic costumes from the 1890s, and are judged on talent, beauty, and "how well they can carry on a conversation with strangers"—apparently an important skill in Pecos. The winner is awarded $500 in scholarship money and goes on to the Miss West Texas competition. (June, Pecos)

MISS MEXICO OF PORT ARTHUR, LITTLE MISS MEXICO OF PORT ARTHUR

One of the few beauty pageants for both small children and teens. Authenticity is the key; each entrant's family background is checked closely to ensure that at least one natural parent is Mexican-American. Once bloodlines have been okayed, the girls are judged on poise, beauty, personality, and their Mexican costumes. Both the Miss and the Little Miss get a crown, a title, and a savings bond. For Port Arthur Hispanic misses only. (September, Port Arthur)

TYLER ROSE QUEEN

Not exactly a beauty pageant, but has all the trimmings. An important social event. The queen, her ladies-in-waiting, and her out-of-town duchesses are selected according to their families' "contribution to the welfare of Tyler"; i.e., personal wealth. This upper-crust event is a kind of coming-out party for college sophomore girls. At one time, a plane flew over the festivities showering rose petals onto the streets. Most famous Rose Queen: Margaret Hunt (H.L.'s daughter), 1935. (October, Tyler)

QUEEN CITRIANA

A salute to the Rio Grande Valley citrus industry. First, thirty young women get dressed up in antebellum gowns in colors representing the fruit, flower, or whatever is grown in their native region (an orange dress for oranges, a red dress for poinsettias, etc.). Then there is an extraordinary product costume show, in which the women wear clothes decorated with the actual fruit or flower. According to the pageant's director, "These girls can take onion skin and make it look just like lace." For Valley girls only. (January, Mission)

MISS BLACK-EYED PEA

A pageant so beloved of Athens townsfolk that a local dentist was once moved to make a gold black-eyed pea necklace for the queen. Winner must love to eat black-eyed peas. Held in conjunction with the Black-Eyed Pea Festival, pageant annually attracts about twenty entrants. (July, Athens)

MISS CAVOILCADE

A tribute to the oil industry of Port Arthur. Not what you might think—there are no tiaras with miniature rhinestone oil rigs, not even a gift of stock in an oil company—just a straight beauty contest. Only high school seniors from Port Arthur may enter, and over fifty do every year. Winner gets the title, a crown, and a $1,000 scholarship. (October, Port Arthur)

RICE QUEEN

Approximately thirty young women vie for this title, honoring the rice harvest in the Gulf area. All contestants must be sponsored by local civic groups. No talent is necessary, but each contestant must be willing to be identified by number for the duration of the event. (October, Bay City)

WATERMELON THUMP QUEEN

Titleholder chosen at Luling's annual Watermelon Thump competition presides over such events as the watermelon eating contest and the seed spit-off (all Thump Queens are exemplars of femininity and therefore are not required to spit any seeds themselves). At her coronation, the queen wears a gown with a train covered in sequined watermelons; she then poses for pictures with an escort in front of a giant watermelon wall hanging. (June, Luling)

TWENTY FAMOUS FACES
Miss America
& Other Texas Beauties

Every year, it seems, Texas has a finalist in the Miss America Pageant. The mother of Phyllis George Brown once said, "I think Texas would win every year if they'd let us." Of course, not all Texas beauties have taken the pageant route to fame. Here's a sample of the Lone Star state's most prized natural resources.

PHYLLIS GEORGE BROWN
MISS AMERICA 1970,
TV PERSONALITY
DENTON

CYD CHARISSE
DANCER, FILM STAR
AMARILLO

CANDY CLARK
FILM ACTRESS
FORTH WORTH

JOAN CRAWFORD
FILM STAR
SAN ANTONIO

SHIRLEY COTHRAN
MISS AMERICA 1974
DENTON

LINDA DARNELL
FILM STAR
DALLAS

JO-CARROLL DENNISON
MISS AMERICA 1942
TYLER

MORGAN FAIRCHILD
TELEVISION STAR
DALLAS

FARRAH FAWCETT
TELEVISION STAR
CORPUS CHRISTI

GREER GARSON
FILM STAR, RANCHER
FORT WORTH

JERRY HALL
MODEL
MESQUITE

DOROTHY MALONE
ACTRESS
DALLAS

ANN MILLER
DANCER, ACTRESS
CHIRENO

SUZY PARKER
MODEL
SAN ANTONIO

VALERIE PERRINE
FILM ACTRESS
GALVESTON

PAULA PRENTISS
ACTRESS
SAN ANTONIO

DEBBIE REYNOLDS
ACTRESS
EL PASO

GINGER ROGERS
DANCER, FILM STAR
FORT WORTH

JACLYN SMITH
TELEVISION/FILM STAR
HOUSTON

SISSY SPACEK
ACTRESS
QUITMAN

BRENDA VACCARO
ACTRESS
DALLAS

Texas Type No. 4
BEAUTY QUEEN

rhinestone tiara — attached with bobby pins digging into scalp

sparkling eyes (Murine)

hair rinsed in beer for more body; fluffed up and out, sprayed twice with Aqua Net before going on stage (was waist-length last year; shorn hair is in keepsake box at home)

hot pink lipstick and peach blusher; eyelashes curled three times; three coats of mascara

white teeth — she puts lemon juice on them and sits in the sun with mouth open to bleach them even whiter

smiling; she won

lips coated with Vaseline — helps make lips glide over teeth for a longer-holding smile

relaxed shoulders

under arms: slight underarm perspiration

back straight, practices the three Bs — "bust out, belly in, butt under"

in arms: scepter, spray of Tyler roses

Cole of California pink spandex bathing suit; bought at cost from former Miss Texas entrant who wanted to unload it

short nails

plays piano — Grieg Piano Concerto in A Minor (much dramatic arm movement, not much skill)

in left hand: ammonia ball to sniff when she feels faint

thighs touching slightly

in suitcase backstage: evening dress; makeup kit; pink plastic rollers; two cans of Aqua Net; travel iron; sewing kit; Kim Dawson's Dallas modeling agency phone number; dog-eared copy of Cheryl Tiegs's The Way to Natural Beauty; box of Kleenex; diaphragm

sheer, nude L'eggs panty hose

in background: applause and "A Pretty Girl Is Like a Melody"

plain white kidskin pumps from Chandler's

Chapter 3

CATTLE &
SADDLE

HOMES ON THE RANGE

Ranching as a Way of Life

The first thing a Texan does when he gets some extra money is buy a ranch. It may be a piddling ten or twenty acres or a massive spread of several hundred thousand. But owning land is crucial to a Texan's ability to acquire inner peace. Even the most citified Texan feels nostalgia for the rugged West and longs to sink his or her toes into real country soil, though many are probably more familiar with dog droppings than cow chips.

While many people in the East have second homes at the shore or in the mountains, the Texan's home away from home is the ranch. It offers him the opportunity to play cowboy, a chance to feel wholesome after a week of being J.R. in the big city.

People have ranches for a variety of reasons. There are pretend ranches, the ones that serve merely as social accessories. At these ranches people may have some livestock on hand for decoration, but the main function is as requisite country setting for barbecues for two hundred.

And then there are dude ranches, those countrified resorts where Yankees have a chance to wear their Billy Martin boots and get saddle sores. Authentic Texans wouldn't be caught dead at one of these places, but they do get a chortle out of taking out-of-state folks for a ride.

True to the reputation Texas enjoys internationally, there *are* a number of genuine working ranches, where real cowboys cluck "Get along, little dogie." At these spreads, ranching is a business. There are chemistry lab-like barns devoted to artificial insemination, in vitro fertilization, and other highfalutin' scientific processes. The land is cultivated with just the right kind of grass to transform a cute little heifer into a hearty cow that'll "make a good mother."

Despite all of these real-life ranch functions, *being* a rancher is loaded with mystique, and ranchers like to keep it that way.

Ranching is more of a frame of mind than something that can be put into a job description. In fact, nobody really knows *what* ranchers do. Some of them claim to be minding the cattle "bidness" or

THE LITTLE SPREAD VS. THE BIG SPREAD

To no one's surprise, Texas leads the nation in number of ranches. They may be little or big but, since most people who buy a Little Spread hope to expand to the larger variety, there are some similarities between the two—both probably have the blue-and-white enamel Texas & Southwestern Cattle Raisers Association sign nailed to the gate. Here are some ways to tell them apart.

MEMBER
TEXAS & SOUTHWESTERN
CATTLE RAISERS
ASSOCIATION

	LITTLE SPREAD	BIG SPREAD
ENTRY	Close to highway. Has lots of ranchy things around gate: wagon wheels, lopsided wooden fence, a few extra cactuses, a hand-painted sign that says "Howdy!"	Can't be seen from highway. Wrought-iron arch with ranch name and/or brand on it. Large picture of breed out front. No welcome sign.
HORSES	Several different-colored horses grazing haphazardly out front. You want to look like a serious rancher.	Several same-colored horses grazing in symmetrical pattern out front. You are a serious rancher.
ROADS	Rugged, rutted roads that are nothing more than glorified cattle trails. The kind your Chevy sedan gets stuck in during next rainstorm.	Fancy paved or graded dirt roads for Caddy or Lincoln tour.
FLAGS	Lone Star waving out front. Sign of state pride.	Lone Star *plus* flags of home states or countries of visiting cattle people.
AIR TRANSIT	Wind sock on field where the animals graze. You never know when the Big Spread rancher who's heard about your heifer will drop in.	Paved airstrip. Control tower optional. Little Cessna for crop-dusting and for taking the wife shopping at Grace Jones in Salado.
ACCESSORIES	Cute farm knickknacks, EGGS FOR SALE signs.	Nothing cute. This is a business.

checking out the hay supply, but chances are what they're really doing is going deer-watching or riding around looking at the bluebonnets. Nothing gives a rancher more pleasure than to be asked what he's going to do over the weekend because it gives him the chance to spread the mystique even thicker. "Why, Bubba, I'm goin' ranchin'."

BRANDING IRON	Used on charcoal steaks and as wall decoration.	Used on cattle only.
TRANSPOR-TATION	Plain old beat-up truck with loose bailing wire sliding around back. Used to drive into town for that air of ranching authenticity.	New pickup with ranch name and/or brand painted on side in ranch colors. Used to drive around spread when you don't want to get the Caddy dirty.
CATTLE GUARD	One at gate. Lets people know when they come to visit that they have just entered a real ranch.	One at every pasture entrance. Slows down your fourteen year old who's learning to drive.
WINDMILLS	Rusted; it's there mostly for decoration. Water trough nearby is filled with algae, but cattle still drink from it.	Shiny, new; mostly for decoration. To gross out her parents, debutante daughter jumps fully dressed into water trough after all-night party.
SALT LICK	Next to water trough. After the cattle get a swallow of briny trough water, they'll need something to kill the taste.	One in every pasture where cattle are grazing, right next to herd's bins of minerals, vitamins, and assorted drugs.
DEER FEEDER	Next to salt lick. You need to keep the deer healthy so they'll look pretty when people come to visit.	Scattered all over ranch. You need to keep the deer fat so when people come to hunt they'll get a nice big buck.
RAIN GAUGE	Filled to brim with water from last summer's rain.	Attached to side of AI (artificial insemination) barn. Measured religiously: rainfall could affect bulls' output.
PASTURES	Have an unkempt look. Lots of miscellaneous weeds and bluebonnets.	Neatly trimmed, with syncopated sprinkler systems. Ranch wife cultivates bluebonnets, then has *House & Garden* photograph them.
LONGHORN	Only one on spread. Used as a decoration — like a bandana or wagon wheel — whenever you throw a barbecue.	Only one on spread, kept to himself. Bought solely to show to out-of-state and foreign visitors, proving that longhorn is a near-deity to Texans.

Texas Type No. 5

THE RANCHER

His spread is his kingdom.

Stetson's "Little Dogie" hat

smiling; his prize bull fetched big bucks at Western Heritage Sale

leathery, sunburned face

bolo tie ordered from his breed association

Stelzig's cotton oxford cloth shirt with gull-wing Western yoke; ranch brand monogrammed on flap pocket

hand-tooled leather belt, white buck-stitching; ranch brand hand-stamped on back

German silver buckle with enameled Red Brangus

tan gabardine twill pants, ranch-style cut — ordered by the dozens from Stelzig's, no longer wears jeans

back pocket contents: keys for Big Spread; hand-tooled leather checkbook cover, checks personalized with ranch brand and Red Brangus head; Texas & Southwestern Cattle Raisers Association membership card; small plasticized map of ranch to give away to visitors

M. L. Leddy's "Cattle Baron" alligator lizard boots — diamond-design tops with shallow scallop, walking heel; manure on sole

THE COWBOY

High plains drifter.

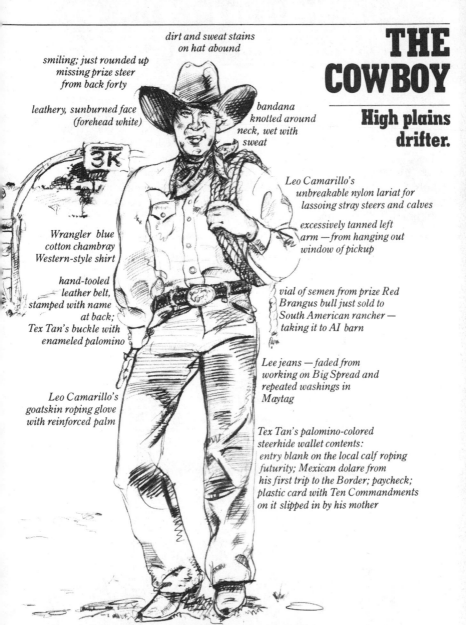

dirt and sweat stains
on hat abound

smiling; just rounded up
missing prize steer
from back forty

leathery, sunburned face
(forehead white)

bandana
knotted around
neck, wet with
sweat

Leo Camarillo's
unbreakable nylon lariat for
lassoing stray steers and calves

Wrangler blue
cotton chambray
Western-style shirt

excessively tanned left
arm—from hanging out
window of pickup

hand-tooled
leather belt,
stamped with name
at back;
Tex Tan's buckle with
enameled palomino

vial of semen from prize Red
Brangus bull just sold to
South American rancher—
taking it to AI barn

Lee jeans—faded from
working on Big Spread and
repeated washings in
Maytag

Leo Camarillo's
goatskin roping glove
with reinforced palm

Tex Tan's palomino-colored
steerhide wallet contents:
entry blank on the local calf roping
futurity; Mexican dolare from
his first trip to the Border; paycheck;
plastic card with Ten Commandments
on it slipped in by his mother

Nocona's suede roughout boots—scarred, cracked,
worn; manure on soles

DOING UP THE DEN
Cow Skulls, Cowhides, Cow Chips

Next to the patio, the den is the most important room in a Texan's house. Different from the living room, a.k.a. the "looking room," as it is called in Texas — "Go look at it. Isn't it purdy?" — the den is where you corral family and friends. The decor is Early Kicker, combining Texas artifacts and antiques; the major design concept is bringing the outdoors indoors. Even the beloved cow contributes — horns for a hat rack, a hide for in front of the fireplace, patties for framing. Decorating Texas-style aims for a look combining the bunkhouse with the taxidermist's shop.

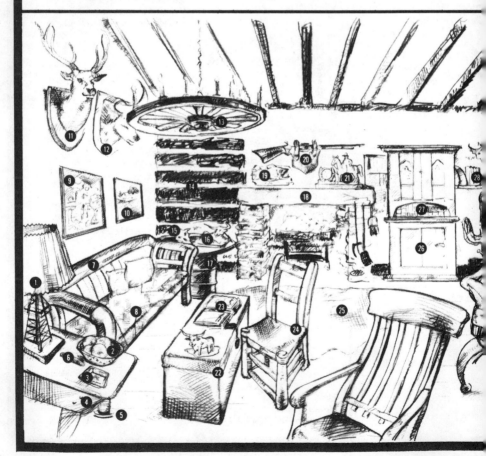

1. Brass oil derrick lamp.

2. Spongeware bowl filled with Stonewall peaches; purchased at fruit stand near LBJ Ranch.

3. Ceramic ashtray with saddle imprint. Always full.

4. Hickory side table. Carpenter's bench in former life. Mama propped up the wobbly shorter leg with an antique Texas ant catcher.

5. White crockery ant catcher. Filled with water. Ants crawl in and drown.

6. Neiman's "Red River" cigar made by Alfred Dunhill. Gift from the oil-lease man.

7. Biedermeier-ish pine couch. Made in Texas, 1840; bought in Fayette County antique store.

8. Quilt. Lone Star pattern in red, white, and blue. Granny pieced it when Mama and Daddy got married.

9. Oil painting of the Alamo. Done by an aunt who was a charter member of the Daughters of the Republic of Texas.

10. Oil painting of bluebonnets by Porfiro Salinas. Everyone remarks on what a "good investment" it is.

11. Mature eight-point white-tailed deer shot by the oldest boy last October.

12. Ibex shot by Daddy on his first hunting trip on the Y.O. Ranch.

13. Wagon wheel light fixture with candle flame-like bulbs.

14. Chinked wall.

15. Cow skull. Mama's favorite cow wandered out of the corral, couldn't find the water troughs or creek, and dehydrated.

16. Bronze sculpture of the foundation Santa Gertrudis bull.

17. Side table. Round piece of glass atop oil drum.

18. Austin limestone fireplace with yellow pine beam mantel.

Boot-shaped stockings hung here at Christmas.

19. Bigmouth bass caught two summers ago at Lake LBJ by youngest boy.

20. Indoor gun rack. Deer hooves hold great-grandpa's 1873 Winchester cartridge rifle. Loaded.

21. Mounted-cowboy-and-horseshoe clock. Ticks loudly.

22. Coffee table. Leather trunk carried on the Chisholm Trail — or so the decorator from Houston said.

23. Magazines. The family subscribes to but doesn't always read: *Texas Monthly*, *Texas Homes*, *Texas Highways*, *Texas Longhorn Journal*, *The Cattleman*, UT *Alcalde*, *Paint Horse Journal*, *Time*, and *National Geographic*.

24. Handmade ladder-back chair with cowhide seat.

25. Longhorn hide throw rug. Good pattern; sheds a lot; skids.

26. Pie safe. Made in Texas around 1848. Wooden cabinet with Lone Star design punched into tin inserts. Houses bar and the Pioneer stereo.

27. Bar. Stocked with leather ice bucket hand-stamped with famous cattle brands; 14-karat gold barbed wire swizzle sticks; bottles of tequila, Triple Sec, mescal, Lone Star, and cans of Tecate beer; salt shaker; bowl of limes; bandana cocktail napkins.

28. Bookshelf: *The King Ranch*, volumes I and II (leather bound) by Tom Lea; UT *Cactus* yearbooks; J. Frank Dobie's *The Longhorns*; Edna Ferber's *Giant*.

29. Mounted Santa Gertrudis weather vane.

30. Saguaro cactus. Put it in the corner after too many guests who had had too many longnecks and margaritas kept running into it.

31. Longhorn chair, upholstered in red velvet. Mama saw one just like it in San Antonio Museum, and now won't let anyone sit in it.

32. Window. Twelve-paned; no curtains — Daddy and the boys want to keep an eye on the herd.

33. Cow pattie. Framed and protected by double-strength glass. Laid by the spread's foundation bull. Brass plate is engraved with date and bull's name.

34. Old barbed wire specimens from famous Texas ranches mounted on plywood.

35. Hat rack. Made of a fine spread of longhorn horns. Every evening Daddy tosses his Stetson up here and misses.

36. UT diploma. Framed with burnt orange mat.

37. UT Ex-Students Association life membership. Framed same as diploma.

38. Branding iron.

RANCHOS GRANDES
The Really Big Spreads

The biggest and oldest of the Great Ranches date back to the last century, to the time when the Texas State Legislature — eager for things to tax (i.e., cattle and people) — signed away 146 million acres to settlers. The smartest ranchers, like Captain King, energetically seized land, discovered oil on their property, and sired heirs who didn't feud too much, thus building prairie empires that still exist today. Other, more contemporary Texans, eager to acquire the honor of the hyphenated profession (oilman-rancher, businessman-rancher, president of the U.S.A.-rancher) built up spreads they already owned, or just bought new ones outright.

THE XIT RANCH
3,000,000 ACRES

Not a ranch anymore, just an awesome memory. When, in 1885, the state of Texas declared itself willing to give land to anyone who could erect a capitol building in Austin, the Capitol Syndicate of Chicago stepped forward. The domed behemoth they built was then the seventh-largest building in the world. The spread it was swapped for covered three million acres, four times the size of Rhode Island. The XIT was broken up in 1912.

THE WAGGONER RANCH
500,000 ACRES

South of Vernon. The largest single piece of privately owned land in the state. It was founded in 1859 by Daniel Waggoner, a real kicker. In 1911 his son W. T. couldn't figure out what to do about the oil seepage on the land. ("Damn it, cattle can't drink that stuff.") That seepage saved the ranch.

THE BURNETT RANCHES
451,000 ACRES

Base of the Panhandle. In 1875, cowboy Samuel Burk Burnett won some land in a poker game. The winning hand: four 6s. The Burnetts have oil as well as luck, and branch ranches in New Mexico and Oklahoma. The Burnett empire is ruled by a matriarchy. Sam's son Tom bypassed his son to give it all to his granddaughter Anne Valliant (wife of Charles Tandy), who handed the ranch over to daughter Anne Windfohr Philips.

THE W. B. BLAKEMORE RANCH
455,000 ACRES

West Texas. Built by J. M. "Silver Dollar Jim" West, a Houston lumberman whose ailing, delicate daughter Marian married W. B. Blakemore II. The most romantic of ranches; besides La Primavera, the half-acre-sized house Blakemore erected for Marian, there is also her tomb, visible for miles around on its Iron Mountain site. Despite all the fluff, the Blakemores are very tight-lipped businessmen.

KENEDY RANCH
450,000 ACRES

Southeast Texas. Located smack dab in the middle of the King Ranch's four sections (Mifflin Kenedy was Richard King's original partner), the ownership of the Kenedy spread has been in dispute ever since 1961, when Mifflin's granddaughter Sarita K. East died, leaving her estate — half the ranch — to be executed by a Trappist monk.

CATARINA (THE DOLPH BRISCOE RANCH)
414,000 ACRES

Southwest Texas. Mrs. Briscoe always keeps a pot of ranch beans on the stove, hot and ready for guests, but ol' Dolph is less than friendly when it comes to telling people how much of Texas he really owns. The rumor is that the former governor has scarfed up more than a million acres. Mrs. Briscoe has redecorated the family bank in Uvalde.

THE BIG BEND RANCH
212,000 ACRES

Oilman Robert O. Anderson owns this spread on the Rio Grande; it has the most spectacular riverfront property in Texas — a couple of waterfalls and a handful of canyons. The General Land Office wants Big Bend for a state park. Anderson wants $20 million.

THE HK
20,000 ACRES

Victoria, south Texas. The HK has the oldest herd of Brahmans in the state and an owner, Henry Clay Koontz who, with wife Mary Kay, gives parties that get featured in *People* magazine (movie stars, Indian princes, quail shoots).

THE LBJ RANCH
3,500 ACRES

Stonewall, near Austin. Not all that big, but it did its bit during Vietnam and the Great Society. Here many preppy Cabinet-level officers were introduced to the social form known as barbecue. LBJ loved to round up the herd using his Lincoln Continental as a cutting horse.

THE JOHN CONNALLY RANCHES
10,000 ACRES

Floresville. Managed by Connally brothers and children. Airstrip in back of house. Through grassy knolls, changes of party, and dairy problems, Big John's wife keeps making Nellie's Jellies. Real good, too.

THE Y.O. RANCH
50,000 ACRES

Near San Antonio. Captain Charles Schreiner, who founded the ranch in the heart of the Hill Country in 1888, had a close business relationship with longhorns that survives at the ranch, where a herd of these cows still roams free (they were used in the first Marlboro Man commercial, shot on the ranch more than twenty years ago). Now the Y.O. is a wildlife preserve, youth camp, and dude ranch. The Wild West has been tamed.

THE KING RANCH
"Buy land and never sell."
CAPTAIN RICHARD KING

Not only is the King spread the biggest ranch in Texas (825,000 acres) it is also the biggest Texas ranch on earth (branches bring the total to 4.3 million acres on five continents). The home base a few miles outside Kingsville sets the standard for Lone Star spaciousness; you could put all of Rhode Island inside it, and still manage to squeeze in a corner of Cape Cod. It's the King Ranch stories — of dynasty-building, family feuds, potent bulls — that barely fit.

CAPTAIN KING

Richard King was a steamboat captain on the Mississippi and later on the Rio Grande. When he decided to buy land in 1853 on the south Texas coast, the area was called the Wild Horse Desert. The land-owners lived as far away as Monterrey, Mexico; none of them had ever expressed much desire to see the remote property, which had on it lots of Indians and no water. Captain King

The Captain.

methodically (and honestly) bought up all the deeds, and named his ranch Santa Gertrudis after one of the titles he acquired, which had been originally issued by the King of Spain. After his death in 1885, King's son-in-law Robert Kleberg, along with the Captain's widow Henrietta, took charge of the ranch. The ranch grew to its peak size in Texas of 1,250,000 acres, and Kleberg continued the King tradition of casually doing stupendous things, like getting a railroad built into Brownsville, stamping out cattle disease, and drilling wells in South Texas that actually had water in them.

THE RUNNING W

Arguably the most famous brand in Texas. Some say it stands for the winding Santa Gertrudis Creek, others that it symbolizes the rattlesnakes that give cattle such a bad scare on the ranch. No one knows for sure. But the running W is versatile — it looks good on cattle and luggage, and it's recognized as the King Ranch symbol in all 254 counties of Texas.

JUST FOLKS

Monkey.

Family feeling runs strong on the King Ranch. Most of the Ranch's Kineños are descended from the inhabitants of the Mexican village Captain King uprooted and carried back with him to his spread in the 1850s. Their children still attend classes in the ranch's two schools.

As for the Captain's own descendants, his widow Henrietta made sure all the heirs got a fair share of the land. And ever since Humble Oil discovered crude on the ranch, there's been a lot more than acres to hand around among the fifty-member family corporation.

Sometimes oil and cattle don't mix. Two Kleberg heirs, Robert Shelton and Belton Kleberg Johnson (known simply as "B"), have sued both the family and Exxon for royalties they claim Exxon never properly paid. It's just a little squabble over $60 million. Says a King Ranch lawyer, "These things happen in big, successful families."

named Monkey. His brother Richard wanted to send the critter to the slaughterhouse. A horrific argument ensued. Monkey was saved—and lived to sire over 150 bulls, who then helped him establish the Santa Gertrudis breed, an American kind of cattle that could take the Texas heat and still yield tender meat to human carnivores.

In fact, Monkey is the only animal officially recognized as the sole foundation sire of a breed (*bos taurus*). Not bad; even Adam can't claim these kinds of credentials.

The homestead and a Kineño.

A BULL NAMED MONKEY

By 1900 Americans were literally fed up with the tough, stringy meat of the famed Texas longhorn, the staple breed of the King Ranch. The Klebergs began crossbreeding Brahmans and Shorthorns to obtain a more commercially valuable breed. In 1920, Robert Kleberg thought he had achieved a particularly good mix in a young bull

SOME FACTS ABOUT THE KING RANCH

THE SPREAD: 825,000 acres, divided into four sections: Santa Gertrudis (headquarters), Laureles, Encino, and Norias.

CATTLE: 60,000 head. The feedlot holds 20,000.

FENCE: 2,000 miles of it.

OIL AND GAS: 2,730 wells. Nice for the cash flow.

WINDMILLS: 350 (for pumping water from wells; repairs keep 20 men busy full-time).

THE EVER-HANDY NEW ENGLAND METAPHOR: The King Ranch, world holdings included, is bigger than Massachusetts and Connecticut combined.

NEATNESS: Kineños (King Ranch hands) are the neatest kickers in Texas: straw hats, white shirts, khaki pants. Usually of Mexican descent, many are the third or fourth generation to be born on the ranch.

BIG HOUSE: The official heart of the King Ranch is the Spanish colonial hacienda overlooking Santa Gertrudis Creek. Built in 1912, its living room is almost as big as a standard-size tennis court.

ON THE HOOF
The Longhorn Legacy

Cows are to Texas what swimming pools are to Beverly Hills — you must have at least one in your backyard. And if you can have only one, it should be a longhorn.

This rugged yet elegant doyen of Texas cattle breeds has a history that goes back hundreds of years. The longhorn's ancestors were the Spanish cattle that Christopher Columbus brought to Santo Domingo. After Columbus discovered America, the longhorn discovered Texas, made it his home, and became the first genuine Texan.

The longhorn didn't get much attention until after the Civil War, when ex-soldiers decided to become trail drivers and cowboys. To earn some greenbacks, they rounded up the cattle roaming wild on the sagebrush plains and drove them to the stockyards of Kansas City and Abilene. Soon after, longhorn steaks were all the rage in East Coast restaurants.

Then someone figured out about bringing the railroad closer to the cattle so they wouldn't get their fat driven off on the trail. Soon the very qualities that had once made the longhorn a sur-

vivor were putting him out of business. His horns (sometimes as much as eight feet from point to point), which were his defense in the wild, made him a pain on the ranch and real difficult to load efficiently into cattle cars; his trim and fit physique, which meant he did not drop from exhaustion halfway to Abilene, also meant that he did not yield the plump side of beef the public was clamoring for. By the turn of

the century, after turning Americans into steak-lovers and Texans into ranchers — and being brought closer to extinction than the buffalo for his trouble — the longhorn was in forced retirement.

Shunned for decades, the longhorn is currently enjoying a renaissance in popularity. Many ranchers, bowing to tradition, now boast at least one longhorn in their herd. (City folk who don't have a ranch can settle for hiring a longhorn limousine to drive them around town. These white Cadillac convertibles with the distinctive horns attached to the grille are particularly popular when

A model longhorn.

★ THE MAJOR TRAILS

Cities in the East wanted meat. Railroads were heading West. Cowboys in South Texas simply had to drive their longhorns up through the state to meet the advancing railheads, and they would have it made. Thus, the cattle drive. There was one false start. (The Shawnee Trail to Sedalia, Missouri, lasted just a year, because the country was well-nigh impassable and the longhorns gave the more delicate local herds tick fever.) But by 1867 the Chisholm Trail, blazed before the war by a Cherokee cowboy, was bringing hundreds of thousands of head of cattle to Abilene, where they were shipped to slaughterhouses in Kansas City and Chicago. American carnivores were happy, and the long drive was a success. To accommodate demand, other trails were opened: the Western, over which herds traveled to Dodge City (farther west than Abilene) and the grazing lands of the Dakotas; and the Goodnight-Loving, which wound its way over the Staked Plains to Denver and Cheyenne, where government agents bought the cattle to feed the Indians on the reservations.

Yankees come to visit.) And, of course, the University of Texas's choice of the longhorn as its mascot is helping to keep the breed in the limelight.

But the Y.O. Ranch, which boasts the world's largest herd of high-quality longhorns, is probably doing more than anyone to preserve the legacy. As their back-to-basics slogan says, "We breed Texas longhorns because they make money for us."

MINI LEXICON No. 1

RANCH TALK

A cattle ranch is a factory; its product is a three-year-old steer that will end up as beefsteak on your plate. Americans have always craved red meat, but otherwise things have changed in the cattle business since the great drives ended around 1884. Cowboys still ride the range, still brand yearlings, still suffer from saddle sores, but nowadays they may actually take courses before they ever get near those dogies. And they're not "dogies" anymore, they're calves who have been second-crossed to improve cutability and dressing percent. On the modern ranch, genetic engineering definitely has the edge on "Rawhide".

anthrax Kills cattle and cripples people, but is now largely under control.

bull prepotency Yes, it has something to do with sex. A prepotent bull's favorable traits are consistently dominant in the calves and heifers it sires. Full-profile shots of bulls in magazines like *The Cattleman* and *The Santa Gertrudis Journal* all show animals admired for their prepotency—a prize prepotent bull can fetch as much as $135,000. These bulls have names like Mr. Corrector, Dynamo, and Choctaw Chief, and their bovine eyes stare arrogantly out from the page. Studs.

barbed wire Joseph Glidden of Illinois developed barbed wire in 1873. It spread rapidly to the West, where wood and stone for fencing were scarce, and the new invention was the perfect thing for cheaply enclosing those millions of acres.

classification "S" For owners of a Santa Gertrudis herd, the brand placed on bulls and cows whose pure traits mark them as producers of future generations. It takes years of experience to spot the cattle which should be branded "S."

cutability How much beef of prime-cut quality a carcass will yield. Any steer can get fat—the trick is to accumulate flesh in the areas where T-bones and porterhouses come from.

conformation Cow or bull traits and the degree to which they conform to the ideal standard of the breed. Cattlemen, who have to look at these beasts all day, breed for aesthetic satisfaction as well as marketability. Cattle chic doesn't vary much: glossy coats and large, soulful eyes are always in, dropping rump and ranginess forever out.

double poll The polled bull or cow has been bred to have no horns. Both parents of a double-polled cow were polled cattle; this increases the genetic chance of producing several generations of polled beasts. Breeding out horns serves safety as well as aesthetic needs; the non-horned bull does not gore—other animals or the cowboy—and those smooth, brown heads just look pretty.

dressing percent Most important equation a cattleman can figure. If a 1,000-pound live steer yields 600 pounds of carcass, its dressing percent is 60 (65 is considered a very good dressing percent). You want to get as much "paying beef" in the store as possible.

finished beef Steer who has gained enough weight to be slaughtered. It's a bit like horse racing: cattlemen are always looking for steers that finish fast—that gain weight so rapidly and correctly that they will reach the slaughterhouse in less than the average time.

foundation sire Bull whose prepotency sires a breed. Usually several foundation sires are involved in the making of a breed.

high gainer Member of the herd that gains weight rapidly. A yearling gains weight at an average of two and a half pounds a day.

maverick Now just a romantic term. Mavericks were cows and bulls that had somehow escaped the rancher's branding iron. When cattle roamed free on the open range, mavericks were a common cause of headache. Now that cattlemen keep tabs on their herds by feeding data into a computer, few cattle enjoy such freedom.

open herd book Ranchers keep open herd book by crossing different breeds for several generations—e.g., Brangus cows bred with Santa Gertrudis bulls. This practice maintains a desired mix in some herds. If a breeder just mates Santa Gertrudis bulls with Santa Gertrudis cows, he is keeping closed herd book.

performance record Just what it says. All the dope on a cow or bull—its conformation, gain rate, ancestry, disposition, adaptability to climate. (A lot like a tout sheet.)

riding herd More vanished romance. Cowboys used to ride herd on cattle—drive them ahead in a pack by riding behind and to the sides—if there was a roundup for shipping or branding.

semen sales Cattle trade journals run ads for these transactions constantly, and no one snickers. A small vial of a prepotent bull's semen, selling for somewhere around twenty-five dollars, can get dozens of cows profitably pregnant with future high gainers; thus in one year a single bull can sire thousands. The bull's owner makes his money by charging for the breeding certificate, which must accompany every insemination.

squeeze chute Portable, narrow pen into which cattlemen drive heifers and calves so they can be branded.

Standard of Excellence Set of traits, minutely described, to which every Santa Gertrudis calf and heifer aspires. The rewards are high; if a Santa Gertrudis bull scores perfectly on the Standard of Excellence chart, he has an active sex life, travels extensively to cattle shows, hears human beings bid huge prices for him, and dies at the age of twenty. If he scores only the median, he gets castrated and ends up in a freezer at the A & P.

THE BEST OF THE BREEDS
Know Your Bloodlines

ANGUS *Like many Americans, gains a lot of weight on relatively little feed. Soft black or red coat, polled. Especially classy: the Marcus family owns them.*

CHAROLAIS *French origins, white or light straw color. As with silver and oil, Bunker Hunt has some of the best in the business.*

BEEFMASTER *Sexy, known for high reproduction yield. Comes in almost all colors. Breed's slogan: "Not perfect, but close."*

HEREFORD *Just like the UT homecoming queen, sweet-faced and sweet-natured. White face, red body. Enjoying a resurgence in popularity.*

BRAHMAN *Extreme hump and lots of loose skin. Breed of choice for rodeo bull riding. Light gray or red to almost black.*

LIMOUSIN *As the name suggests, loaded with class. Red-gold color, French origins, relatively small frame. Known as "the butcher's animal" for its high meat yield.*

No one wants to be in the embarrassing position of not knowing which breeds of cattle your friends raise—what could be worse, after finally receiving that prized invitation to the Connally ranch, than not being able to remember whether they have Red Brangus or Santa Gertrudis? If you play a lot of cattle-oriented "I Spy" as you tool along the interstate a basic familiarity with Texas's major breeds is required. To help you make it through the quirks of cattledom, here is an illustrated guide.

PINZGAUER *Absolutely huge. Black with white underbelly and backside. Easy calvers. Breed slogan: "Bred in the Alps, proven in the Tropics."*

SHORTHORN *Rectangular, boxy shape; wide between the eyes; red, white and roan coloring. Females are "large milkers." First European breed imported to United States.*

RED BRANGUS *Part Angus, part Brahman. Despite his nickname, "big red muley," the bull is known for his virility. Large in stature, red in color, polled.*

SIMMENTAL *Advertised in breed brochure as "excellent producers of milk, butter, and cheese." (We haven't figured out yet how they get all of these straight out of the cow.) Red and white coloring.*

SANTA GERTRUDIS *America's first beef breed, founded at the King Ranch. Cherry red. Heifers said to "make good mothers." Greer Garson owns Santas.*

ZEBU *Bears strong facial resemblance to Iran's highest-ranking clergy. Asian origins, gray coloration. Extremely large hump, droopy ears, sad face.*

CATTLE AUCTIONS
The Real Meat Markets

Beef on parade.

The cattle auction is as steeped in tradition as it is in big bucks and dung. It is the country boy's country club, for it magically combines serious wheelin' and dealin' with enough social horsing around to make it fun. It's the one place where the average country rancher can rub business and social elbows with the cattle aristocracy.

People — or "cattle people" as they like to be called — go to auctions for a whole slew of reasons. For most of them, the lure is the opportunity to do some matchmaking for the heifers back on the spread. For others it is the chance to add a little human camaraderie to their lives — a cattle auction gives the average cowpoke a sense of belonging to a world outside the ranch. And for the cowboys-come-lately, it's a chance to show off how much they know about their chosen breed. And how much money they have.

WHERE THE BULLS ARE

AMARILLO. The Western Stockyards here is the proud setting of the world's largest cattle auction — and the original Dr. Pepper clock. It is a veritable bull-a-rama, with more than 600,000 head sold annually. The Hereford is the sweetheart of the ring and the sweetbreads are the favorite in the cafeteria. (Mondays and Tuesdays, year-round.)

FORT WORTH. The Fort Worth Stockyards Exchange is the granddaddy of cattle auctions. It once handled two million head a year, and though it's slumped to a mere quarter of a million, it's still where the West begins. You can smell it from blocks away. (Mondays and Thursdays, year-round.)

KINGSVILLE. The King Ranch sale has maintained its reputation for more than thirty years as one of the classiest private auctions. They sell only twenty Santa Gertrudis bulls and twenty horses, but as many as 3,000 people show up for the event. Robert Redford started his horse ranch by buying stock here. (Once a year, usually in October.)

HOUSTON. The Western Heritage Sale is where man meets beast in a hotel ballroom. Twelve hundred invited guests troop to the Shamrock Hilton each year in long gowns and Western-cut tuxes (some black, some powder blue double knit) to bid on cattle, horses—and art. No one can say these duded-up ranchers don't take culture seriously; last year they spent more than $2.5 million on paintings of cowboys, heifers, and Indians. Most overheard question: "Is John here?"—referring to sale organizer and superstar John Connally. (Once a year, invitation only.)

AUCTION ETIQUETTE

There is a clubby atmosphere around a cattle auction. From the moment you enter the sales arena, the rapid-fire, twangy gibberish of the auctioneer is enough to confuse the untrained ear. Familiarity with auction protocol, in both attire and bidding technique, is vital to even the most casual of cattle people.

HATS. Worn at all times during auction. Important bidding tool. A rancher who knows the ropes always has just the right hat — a Panama straw. The hat is sweat-stained and shows lopsided creases he's made himself if he's a real working cattleman. It's unsullied if he's more of a gentleman rancher; this proves he's got enough money for more than one hat.

BOOTS. The genuine cattle tycoon always sports a pair of expensive, usually hand-tooled, reptile boots. Lizard and python are popular, but only in the right colors: black or brown. *Never* wear red or patchwork leather cowboy boots to an auction. If you do, your bid will probably be ignored.

WOMEN'S ACCESSORIES. For those in the know, appropriate jewelry is a must. It is your duty as ranch wife to familiarize the world with your brand. Also, always carry your King Ranch handbag, with either your initials or your ranch insignia in hand-tooled letters on the side.

BIDDING TECHNIQUE. Subtlety is everything. All you need to do is touch the brim of your hat or gently lift your auction program to place a bid. *Never* call out or wave to the ring man or auctioneer — it's the bull's turn to be in the spotlight.

SEATING. The lowest tier of seats is reserved for the serious, big-spending ranchers. *Do not* take one of these seats unless you are a member of the "club."

GENTLEMAN'S AGREEMENT. If a fellow rancher has done you the favor of buying some of your herd at a prior sale, it is your duty to buy some of his herd at a later sale. Gentleman ranchers always look after one another.

AUCTIONEERS. If you're going to have a sale of your own at your spread, make sure you get a good auctioneer. One unlucky cattleman hired an auctioneer who made the mistake of revealing a little too much information about the bull he was trying to sell — the bull's lineage sounded like a *Who's Who* of dwarfed cattle. By the end of the bidding, the careers of both bull and auctioneer were over. Callers advertise in the back of *The Cattleman*, which you've subscribed to for years.

THE TEXAN'S COAT OF ARMS

A brand implies all that is good — vast acres, numerous herds, membership in the Texas and Southwestern Cattle Raisers Association. The association's registry in Fort Worth (they have 200,000 brands on file) is the *Debrett's Peerage* of Texas. (You're cattle royalty if your brand was registered before 1900.) Burned with a hot branding iron into the left rump of young cows, the brand is still the most reliable way to establish the ownership of an animal that has strayed or been rustled.

The most prestigious place a Texas cattleman or cattlewoman can put his or her brand is on the "branded stairway" at Texas A & M's Kleberg Center. Some of the most famous cattle brands in Texas include the following — and nearly all have been burned into the famous stairwell.

HK. Recorded in 1859 in Nueces County and used by Henrietta King when she ran the King Ranch. Now used on the King Ranch's La Puerta de Agua Dulce section.

PITCHFORK. Used on the Herefords raised commercially on the 163,000-acre Pitchfork Land and Cattle Company spread outside Guthrie. Originally registered in south Texas about 1836.

LBJ. The personal brand of the thirty-sixth president of the United States. Ranch manager Dale Malechek continues to use this brand at the LBJ Ranch in Gillespie County.

SAM. Brand of Sam Houston, president of the Republic of Texas. Used for only a short period of time at his Washington County spread.

XIT. Designed and first used in 1885 at Buffalo Springs, largest of the seven ranch headquarters of the famous three-million-acre XIT Ranch.

CIRCLE G. First registered in 1835 by Peter Gallagher, rancher and builder of San Antonio's Menger Hotel. Still used on the original ten-thousand-acre Bexar County ranch, now owned by Mrs. V. H. McNutt.

HAT. The Hat Ranch brand was registered in Mitchell County in 1892. Ranch was owned by A. B. "Sug" Robertson, granddaddy of actor Cliff Robertson.

YO. Brand used at the Mountain Home Ranch in Kerr County by the Schreiner family cattle and hunting operations.

ROCKING Y. Owned by Robert and John Yturria of the Bexar County Yturria Ranch. Registered before 1845 to Manuel Yturria, who came to Texas in 1803. Ranch was originally part of a Spanish land grant, and the brand is still being used.

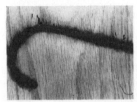

LAZY 9. Used on Hereford cattle at the Merle T. Waggoner Ranch near Decatur. First registered in Wise County in 1895.

JN. Brand used by John and Nellie Connally on their Floresville cattle and horse ranch in Wilson county. The Connallys once had a brand shaped like the state of Texas.

12 Places Besides a Cow to Put It

Better than any monogram, your cattle brand should not be confined to the backside of some old cow. Now that you've got it all designed and ready to go, there are a number of swell places to display it.

1. Printed on watermarked vellum stationery. Crane's is preferred. Frost's and Neiman's will make dies.

2. Embroidered on the pocket or cuff of a Western shirt.

3. Hand-stamped on the back of a tooled leather cowboy belt.

4. Painted on the doors of the pickup truck or sides of the horse trailer.

5. Placed on a steak-branding iron for personalized T-bones.

6. Stitched on top of a gimme cap.

7. Knitted into a design on the back of a handmade sweater.

8. Engraved on the family's Georgian silver tea service.

9. Appliquéd on custom-made chaps from Ryon's.

10. Worked into an inlay and an overlay on custom-crafted boots.

11. Printed on checks to distinguish the ranch account from the city account.

12. Engraved on cuff links, belt buckles, collar tips, heel guards, spurs.

HORSE POWER
16 Hands & a Lotta Heart

While a custom-made barrel racer's outfit from Ryon's may be a cowgirl's best friend, the horse remains a cowboy's closest companion and most revered possession. This special friend and fellow worker is the object of much fuss—especially when it comes to selecting the ideal soul mate. For the strict cowpoke, likely as not it will be a quarter horse, first bred in Texas and one of the few things in the horseman's life guaranteed to obey its master. For those riders with a touch of flair, the selection would probably be the more exotic Appaloosa. After all, a spotted rump on virtually any walking creature is bound to turn some heads. For ladies and gentlemen who prefer blonds, the palomino is the pleasure horse of choice. And for those who lead more unpredictable lives, the crazy-quilted paint horse hits the spot. Of course, horses do not exist for cowboys alone. The modern Texan finds that these four-legged critters come in handy in lots of situations.

Gifts. Horses always make a nice present, especially for that daughter or son who already has

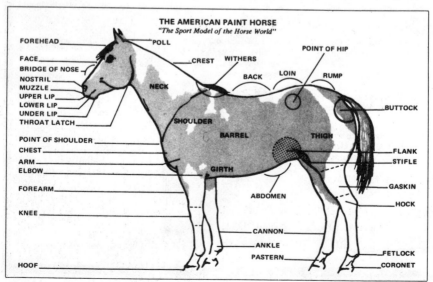

THE AMERICAN PAINT HORSE
"The Sport Model of the Horse World"

FOREHEAD — POLL — POINT OF HIP — FACE — CREST — WITHERS — BRIDGE OF NOSE — NOSTRIL — BACK — LOIN — RUMP — MUZZLE — NECK — UPPER LIP — LOWER LIP — UNDER LIP — BUTTOCK — THROAT LATCH — SHOULDER — POINT OF SHOULDER — BARREL — THIGH — CHEST — FLANK — ARM — STIFLE — ELBOW — GIRTH — FOREARM — GASKIN — ABDOMEN — HOCK — KNEE — CANNON — ANKLE — FETLOCK — PASTERN — CORONET — HOOF

everything. Gets them back to the soil.

Transportation. When you've left the pickup back at the spread and the Caddy's in for repairs, your horse will do just fine.

Decoration. Many Texans use horses as ornamentation for the spread. These are the folks who watch the animals from the veranda at sunset, the strains of "Sugarfoot" running through their heads.

Tax deduction. Comforting and practical. A herd of lovely creatures can often prove enough of a loss to write off on your income taxes.

Work. Though it's part of a dying breed, the work horse continues the thankless job of working the land on the spread.

Rodeos. The festival atmosphere of the rodeo is the ideal place to show off the work horse. These special beasts are the Dallas Cowboys of the horse family.

Sex appeal. Horses are used in some quarters to provide an excuse for acquiring a team of cowboys to ride them.

Wardrobe accessory. Once you've gone to the trouble of buying handmade python boots, sterling silver spurs, and a suede and leather hand-tooled saddle, you've got to have something to use them on. The horse continues to be the most practical yet stylish accessory in anyone's Western wardrobe.

THE BEST HANDMADE SADDLE IN TEXAS

The Bob Kleberg Special from the Running W Saddle Shop ("Western Wear for Horses and People"), in Kingsville. Fully handmade to provide maximum strength, durability, and comfort, this saddle is as easy on the horse as it is on the rider. A working cowboy can spend hours mounted up and not get saddle-sore. Created for the real cowboy, not a saddle for pleasure or for show.

Made of number one skirting leather, the Bob Kleberg Special features a rawhide-covered mountain-pine tree, steel horn and hardware, riggings, and covered stirrups. A good-looking pair of saddlebags in matching leather is a smart option. Stamped under the cantle is the famous ranch's registered trademark and its Running W brand. (*Running W Saddle Shop, P.O. Box 1594, Kingsville 78363*)

RODEOS & ROUNDUPS
Riding Herd on the Circuit

Losing it.

A Texas rodeo (pronounced "roadie-oh") is a field day for cowboys — a sort of cowpunchers' Olympics. However — soft drink ads aside — it is not always clear why cowboys would want to participate in these gladiatorial contests of the old West. For some it is the opportunity to show off those special skills learned back at the ranch. Chances are that the folks who come to the arena will have more appreciation for cowpoke flair and guts than the jaded old hands at the spread. Rodeos also provide an excellent opportunity to impress that sweet little angel from Diboll or Cut 'n Shoot — if your charm and personality don't catch her eye, maybe risking your life and limb on the back of some ornery Brahman will. Of course there are the trophy saddles and cash prizes, but $1,500 hardly explains the cowboy's eagerness to break his back. The desire to pile up serious macho credentials does.

GRAND ENTRY

All rodeos open with something called the "grand entry," which is nothing more than a horse traffic jam made up of folks who couldn't make the cut for the *real* rodeo events. It's basically an equestrian family affair where everyone has a chance to be in the center ring and get noticed. Sometimes there are more people in the ring than in the stands. The grand entry also gives you the chance to wear those rodeo-bright day-glo shirts that are a bit too gaudy to wear anywhere else. The Texas flag is all-important to this occasion; as each of the dozens of riders trots past the flag, hats are removed and placed over hearts in a gesture of undying love for the Lone Star state.

Anyone who participates in a rodeo is clearly made of stronger stuff than the average cow-puncher. You've got to be more than tough: you've got to be mean. A rodeo cowboy has to ride that bull or bronc with a ven-geance, as if his life depended on it ... and it often does. These life-threatening events come in two categories.

ROUGH STOCK EVENTS

Where you show your tenac-ity—otherwise known as insan-ity—over a set period of time. In the rough stock event, the cow-boy is given eight seconds to stay on a bucking bronc (horse) or bull. The bronc-riding events are per-formed both with and without a

Getting numbered.

THE TEXAS PRISON RODEO

Notorious as the ultimate in pent-up (and unpent) emotions. Every Sunday in October, boots and hats are added to the more traditional black-and-white uni-form as some fifty Huntsville State Prison inmates become rodeo cowboys—the toughest, meanest cowpunchers behind bars. One of the favorite tests of these incarcerated cowboys is called "hard money." About forty convicts get in the ring with a 1,500-pound Brahman bull. The goal is to cozy up to the beast and remove from between his horns a small bag of money. Whoever gets the bag gets to keep the money. A difficult way of making some loose change. Other amusements:

    1. Music. The convicts sell original records and tapes re-corded by their own C&W band.

    2. Humor. Inmate stand-up comics entertain crowds with their special brand of humor.

    3. Beauty. In the best Texas tradition a Miss Texas Prison Rodeo is selected on the first rodeo Sunday.

saddle. And, as if the ride weren't spirited enough, the rider is required to press his spurs into the horse's sides and shoulders. (The spurs are supposed to be dulled to protect the horse.) Bull riding is the toughest of the rodeo events. Here, the cowboy is not *required* to dig his spurs into the Brahman, but can gain extra points if he proves crazed enough to do so.

TIMED EVENTS

Where you prove your prowess in as short a time as you can muster. Timed events are somewhat closer to the activities you'd find on a working ranch: calf roping, steer roping and wrestling, team roping. In these events, the race is against both the clock and the other contestants. Calf and steer roping are essentially the same thing — the cowboy ropes the animal, jumps off his horse, then ties together any three of the animal's legs. Team roping is for two riders. The goal is for one cowboy to rope the calf while the other ropes its hind legs; neither horseman leaves his mount. Steer wrestling, otherwise known as bulldogging, is a pure test of brawn. The cowboy, mounted, charges after the steer, jumps off his horse, then literally takes the bull by the horns and tries to drag the animal down, all in a matter of seconds.

SPECIALTY EVENTS

Lots of flash, lots of skill. Slapstick comedy with a Texas twist. To keep the kids from begging for another Coke and hot dog. Among the most popular are the cow milking event and "snubbin' and buckin'." In snubbin' and buckin' a "ghost rider" leads into the ring an unsaddled bronc with a gunnysack over its head. Another cowboy, dressed in wooly chaps and Tom Mix hat, rushes in and saddles the horse, which is by this time bucking wildly. He then jumps onto the back of the ghost rider's horse, and from that precarious position launches himself onto the newly saddled buckin' bronc. The cowboy rides the bronc for a set period of time and is judged on style and flash — if he has survived the previous steps.

Calf scramble.

Bucking the bronc.

BARREL RACING

There is a place for women in these male-dominated rodeos: barrel racing. In fact, no men participate in this event at all. The sweethearts of the rodeo race individually on horseback around a configuration of barrels, trying to get as close to the barrels as possible without knocking them over. Sue Pirtle and Martha Josey are the acknowledged champions.

OTHER GOINGS ON

Apart from the scheduled events, there is considerable behind-the-scenes activity. For some cowboys there just aren't enough opportunities in life to get into a good fistfight. The action under the grandstand and behind

THE ALL-GIRL RODEO

It's the women's roller derby of the country crowd, the sport for the Texas tomboy. Cowboy skills learned growing up on a ranch become competition for tough, gritty women who ride, rope, and wrangle in events just like the boys. They like to be called "just a bunch of ranch girls," but most of the contestants in the ten or so all-girl rodeos held in Texas each year work nine-to-five jobs during the week. Femininity remains a concern; rather than get their nails dirty bulldogging, they practice "steer undecorating," pulling a ribbon from the steer's horns instead of wrestling the animal to the ground.

These rodeo queens do participate in the toughest event of them all, bull riding. However, the all-girl group rides the Brahman for only six seconds, and they can hold on with both hands. As one Cowgirl Hall of Famer puts it, "We're ladies. We like to stay in the ladies' place."

the horse trailer is second only to events in the ring. A rodeo just wouldn't be complete without brawls, cheating around, and budding love affairs—after all, where did television's torrid romance between Sue Ellen Ewing and Dusty Farlow first get kickin'? A lot of folks attend rodeos solely for the entertainment value of these cowboy soap operas.

Texas Type No. 6

RODEO RIDER

The cowboy daredevil.

RCA felt hat

smiling; posted a high mark to win (stayed on more than eight seconds); has just been asked t endorse a line of jeans

pinch of Skoal snuff wedged between cheek & gum; five o'clock shadow, grizzly

bandana tied in front, knotted at center of throat

Larry Mahan shirt with floral yoke, cuffs, contrasting stitching, snaps, & arrowhead-trimmed inset pockets

Tex Tan's bull rope, plaited leather grip

Leo Camarillo's deerskin roper gloves; black rosin on palm

pocket contents: PRCA membership card; receipt entry fee; prize-money che

embossed cowhide belt with oak leaf motif & white buck-stitching, nickname hand-stamped at back

trophy buckle of German silver, engraved with bull rider motif and year he won it

boot-cut Wrangler jeans

bowed legs from riding real bull

injuries on body: scraped skin from climbing up chute gates; separated shoulder; torn hamstring muscle

M. L. Leddy's custom-made batwing chaps

silver-mounted personalized spurs with mahogany skirting, leather straps

Rio of Mercedes' eel-skin boots with cutting heel scratched up from rubbing against chutes

BARREL RACER

Never lost her tomboy ways.

hair in side ponytail held with horseshoe-shaped embossed leather clip

smiling; just been signed to design a line of rodeo equipment that will bear her name

Western crossover tie

embossed German silver circle medallion

Ryon's custom-made "Supreme" blouse; solid hot pink body to match pants, contrasting plaid yoke and cuffs, double yoke in back

embossed floral cowhide belt with white buck-stitching, name at back

fractured finger; several bruises and bumps

in hands: racing bat; another trophy buckle; winning check; ribbon

hot-pink gabardine pants, custom-made at Ryon's; flared legs, almost bell-bottomed; fit snugly around thighs and hips

huge oval trophy buckle, German silver, engraved with barrel racer; won at last barrel racing event

several bangle bracelets from Montgomery Ward's — she puts them on after her ride

pocket contents: Women's Professional Rodeo Association membership card; picture of Tee Wolman

M. L. Leddy's custom-made red suede calfskin chaps with deep side fringe

stain on chaps — sweat and drop of neat's-foot oil from polishing her tack before events began

Connie Combs's barrel racing saddle

Martha Josey's shin guards — strapped underneath

TOP TEXAS RODEOS

Summertime in Texas is known as "cowboy Christmas" because there are so many rodeos scheduled—open, amateur, and professional. The professional circuit is managed by the Professional Rodeo Cowboy Association (PRCA). Prize money counts toward points, enough of which will lead to the Lone Star Circuit finals in Fort Worth and the National Rodeo finals in Oklahoma City.

ALL-GIRL RODEO, *Hereford.* Country's largest all-girl rodeo. Because the National Cowgirl Hall of Fame is located in Hereford an impressive induction ceremony always takes place. Draws top Women Professional Rodeo Association (WPRA) riders from all over the U.S. (Second weekend in May.)

BLACK RODEO, *Brookshire.* Emancipation Day in Texas, June 19, used to be the only day that black cowboys and farm hands got together to rodeo. In recent years more and more rodeos with black participants have started up. This is one of the best. Rufus Green, "Treetop," and Calvin Greely are the crowd-pleasin' stars of soul rodeo. (Sunday afternoons, at least eight months of the year.)

COWTOWN RODEO, *Cowtown Coliseum, Fort Worth.* Family-oriented, authentic rough-and-tough rodeo. PRCA-approved, the Cowtown schedules all the basic rodeo events plus special features: calf scramble for kids, wild-horse race, specialty acts, and a wild cow milking. (Every Sunday night; March–May and September–November.)

KOW BELL RODEO, *Mansfield.* America's only weekly indoor year-round rodeo. Started in 1958, it's a family affair with local ranchers, their wives and kids leading the grand entry. Good clowns. Very popular with foreign tour groups. Fifteen miles south of Fort Worth. (Every Saturday.)

LONE STAR CIRCUIT FINALS RODEO, *Cowtown Coliseum, Fort Worth.* Where all the top Texas cowboys come together. Having finished their year on the Lone Star Circuit, winning PRCA cowboys compete for the Top Texas Cowboy championship. In these grueling finals a cowboy must enter in events all four nights to qualify. Top cowgirl barrel racers are entered here too. So popular that tickets must be bought in advance. (Four consecutive nights in late December.)

MESQUITE CHAMPIONSHIP RODEO, *Mesquite.* Adjacent to city limits of Dallas in a covered arena. Where Don Gay, six-time world champion bull rider and Monty Henson, two-time world champion saddle bronc rider got their winning starts. Out back a "kiddie korral" where budding buckaroos can pet young ranch animals and ride real ponies. (Every Friday and Saturday night from April to September.)

PECOS RODEO, *Pecos.* Home of the world's first rodeo. Staged here in 1883 as an informal contest among cowboys of early ranches like Hashknife, the NA, and the Lazy Y, now a PRCA-sanctioned rodeo. (Every July 4th.)

TEXAS COWBOY REUNION, *Stamford.* Nation's oldest and largest open rodeo. Sponsored by an organization of retired cowboys, it has been held every year since 1930. The color and excitement of the old West. All basic rodeo events plus wild mare race and breakaway calf roping for men sixty-five or older. (First week in July.)

SOUTHWESTERN EXPOSITION AND FAT STOCK SHOW, *Cowtown Coliseum, Fort Worth.*/**HOUSTON LIVESTOCK SHOW AND RODEO,** *Astrodome, Houston.*/**SAN ANTONIO LIVESTOCK EXPOSITION AND RODEO,** *Joe Freeman Coliseum, San Antonio.* For nearly two weeks each year city slickers in these three Texas cities don their Noconas and Resistols and play cowboy and cowgirl. Children take off from school because the rodeo has come to town! On opening day in each of these cities hundreds of horses, riders, and chuck wagons parade through the main streets in a colorful procession, known as a trail ride. Famous C&W singers headline the rodeos. Pickup trucks are raffled off. (Southwestern: late January–early February; Houston: mid-March; San Antonio: February.)

Chapter 4
STRIKING IT RICH

15 NAMES TO REMEMBER IN OIL CITY U.S.A.

Nobody has to be told that Houston is the town that oil built. But if you think it's all Gulf and Exxon, take a look at this list of Oil City's top fifteen petroleum companies (the first is the easy one). Then try to wangle a lunch at the Petroleum Club atop the Exxon Building and head straight for the Wildcatter's Grill. That's where you get the bottom-hole information: kickbacks in Indonesia, that SEC investigation of Mobil, takeovers real and false. (Two oil CEO's had lunch at the Petroleum Club. By the time they got back to their offices, Wall Street was talking merger.)

COMPANY	1980 EARNINGS
SHELL OIL	$1,541,600,000
TENNECO	726,000,000
THE COASTAL CORP.	109,500,000
TEXAS EASTERN	219,754,000
UNITED ENERGY RESOURCES	165,454,000
EL PASO CO.	302,995,000
TRANSCO	112,500,000
HOUSTON NATURAL GAS	219,846,000
PENNZOIL	308,509,000
PANHANDLE EASTERN	183,700,000
SUPERIOR OIL	334,458,000
ZAPATA	43,627,000
HOUSTON OIL & MINERALS	79,550,000
POGO PRODUCING	54,030,000
INEXCO OIL	22,576,000

THE BIG BOOM
Oil Blows In & Texas Takes Off

On the morning of January 10, 1901, Lucas Number 1, a well on Spindletop Hill near Beaumont, started coughing up mud and pieces of broken pipe. It was just clearing its throat. At 10:30, the well gushed out a seventy-five-foot geyser of rich, black oil.

Thus Texans found out that God had given them the Big Boom.

Lucas Number 1 rained crude at the rate of 75,000 barrels a day. By the time it was capped, that well had completely transformed the state. Before Spindletop came in, Texans were famous for two things—cattle and the Alamo. That was fine; everyone could go around pretending he had cow patties on his boots and that his ancestor was Colonel Travis. But it wasn't enough. What was desperately needed for Texas to come into its own were large amounts of quickly obtained, riotously spent, democratically distributed, all-American cash.

Which is exactly what Spindletop and the fields that opened up provided.

Every time a new wildcat turned yet another hick town into the center of the American oil industry, more sons of Texas could strike it rich, after a few drunken, hardworking months in the oil patch. Then the newly wealthy could concentrate on the important things: buying islands in the Bahamas, flying personal Lear jets, acquiring football teams, and driving all the Old Money in the state (and the world) absolutely batty with their ostentatious vulgarity, common origins, and oil depletion allowances. Thanks to Spindletop, Texans not only had money, they also had a new folk figure, The Oilman. The Big Boom keeps Texans dreaming of when they'll be Oilmen, too.

It also keeps them all working. The Big Boom has a tremendous transitional value. All those oil boom towns ensure that Texans always have some other kind of boom to get rich on. The real estate boom in Houston. The aircraft boom in Dallas. The insurance boom. The commodities boom. The construction boom. But no Texan ever, ever forgets the one boom that's responsible for it all—the one he'll cash in on someday. God meant it to be.

FROM SPINDLETOP TO SPINOFFS

The Evolution of Black Gold:

Four hundred million years ago the shallow seas of the Ordovician period covered Texas with microscopic marine life. The seas receded, and layers of sandstone and limestone weighed down on the fossils of those itty-bitty creatures and crushed them into hydrocarbons — petroleum. There's a whole lot more — about anticlines and overhangs, salt domes and chalk — which is why taking at least one geology course at UT is not a bad idea. Suffice it to say that Mother Nature left Texas sitting on an ocean of oil.

And there she sat for a few score million years. The Indians were no help to development— they either used oil seepage as an ointment, or they drank it. DeSoto's men used it to caulk their boats.

Then the Industrial Revolution came.

City populations soared. Peo-

The Schlumberger ("slum' bər zhay"), or wire-line logging truck. It can tell you whether you have a duster or a gusher.

ple needed kerosene for their lamps and stoves. In 1859 Colonel Lewis Drake drilled the world's first oil wells in Titusville, Pennsylvania. He became rich. In 1865 Lynis T. Barnett drilled for the first oil in Texas. He became poor. But he did obtain a lease for drilling rights, making an invaluable contribution to the growth of the Texas legal industry.

Meanwhile, the Pennsylvania oil boom just didn't seem authentic. The fields developed slowly.

What *was* authentic was Pennsylvania money. A Pennsylvania oilman, John Davidson, was behind the first successful oil well drilled in Texas, at Corsicana in 1894. *Successful* is a relative word. The first Corsicana wells yielded a few barrels a day. Six years later, the Pittsburgh wildcatting firm of James Guffey and James H. Galey provided the capital so that two Texans, Patillo Higgins and Anthony Lucas, could drill into the Spindletop salt dome near Beaumont. When Spindletop hit its stride, it yielded a very satisfactory hundred thousand barrels a day.

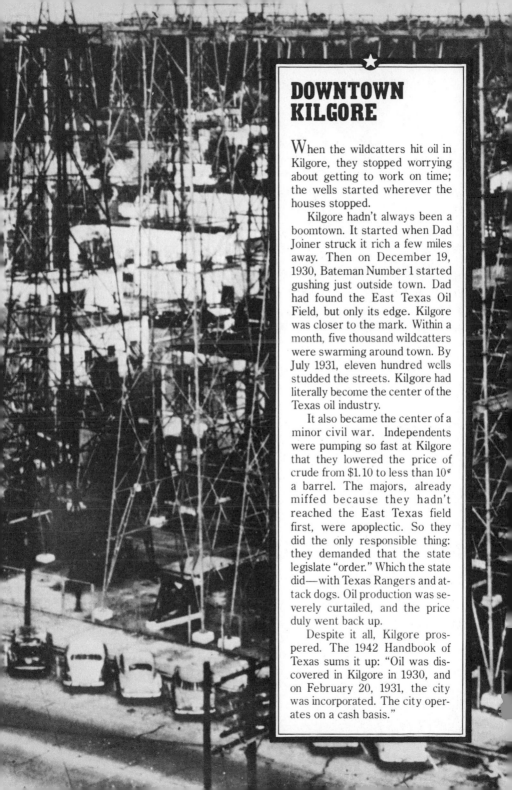

DOWNTOWN KILGORE

When the wildcatters hit oil in Kilgore, they stopped worrying about getting to work on time; the wells started wherever the houses stopped.

Kilgore hadn't always been a boomtown. It started when Dad Joiner struck it rich a few miles away. Then on December 19, 1930, Bateman Number 1 started gushing just outside town. Dad had found the East Texas Oil Field, but only its edge. Kilgore was closer to the mark. Within a month, five thousand wildcatters were swarming around town. By July 1931, eleven hundred wells studded the streets. Kilgore had literally become the center of the Texas oil industry.

It also became the center of a minor civil war. Independents were pumping so fast at Kilgore that they lowered the price of crude from $1.10 to less than 10¢ a barrel. The majors, already miffed because they hadn't reached the East Texas field first, were apoplectic. So they did the only responsible thing: they demanded that the state legislate "order." Which the state did—with Texas Rangers and attack dogs. Oil production was severely curtailed, and the price duly went back up.

Despite it all, Kilgore prospered. The 1942 Handbook of Texas sums it up: "Oil was discovered in Kilgore in 1930, and on February 20, 1931, the city was incorporated. The city operates on a cash basis."

Lucas #1 blows in.

In 1908, Henry Ford introduced the Model T, the first mass-produced American car with a gasoline-burning internal combustion engine. The gasoline was made from Texas oil. Fifteen million Model Ts were produced.

In 1911, Standard Oil of New Jersey lost its monopoly on the oil industry. Independents and larger outfits like Gulf and the Texas Company were free to grab for all the Texas crude they could get.

In 1913, Congress created the oil depletion allowance, the sweetest piece of legislation the Yankees ever devised. The allowance meant that oilmen could deduct as much as 27 percent of their income before paying taxes. (Made sense; the more oil Texas gave America, the less was left in the ground.) The allowance remains sacred to Texans.

In 1917, the Texas legislature decided that oil pipelines were common carriers and that, by extension, oil and gas in all phases of production and transport were to be regulated by the Texas Railroad Commission. The Commission rapidly became an oilman's best friend.

In 1920, John L. Lewis became president of the United Mine Workers. Under Lewis the UMW started going on strike every spring. American industrialists made a twofold discovery. Oil could take the place of coal in many machines. And oil, flowing in pipes, *never* goes on strike.

In 1930, the Depression was forgotten in East Texas. The field needed more men to work it than were available. Henceforth, oil production made sure all business fluctuations stopped on the far side of the Red River. (During the 1974 recession, Texas oil prices soared and unemployment went down.)

In 1946, the Petroleum Club was founded in Houston. After the Texas Railroad Commission, it became the best club an old wildcatter could join.

In 1955, nearly four million gas guzzlers rolled off assembly lines in Detroit. America's love affair with the automobile was reaching fever pitch.

Texas oil was here to stay.

MINI LEXICON No. 2
OIL

Getting a job on a rig is easy; around seven in the morning, go to a coffeeshop in Giddings—or anywhere else in the Chalk—flex your muscles, and look broke. But first memorize this lexicon.

boll weevil First-time oil field worker. Giddings is a-crawl with them.

blowout Gusher. When too much pressure builds up from the presence of natural gas, the oil blows out of the hole.

bulldog Tool used to fish broken pipe from the hole. Canine metaphors abound in oil talk.

the Chalk The Austin Chalk, the hottest new oil patch in the state.

doghouse Shack on the drilling floor that doubles as an office and a storage space.

doodlebug Amateur geologist who promises that if he can't smell the oil out, his divining rod will do the job. An object of some, but not total, derision.

dry hole "Duster," a well with no oil or gas at the bottom.

fracing Or fracturing, in plain English. Extracting more oil from well by widening openings in well's rock deposits.

mousehole Opening through the rig floor through which extra lengths of pipe are inserted.

pebble pup Assists rockhound.

pig Scraping tool sent through a pipe to clean it out.

rockhound Field geologist. Responsible for figuring out where to drill. Often wrong.

roughnecks Men who drill well. Crew hierarchy: tool pusher (responsible for several crews), driller (on-site straw boss), tool dresser, derrick man, lead-tong man, backup, motorman.

roustabouts Workers who manage well once it's pumping and fun of striking it rich is past. You do not want to be a roustabout.

spud in Start drilling a well.

turn that bit to the right "Keep drilling." Usually twenty-four hours a day, since rigs and equipment are rented on a twenty-four-hour basis.

suitcase rock Geological heartbreaker. Layer of rock beyond which drill won't go. Time to pack your suitcase and move on.

tightholer Oilman who doesn't talk about his projects.

tower Corruption of "tour," or shift, of which there are usually three.

twist-off Length of pipe that breaks in a well. Also partying, roughneck style.

wildcatter Noncompany man. Adventurer who tries to find oil where no one else has looked. What Texas is all about.

Texas Type No. 7

THE WILD CATTER

Tenacious gambler; knows he's got a gusher this time.

Vogt's hand-braided natural rawhide hatband with eight sterling silver ferrules

Resistol's "Las Vegas" hat in whiskey, 3XXX beaver with four-inch brim

smiling; just received some very good "bottom hole" information; acquired large wildcat lease block in Austin Chalk; also, the gauge on nipple valve is showing extraordinary pressure

rough, tough, and ready; handsome hustler

Texas Colonel clip-on tie

M. L. Leddy's hand-engraved sterling silver collar tips with 14-karat overlays

shirt pocket contents: solid gold Mark Cross pen for signing leases

"Travis Club" cigar made by San Antonio's Finck Cigar Co.

Stelzig's white satin striped shirt with flap pockets, yoke, snap front

alligator belt

Cutter Bill's silver oval buckle with 10-karat-gold oil derrick in center

M. L. Leddy's cuff and jacket buttons with 10-karat-gold oil derricks on solid silver

diamond horseshoe ring; UT class ring with large diamond in center; gold Rolex — the Texas Timex

M. L. Leddy's ostrich attaché case with brass hardware, lined with suede pigskin briefcase contents: oil prospectuses; unsigned leases; can of pork and beans (a reminder of when he was hitting dry holes before the big well came in); copy of Wall Street Journal; *Gucci phone book with Red Adair's number circled in red; Mark Cross appointment book (year's supply of Petroleum Club lunches)*

in pocket: keys to Lear jet (jet has "White Wing Dove" painted on side doors); keys for the Big Spread; money clip with $3,000 in cash

Cutter Bill's alligator wallet contents: royalty check from current well; Petroleum Club membership card; picture of favorite well; gold American Express card

classic Western-style suit, custom-made, tan gabardine twill, yoke pockets, five-button vest, keystone belt loops

Lucchese boots, bought before the company stopped hand-making them; still has his last in San Antonio

THE ROUGH NECK

Natural-born troublemaker, but gets the job done.

handsome in a rough, cocky way

silver hard hat with name in Magic Marker, covered with decals: picture of a pit bull; "Oil Field Trash and Proud of It"

Fu Manchu mustache

hair on the long side; greasy

smiling; the Schlumberger truck is on its way

very tan; sunburned, peeling shoulders

no shirt — lifeguard mentality in effect

bandana in back pocket to wipe oily pipes

in hands: protective gloves; safety goggles; spud pipe

pocket contents: keys to pickup; keys to motel room he rents down the road; $203.50 fine for disorderly conduct (started fight with another oil worker on nearby rig last night); Red Adair's phone number; $1,000 in cash, rolled up

spots of dried mud and oil; he is dirty

Sears heavy-duty cotton pants; once were gray, now very dirty & caked with mud, caustic soda, oil

steel-toed leather lace-ups, spots of caustic soda on them, some of shoe eaten away by soda

THE SUPERBARONS
Risk-Takers, Lease-Stakers, & Profit-Makers

Ordinary people (i.e., those with incomes of less than $900,000 a year) share the same images of Texas's oil rich: jewel-covered wives, two Congressmen in every pocket, fleets of private cars, private jets, private orchestras, private *everything*—all marked by a capital-intensive rambunctiousness as crude and expensive as the stuff they pump out of the ground.

It's absolutely true. But let the deeds of the Superbarons speak for themselves (from flamboyance to utter flamboyance).

GLENN McCARTHY

The original, many think, of Jett Rink in Edna Ferber's *Giant*. Barrel-chested, heavy-drinking, devoted to his mother, he made the cover of *Time* in 1950. A millionaire at twenty-six, McCarthy built the Shamrock Hotel in Houston so he could ride his horse through the lobby. He also founded Houston's greatest nightclub—the Cork Club—and imported the first jet-setters to Oil City. Glenn later ran into some trouble with dry wells in South America—he sold the Shamrock and the Cork Club was closed. Houston hasn't had a really hoity-toity place since. While wildcatting his first well, he told the crew, "Anybody leaves this rig, I'll beat the hell out of him." No one left.

Glenn McCarthy.

MICHEL HALBOUTY

The Thinking Man's wildcatter. Combining an A&M degree in geology with a natural feel for sweet pots, Halbouty has enjoyed an extraordinary career as an independent (he discovered the Lake End field and invented a high-class form of mud). Halbouty is also possessed of a certain eloquence, which his enemies would uncharitably call a big mouth. Favorite topics: OPEC and deregulation, the federal government and deregulation, the major oil companies and deregulation, and just plain old deregulation (he thinks it's a good idea).

HUGH ROY CULLEN

Cullen gave so much money to the Houston Symphony Orchestra that they played "Old Black Joe" every time he attended. It was his favorite. His real passion: Godless Communism. Cullen's Liberty radio stations broadcast Cold War polemic in thirty-eight states. And he once gave a $6,000 Cadil-

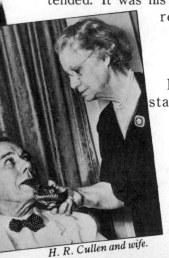

H. R. Cullen and wife.

lac to Joe McCarthy ("the greatest man in America"). In his River Oaks mansion, the stair well is made of Steuben glass.

CLINT MURCHISON & SID RICHARDSON

Founders of the Union Gas and Liberty Oil companies, respectively. These two come as a pair because a day never passed without their making money together (it all started when Clint pulled Sid out of a midnight card game to stake a claim in Wichita Falls). The best example of their offhanded wheeling and dealing: Murchison told Richardson to put up $5 million more to help them acquire the New York Central Railroad, a deal that was keeping the Wall Street folks on edge for weeks. Richardson said okay, then asked absentmindedly, "Say, Clint, what *was* the name of that railroad?" Sid left it all to his nephew, who later built Vail.

HAROLDSON LAFAYETTE HUNT

J. Paul Getty (who made his money in Oklahoma and doesn't count) once said: "In terms of extraordinary wealth, there is only one man—H. L. Hunt." And William F. Buckley, himself the son of a transplanted Texas oil millionaire, commented after Hunt's death: "Hunt gave capitalism a bad name, not, goodness knows, by frenzies of extravagance, but by his eccentric understanding of public affairs, his yahoo bigotry, and his appallingly bad manners." In between those quotes was a lot of man: hobo, dishwasher, cardshark, philosopher (his version of Utopia appeared in his book *Alpaca*). An inveterate gambler, Hunt hired a mathematician from MIT to figure out odds, but once lost $300,000 on a baseball game. In his final years, he ate raw vegetables, "creeped" on all fours, carried his lunch to work in a brown paper bag (mayo on everything), and vowed to live to 167. That was one thing the world's richest man couldn't buy.

TOM WAGGONER

His daughter Electra owned 350 pairs of shoes, but Arlington Downs was his real pride and joy. The estate included a forty-six-million-gallon artificial lake, a million-dollar string of ponies, and a six-thousand-seat grandstand. The state of Texas indulged Tom's passion for the numbers by removing the ban on parimutuel betting for the last year of his life (it was reimposed as soon as he died).

D. H. ("DRY HOLE") BOYD

He drilled fifty-seven holes— and fifty-six came up dry. But the first was a honey. It permitted old D. H. to throw a party every year after the Texas-OU game. More than a thousand people usually attended (he once invited an entire stadium section by mistake). Boyd went to meetings of the railroad commission in his Civil Air Patrol uniform, and gave the world's biggest drum to the UT marching band (eight feet wide, three feet eight inches deep). His bright orange Cadillac had longhorns mounted on the hood and the horn honked—what else?— the opening bars of "The Eyes of Texas."

BILLY BYARS

Though just a drilling contractor, Billy's wealth helped him throw a little reception for his prize bull, 105-TT, in the governor's suite of Tyler's Blackstone Hotel. He had a gold-plated shovel on hand for emergencies.

EVERETTE LEE DEGOLYER

The odd man out. DeGolyer had the biggest private library in Texas, and once saved *The Saturday Review*. But his description of the two kinds of oil rich is classic Texan—the "silver-spoon boys" (who had money before) and the "rabbit's-foot boys" (who ran into a piece of luck). DeGolyer was a rabbit's-foot boy, though a crafty one; he later won prizes for his research in geophysics.

KING OF THE WILDCATTERS

The life of "Dad" Joiner is a textbook case of the typical wildcatter life cycle. It has the humble, hardworking beginning (southern, of course), the gushing moment of truth at the well (which everyone knew would come up dry), and the final, heartbreaking encounter with the speculator who keeps you out of court but leaves you in possession of nought but a pair of mud-caked Levi's. Dad Joiner went through all three stages—in a spectacular way, even by Texas standards. The field in question was East Texas, and the speculator was H. L. Hunt. In fact, Joiner's whole career could be considered a kind of petroleum-based tragedy. Not coincidentally, Dad used to quote Shakespeare by the hour to the rhythm of the rigs.

THE HUMBLE BEGINNINGS

Born near Center Star, Alabama, in 1860, Marvin Columbus Joiner worked his way through college and became a country lawyer. This palled, and in 1897 he went to Oklahoma, where he found he had a nose for oil. An incredibly sensitive nose, it turned out. By 1926 Joiner had made and lost two fortunes in the fields. He moved down to Texas to see if he could smell something there. By the time he reached poverty-stricken Rusk County, he had a suitcase of dirty shirts, a reputation for honesty, and a cockeyed theory that the oil-rich Dallas sand belt stretched, untapped, to the plains of East Texas.

THE MOMENT OF TRUTH

In 1930 Joiner scraped together enough tools and money to "po'-boy" two exploratory wells eight miles east of Henderson. They were dry. Joiner was broke; the only person he could convince to back him anymore was the widow Daisy Bradford. On September 8, 1930, the well named Daisy Bradford Number 3 started gushing. Joiner had fathered the biggest oil field in the continental U.S. Hence the name Dad.

THE FINAL, HEARTBREAKING ENCOUNTER

The trouble started shortly thereafter. In his haste to start drilling, Dad had not bothered to secure airtight leases on the acres he had covered with rigs. The original owners had a convincing case against Dad; an Okie poker player named Hunt who had been hanging around the wells for weeks offered help. H. L. Hunt gave Dad $50,000 in cash, $45,000 in notes, and $1.3 million in future earnings. Hunt became the world's first billionaire vegetarian. Dad (after losing all in real-estate speculation) died broke in Dallas in 1947.

Dad Joiner (in tie).

HELL FIGHTER

After John Wayne portrayed him in the 1968 film *The Hell Fighters*, "Red" Adair traded in his fame on the oil fields for worldwide renown. He even got to make an American Express commercial (whirring helicopter, blazing offshore rig, the works).

But that didn't stop Red from continuing to ply the trade he had begun in the late forties, after service in the Army Bomb Disposal Squad taught him what he needed to know about high explosives and iron nerve. Some of Red's big fires: the 1962 "Devil's Cigarette Lighter" in the Sahara; the 1977 Bravo blowout in the North Sea; the Ixtoc Number 1 disaster in the Gulf of Mexico. Red's hobbies are speedboat racing and writing checks to the Easter Seal Society. None of his workers has ever been killed.

THE BASIC TECHNIQUE

Although Red can get quite imaginative when it comes to taming a wild well (he once had rubber Superballs on hand to plug holes in a gas pipe), he has developed a basic technique that has quenched thousands of oil well fires and blowouts. Some components:

BRASS TOOLS. They don't spark when they strike metal. Very important when the atmosphere is drenched with gas.

NITROGLYCERINE. Packed in a special barrel, the nitro is detonated directly over the center of a wild well, snuffing out the fire—usually—like a hand over a candle (it takes away all the oxygen).

WATER. As much as sixty thousand gallons a minute. To keep everything—men, equipment, and explosives—just below the boiling point.

RED ZIP-FRONT JUMP-SUIT UNIFORMS. It pays to look snappy on the job, they're easy to spot, and they match the color of Red's Cadillac fleet.

(713) 464-0230

Chapter 5
POWER & MONEY

THE IMPORTANCE OF HOLDING ON TO YOUR MINERAL RIGHTS

The part of Texas that's topsoil can give you cotton, rice, and well-grazed cattle. But if you're lucky (and a trifle rapacious), the part of Texas that's oil-rich and underground can earn you an address in River Oaks, innumerable tax loopholes, and an exposé in *Texas Monthly*. The topsoil can be dispensed with; *never* give up your mineral rights.

Fortunately, Texas attorneys have been working on this knotty problem ever since Spindletop. They have devised three basic clauses that will guarantee access to the profits of mineral exploitation of your land even after you've sold the property. All three (they describe different terms and time spans of mineral rights ownership) should be memorized—they're fascinating reading—and applied with equal rigor when you sell land on your ranch, in town, in the backyard, in the front yard—anywhere. (Property values around Rice University in Houston have sky-rocketed thanks to certain geologically significant rumors.) One more thing—have a good lawyer and plenty of title insurance. Where the slick goods are concerned, no one exchanges land in Texas with just a smile and a handshake.

HOW TO GET IT

Nothing Succeeds Like Excess

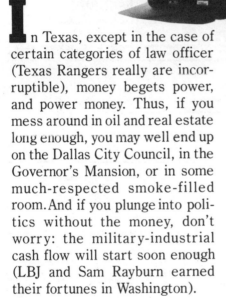

In Texas, except in the case of certain categories of law officer (Texas Rangers really are incorruptible), money begets power, and power money. Thus, if you mess around in oil and real estate long enough, you may well end up on the Dallas City Council, in the Governor's Mansion, or in some much-respected smoke-filled room. And if you plunge into politics without the money, don't worry: the military-industrial cash flow will start soon enough (LBJ and Sam Rayburn earned their fortunes in Washington).

Of course, the trick is to get going. Your main advantage is that in Texas, doing the top-heavy Ivy-League waddle down the corridors of power (Groton, Princeton, Harvard MBA, and Brooks Brothers) is not really necessary. Lone Star style is more casual. Jeans on the job are not unheard of; cowboy boots almost always replace wingtips; and a UT sheepskin or law degree is worth more than a flimsy piece of paper from any out-of-state school.

There are a number of ways to get into the shootin' match. One is to be born into it, the scion of a proud papa whose fortune includes everything from Canadian wheat to a string of radio stations (Texans love to broadcast their opinions over the airwaves).

But the classic way of obtaining power and money is more cinematic (although it's not as easy as it looks). Show up young and penniless at an oil rig, real estate office, or the gates of Texas A&M, work at incredibly menial chores, and send money home to the folks. The next thing you know, you'll own sections of downtown Houston or be defending divorcées at murder trials.

One last thing. Never talk about the fortune you're acquiring—only mention the one you're ostensibly losing. ("Boy, did I lose my shirt in bellies last week!") You have so many fortunes that if one is misplaced, it's not a big deal. But remember that although remarking on your losses is in good taste, *really* losing everything you have is most certainly not.

THE BIG RICH

Profiles in Money

Everyone in Texas is *not* rich. It just seems that way to the rest of the world. Texas, in fact, has one of the lowest per capita incomes in the United States. Nevertheless, Texans are

NAME	NET WORTH	OCCUPATION	MARITAL STATUS
Bill Brosseau *Dallas*	$15–20 million	Independent oil man	Divorced
Melvin Lane Powers *Houston*	$15–20 million	Developer	Single
John Mecom Jr. *Houston*	$25–50 million	Independent oil producer	Married to Katsy Mullendore, daughter of Oklahoma oilman-rancher
Gerald Hines *Houston*	$30–50 million	President, Gerald D. Hines Interests	Married (for the second time) to his former secretary
Oscar Wyatt *Houston*	$40 million	Chairman, Coastal States Gas	Married to Lynn Sakowitz
Mary Owen Greenwood *Houston*	$50 million	Philanthropist	Divorced
Harold Farb *Houston*	$50–75 million	Real estate and apartment development.	Married (for the second time) to Carolyn Friedman, grand-daughter of old-time Houston gambler Jakie Fried
Margaret McDermott *Dallas*	$50–75 million	Philanthropist	Widow
Lady Bird Johnson *Stonewall/Austin*	$50–$100 million	Ex-first lady	Widow

thought of as rich, thanks to the flamboyance and flashiness of those Texans who are. Cross a denizen of Dogpatch with a dandy from the Court of Louis XIV and you'll wind up with something akin to a Big Rich Texan. Most Texas wealth comes from those old reliables—oil and land—or from marrying well and/or divorcing better. To distinguish super-rich Texans from merely loaded ones, a chart through the greenback maze is provided—including a peek at some of the special ways they spend their Big Bucks. Texans go beyond first class; theirs is a supersonic spending. None of these folks will know hard times.

HOW THEY GOT IT	HOW THEY SPEND IT
Owns interests in over 100 wells.	Driven to and from his wells in a Cadillac limousine by his chef-chauffeur; wears monogrammed snakeskin boots with Southwick suits, Turnbull & Asser shirts, and a diamond-studded Corum watch.
Ex-lover and aunt Candace Mossler helped him get started in the construction business.	Built the ultimate Texas statement: a penthouse atop one of his buildings; owns the 100-foot yacht that once belonged to Coco Chanel. Commutes by helicopter. Wears big rings, open-neck shirts, gold chains.
Family-owned Mecom Oil Company.	Owns Stavros Niarchos's plane (complete with his cups and saucers); a private Caribbean island; a mansion on Lazy Lane in River Oaks; a ranch near Laredo; the New Orleans Saints football team. Had a Fleetwood Brougham Cadillac converted into a station wagon so Katsy could make daily trips to Jamail's.
Building Houston (Pennzoil Place, Post Oak Central, One and Two Shell Plaza).	Building more of Houston. And Chicago. And San Francisco. And New York City. Mountain climbing. Maintains a low profile (no politics).
Owning gas fields, piping it into such cities as San Antonio (he couldn't supply enough, in 1974 resulting in a brown-out of the entire area).	Leases Somerset Maugham's villa. Stocking private wine cellar, paying off huge legal fees and fines. Wearing huge, diamond-crowned A&M ring. Wife is always on best-dressed lists. Flies chili and C&W bands over to Southern France. Real-life JR.
Divorce settlements.	Calls herself "just a poor girl from Athens, Texas"; Suzy calls her C.R.C. for cute, rich, and clever. On national board of March of Dimes and other charities; owns impressive suites of jewelry and a big house in New Braunfels. Gives and goes to a lot of parties.
Largest owner and operator of apartments in the U.S. Has built over 23,000 garden-type units in Texas alone.	Cutting records of himself singing Al Jolson and giving them away as dinner party favors. Put up the money for Ultra magazine; owns custom-ordered El Dorado and a Rolls. Wife raises lots of money for charities.
Was married to Eugene McDermott, founder of Geophysical Services, Inc., forerunner of Texas Instruments.	Running two family foundations. Extremely devoted to art collecting (the Dallas Museum of Fine Arts owes her a lot). Affable. Well-liked.
Owns 53 percent of the Texas Broadcasting Corporation, which includes KTBC-TV, and real estate.	Hosting small seminars with guests like Kissinger at LBJ ranch in Stonewall; parties and travels with other socialite pals like Mollie Parnis and Mary Lasker; campaigns for son-in-law Chuck Robb, Lt. Governor of Virginia.

NAME	NET WORTH	OCCUPATION	MARITAL STATUS
Baron Enrique (Ricky) di Portanova *Houston and Rome*	$50–$100 million	Consul General for San Marino to Washington	Married (for the second time) to Sandra Hovis, daughter of Houston furnitu dealer; she changed her name to Alessandra
Perry R. Bass *Fort Worth*	$75 million	President, Perry R. Bass, Inc.	Married
Arthur Temple *Diboll*	$75 million	Vice Chairman, Time, Inc.	Married (to his former secretary)
Trammell Crow *Dallas*	$75–$100 million	Real estate developer	Married
Robert Shelton *Kerrville*	$75–$100 million	Rancher	Married (for the third time) to Fronie Shelton
Dominique Schlumberger de Menil *Houston, New York, and Paris*	$100 million	Philanthropist	Widow
Edwin L. Cox *Dallas*	$150 million	President, Cox Oil Co.	Married
Josephine Abercrombie *Houston*	$200–$300 million	Officer, Cameron Iron Works; markets beef from the South Texas ranch	Divorced (married five times)
George Mitchell *Houston*	$200–$300 million	CEO, Mitchell Energy & Development Corporation	Married (ten children)
Clint Murchison, Jr. *Dallas*	$500–$750 million	Real estate development	Married to Anne Murchison, former wife of Dallas Cowboys' chief scout Gil Brandt
Nelson Bunker Hunt *Dallas*	$1 billion	Owner, Great Western United and Placid Oil. Breeds horses	Married to Caroline Hunt

HOW THEY GOT IT

HOW THEY SPEND IT

HOW THEY GOT IT	HOW THEY SPEND IT
Inherited it: a grandson of the legendary oilman Hugh Roy Cullen. Rumored monthly income $600,000.	Has a private plane named *The Barefoot Baronessa*; villa in Acapulco with thirty-two bathrooms; mansion on River Oaks Boulevard. Has his own soft-porn labels (female torsos with grapes placed over strategic areas) on vintage wines. Tried to buy "21" as birthday present for the Baroness.
Oil.	Buying Santa Gertrudis Cattle for his Floresville ranch. Also owns San José Island near Port Aransas.
Lumber, timber products.	Stock market, politics. Father of Texas Railroad Commission's new member Buddy Temple. Built the Crown Colony Country Club in Diboll when he got bored with the country club in nearby Lufkin. In fact, built the entire town of Diboll.
Started as CPA, ended up as the country's biggest landlord (some projects: Dallas Market Center, Peachtree Center in Atlanta, Embarcadero Center in San Francisco).	Quietly. A film studio at Las Colinas, squash courts at home.
Cashed in his inherited shares in the King Ranch	Collecting expensive cars, and cowboy art. Buying quarter horses and Santa Gertrudis cattle for his numerous ranches across Texas and the United States. Built a 500-foot-long swimming pool at his home; wanted to make sure his eight children would have plenty of room to swim around in.
Inherited it. Daughter of man who founded the world's biggest oil drilling service company.	On art. Houston's #1 art patroness. Has given over $25 million worth of art to the city, including the Mark Rothko Chapel housing the painter's last works and vast sums to St. Thomas and Rice Universities. Lives in striking modern Philip Johnson mansion with its own indoor atrium.
Oil.	Founded E.L. Cox School of Business at SMU in 1978. Lives across the street from the Dallas Country Club but never has to go there — he's got his own sports complex at home, with indoor and outdoor tennis courts.
Inherited it from Daddy, oilman James S. Abercrombie, who founded Cameron Iron Works. She owns 60 percent of the business, a Fortune 500 company.	Has horse-breeding farm in Kentucky; sits on Rice University board.
Struck it rich in the forties in an oil syndicate with partners like Barbara Hutton; bought out syndicate and turned it into the Mitchell Energy & Development Corporation, a Fortune 500 company.	Unobtrusively. Developed The Woodlands, a 47,000-unit planned community near Houston. Owns Pelican Island near Galveston.
Inherited a lot from Daddy; built it up more through various investments.	Much of it goes to the Dallas Cowboys, of which he is the principal owner. Has also invested in the Racquet Club in Palm Springs, Vail Mountain Ski Lodge, and Daytona Speedway. Keeps a low profile, but his wife leads a more public life, having recently written two published Bible study books.
Oil inheritance from Daddy H.L.	Commodities. The silver market continues to quake as a result of the Hunts's 1980 efforts to corral the world's silver. Also spends a lot of money on thoroughbreds for his Roanoke ranch.

SPENDING IT
Or, What to do When the Well Comes In

The way rich Texans spend their money marks them as different from other rich folks. Texas Rich tend to go beyond first class. Theirs is a supersonic, go-for-broke way of spending that outdistances the ordinary wealthy in unequaled inventiveness. A rich fellow in New Jersey would probably not pay a quarter million dollars for a bull, and his wife would probably not get behind the wheel of her pickup truck in a full-length fur coat. Although today's rich Texans do not go around lighting Red River cigars with hundred-dollar bills or throwing money out of car windows as "Silver Dollar" Jim West did, they do go out and have custom-made mink coats trimmed with mink hot dogs to honor the family business. Most Texans with a lot of money still take the good advice of Clint Murchison, Sr., who once said, "Money is like manure. Pile it all in one place and it stinks like hell. Spread it around and it does a lot of good."

Should your well come in there are, of course, the obvious things you must do: trade in the Little Spread for a Big Spread, trade in the Mercedes for a Rolls-Royce, and trade in your Chris-Craft for a yacht. However, to launch you into the creative big-spending mainstream, here are some suggestions.

GET A FAMILY PLANE AND PILOT. Perfect for long-distance errands. You'll want to send the pilot down to citrus country when you develop an uncontrollable hankering for some fresh south Texas grapefruit. Also handy for when Charles Schreiner III invites you to do some weekend hunting at the Y.O. Ranch and for short business trips (your accountant will appreciate the tax write-off).

Mitsubishi's Marquise: won't get stuck on the freeway.

CREATE YOUR OWN HUNTING RANCH. So you, the family, and friends can enjoy hunting all year round. Buy another Big Spread near Kerrville or Laredo, add a private airstrip, hire a personal guide, and stock it with white-tail deer, dove, quail, and exotic animals like ibex, antelope, and mouflon. Raise these animals on a surplus harvest program and occasionally sell one to a zoo. Buy Egyptian cotton brush pants and shirts from Toepperwein in San Antonio and a custom-order Purdy gun from Dallas's Abercrombie & Fitch. Send out Christmas cards of you and the kids wearing your camouflage outfits.

BUILD YOUR OWN PRIVATE HEALTH AND BEAUTY SPA AT HOME. Never again will you have to worry about getting into Maine Chance, La Costa, or The Golden Door. Hire a live-in masseuse, manicurist, pedicurist, skin care specialist, barber, hairdresser, nutritionist, and exercise instructor—all on call twenty-four hours a day.

BUY AN ISLAND. In the Bahamas. Go there for one week only during Easter; take the kids and their friends. Avoid other rich Texan island-owners.

BUY A FAMILY PLOT IN GLENWOOD CEMETERY. On Washington Avenue in the Heights area, this is Houston's oldest, choicest buryin' ground. Even in perpetuity, you and yours will be surrounded by other wealthy Texans, including governors William P. Hobby and Ross Sterling, not to mention that local boy who made *very* good, Howard Hughes.

START COLLECTING FIRST EDITIONS—of early Texas books. You can tell everyone that you own "one of the largest collections in the state." Gives you good credentials for endowing a room with your name on it in Rice University's Fondren Library.

BUY A CONDO IN VAIL OR ASPEN. So you can go there the day after Christmas and show Coloradans that Texans *can* learn to ski. (Take private lessons from the best pro.) Make new friends with the kind of people that are always being photographed for *Town & Country*.

STRIVE TO GET ON THE IN-TERNATIONAL BEST-DRESSED LIST. It will take lots of money, time, and patience to go through all that fitting and refitting. You stand a good chance if you go to the Paris collections each August to order couturier clothes and befriend Manhattan fashion publicist Eleanor Lambert and all *Women's Wear Daily* reporters and photographers. If you make the list, then you can suggest that fashion designers give you their latest clothes at below cost.

FLY TO SANTA FE ... FRE-QUENTLY. A lot of useful things to buy here. Stay at Bishop's Lodge, shop for Fritz Scholder paintings (his bold colors and Indian figures go wonderfully in the den), purchase a John Gaw Mean-designed adobe so you and friends will have a place to stay during the Santa Fe

A poster by the preferred artist.

Opera season (July-August), and buy an antique Zuni concho belt (to wear with your Ralph Lauren prairie skirts.)

PURCHASE A PRIVATE STA-DIUM BOX. At Texas Stadium in Irving or a Sky Box in the Astrodome. This is where the high-lifers gather instead of down near the AstroTurf. Call in Houston's Beverly Jacomini or Dallas's Trisha Wilson to decorate it before the season starts.

Earrings from Cartier.

BUY IMPORTANT JEWELRY. Send for David Webb's Elyse Robbins, Cartier's Fernanda Gilligan, or Bulgari's Nicholas Bulgari to bring down trays of their biggest and best rocks. Real jewelry—the kind that must be locked up in Texas Commerce Bank—sets you glitteringly apart from Texas girls who still wear James Avery dinner rings.

SEND THE KIDS TO SCHOOL IN SWITZERLAND. Kinkaid, Hockaday, St. John's, and St. Mark's are no longer smart enough. Besides, all those Colorado ski lessons can be put to good use when you visit Klosters or St. Moritz. Le Rosey is particularly popular with Texas

The Texas version. Not 1600 Pennsylvania Avenue.

Rich. The eldest son will get to rub shoulders with future oil sheiks and bring them home to the Big Spread.

BUY THE TEXAS WHITE HOUSE. Former Morgan's Point home of Governor Ross Sterling, one of the early Humble (now Exxon) Oil Company founders, this thirty-four-room mansion sits on six acres on Galveston Bay. Offered by Houston realtor John Daugherty/Sotheby's at just under $1,500,000. Looks exactly like the other one in Washington, D.C. No need to ever run for president of the U.S. when you have this to come home to.

TAKE TENNIS LESSONS FROM A REAL PRO. Go to the Puente Romano tennis resort in Marbella, Spain, to brush up your game with Bjorn Borg. The steely-eyed Swede occasionally holds tennis clinics at this chic hotel hideaway on the Southern coast of Spain. Casually mention the pointers Borg gave you when you beat the resident pro at the tennis club back home.

Texas Type No. 8

THE MILLION AIRE

Into real estate, oil estate, & bank estate.

haircut by Jesse at Highland Park Village Barbershop

smiling; just closed a land deal with Canadians; just beat best friend in game of gin rummy at Preston Trails

Bell jet Ranger II four-seater helicopter, customized by Southwest Vert-all —features 24-karat gold seat belts, French burl wood instrument panels; Hermes goatskin seat coverings

custom-made bolo tie, gift from wife on last birthday

pale blue Swiss cotton voile shirt, custom-made with three initials on pocket

pocket contents: keys to Cadillac with Scots sticker from Highland Park football team on rear window; keys to gatehouse at Big Spread; solid gold money clip with coin motif containing $1,500 withdrawn from Bentwood Tree National Bank

crocodile bel.

gold Rolex watch circled with diamonds; star sapphire on pinkie

two Hermes suitcases. Contents: white Mexican wedding shirt; khaki pants; Barry Kieselstein-Cord's "Winchester" belt with solid gold buckle; loaded .38; Stetson

Oxxford suit, gray glen plaid custom-made at Neiman's Men's Shop

custom-made crocodile boots — from boot maker in small Texas town whose name he prefers to keep secret

THE MILLION AIRESS

Into shopping, charities, & getting her name in print.

lots of frosted blond hair done at Mr. Jack's; colored by Brewster; styled to cover face-tucks done by Mark Lemmon; must curl up at ends

makeup by Erno Laszlo (religiously rinses sixty times a day)

mandatory sunglasses on top of head (helps push up hair)

Erace under eyes

smiling; just been named to Crystal Charity Ball's Best-Dressed Hall of Fame

big gold hoop earrings

perfect teeth

necklace with 3-carat pear-shaped diamond drop — made from engagement ring from first husband, redesigned by Neiman's Precious Jewelry department

Bottega Veneta handbag contents: tickets to Crystal Charity Ball style show; swatch of fabric (redoing chairs in their Texas Stadium box); Mark Cross pen; Carlos Falchi appointment book; compact with Laszlo powder and blusher; Norell spray perfume; Erace stick; Face Savers; Valium; Tylenol; Binaca; rattail comb to lift bouffant hairdo; initial key ring; checkbook (prefers to cash checks at Highland Park Safeway); glasses (for reading menus only)

Piaget watch for dress (has gold Rolex for sport) nails done by Isarela at John Phillip Ltd. 6-carat diamond ring from Cartier, diamond band, sapphire guards

wallet contents: gold American Express card; $300 withdrawn from Bentwood Tree National Bank; charge cards: Neiman-Marcus, Sakowitz, Master Charge, Visa, Exxon, Shell, Gulf, Marty's

Vuitton shopping bag; leotards from morning exercise stint at Jenny Ferguson's aerobic dance classes subscription blank to "W"

Ferragamo pumps (F's in band) bought at Neiman-Marcus from Sam Fagin

emerald ring from Richard Eiseman at Joskes

Adolfo suit bought at Lou Lattimore from Diana Bowser

Vuitton suitcase contents: brown custom-made lizard boots; Ralph Lauren prairie skirt; Calvin Klein shirts; Ralph Lauren khaki pants; long cotton dress by Mary Murchison; Ungaro sundress; Barry Kieselstein-Cord's "Winchester" belt with silver buckle

WHERE TO LIVE

The Right Neighborhoods

The ultimate address: the Governor's Mansion.

Part of being rich in Texas is knowing where to live. Residing in a second-rate neighborhood is the one eccentricity a millionaire can't afford. You've got to surround yourself with wealthy neighbors before people will believe you're rolling in dough. So when you strike it rich, move to the turf of the well-heeled. There's a swank address for any fat cat, no matter what part of Texas he lives in.

AUSTIN
WESTLAKE HILLS

Big money in a rough Western setting. The terrain is craggy, the houses are big and rambling. There are two advantages to living in Westlake Hills: (1) the spectacular view of the lakes around Austin; and, more important, (2) the vista of the UT tower turning orange when the Longhorns win.

DALLAS
HIGHLAND PARK

People say they live here for the school system, but it's really for the flash and prestige. Lots of Rolls-Royces parked in front of big houses with de rigueur tennis courts and/or swimming pools in the back. Preferred street: Lakeside.

EL PASO
KERN PLACE

Stucco homes with the requisite view of Juarez dominate this area on the west side of the mountain. Here, the wealthy are quiet about their money. Home interiors have a cross-cultural design influence, with fine Chinese antique furnishings behind many of the Mexican-style facades.

FORT WORTH
WESTOVER HILLS

This neighborhood is actually an incorporated city within Fort Worth, with its own police and fire departments and a stone-pillared entry. Once you've landed an address here, it's important to live on the first of the two hills—that's where the older, more serious money is. The area is characterized by winding streets with lots of trees, vast lawns, and big houses behind rock walls.

HOUSTON
RIVER OAKS

Huge, Tara-like homes with sweeping driveways and yards lined with azalea bushes. Social climbers live on River Oaks Boulevard, but the most prestigious address is on Lazy Lane. It helps your status if you hang out with Middle Eastern and European royalty. River Oaks celebs: John Connally, Denton Cooley.

MIDLAND
RACQUET CLUB

Old, oil money neighborhood; many homes designed by Frank Welch. Eccentricity abounds in Midland: one house has air-conditioned squash/racquetball courts built into the basement, complete with sable throws to keep the spectators warm.

OZONA

This west Texas town is so small and thoroughly ritzy, there is no single exclusive neighborhood. Wealthy goat ranchers and oil-monied families live in huge houses along Main Street.

SAN ANTONIO
OLMOS PARK

Hilly district with big, beautiful houses on winding streets. San Antonio's old guard rich live in these sedate two- and three-story dwellings with naturally landscaped yards.

GAINFULLY EMPLOYED
How to Work for a Living

Access to huge amounts of cash, of course, can never be overestimated as an effective means of snaring power in Texas—oilmen and real estate magnates continue to be the state's primary power brokers. But the dollar isn't always the only thing that's almighty; there are other ways to exert one's influence in the Lone Star state. Thousands of Texans have joined the ranks of the smart set without piling up even a first million, usually by pursuing the following careers:

LAWYER

Always a respectable position, but one that is loose enough so that you can wear your boots to work. Good launching pad to political power; professional haven for politicians (John Connally, Bob Strauss). The work isn't always interesting, but it's a good way to rub elbows with the high and mighty. To get on a different kind of power track, become a district attorney. Dallas D.A. Henry Wade, who became a local celebrity when he prosecuted Jack Ruby, continues to be a favorite dinner party guest.

POLITICIAN

Not a lot of (aboveboard) money to be made, but lots of power, fun, and contact with important people. Ideal job for the Texan who can talk endlessly, has a knack for the absurd side of parliamentary procedure, and is a bit indolent—but don't get too lazy or *Texas Monthly* will attack (they do a Best and Worst list every year). Primary requirements: ability to vary the intensity of one's accent, good bullshit capacity, and knowledge of enough Spanish to get the Hispanic vote.

BANKER

Ideal career for those who aren't loaded with—but still want to spend a lot of time around—money. When you're a banker you have free reign to play the Big Tex act. Bankers like to go to French restaurants and call all the waiters Pierre. They think it makes them sound simultaneously quaint and cosmopolitan.

ASTRONAUT

For those with a scientific bent. Space travel makes you instant star material. Unlike the first astronauts, you won't make a lot of money, but you will become a celebrity and therefore be invited to lots of River Oaks fetes. With some luck, you may get an American Express commercial or a Coors Beer distributorship.

RESTAURATEUR

Texas's devotion to chicken-fried steak, Tex-Mex, barbecue, chili, etc., places this career high in the ranks of respectability. Power comes into play when socialites and politicians visit. Every Mexican restaurant worth its salsa has autographed photos of prominent politicians past and present on its walls. It makes the restaurants seem more American and the politicians more likable.

THE PROFESSIONAL TEXAN

The hidden career of numerous writers, artists, and miscellaneous ne'er-do-wells who live outside the state's borders. The best thing about it is that any Texan can be one. All you have to do is retain your accent, cuss with imagination, and maintain a partying spirit, a grand sense of humor, and a simple Texas wardrobe: boots, bandana, cowboy hat. Popular career among Texans living in New York City. Use downhome phrases like, "I'm just a country dog come to the city" at Elaine's and maybe she'll let you run up a big bar bill.

THE TEXAS RANGERS

Ever since Stephen Austin assigned ten mounted men to range over the settlers' lands in 1835, Texans have been continually grateful to their Rangers for defending them against assorted baddies—Comanches, cattle rustlers, Bonnie and Clyde, bootleggers, others. Some tales that never dim in the retelling:

• The first Ranger report.
Date: August 10, 1876
Name of Offender: Bill Jones
Offense: Stealing Cattle
Disposition: Mean as hell.
Had to kill him.

• The classic. A Texas mayor wired for Rangers to come on the next train and quell a riot. When the train arrived, only one Ranger got off. The panic-stricken mayor asked: "Why only one?" Answer: "Well, you ain't got but one mob, have you?"

• The most poetic description of violent death (i.e., "necessary force"). It was written by a Ranger about a Mexican rustler. "The other day we ran onto some horsebackers and one of them thought he would learn me how to shoot, so I naturalized him—made an American citizen out of him." (He was buried north of the border.)

Nowadays the border is quiet and the remaining Indians are on reservations. But every Ranger unit still has an ample supply of Thompson submachine guns, AR-15 rifles, and riot gear (plus access to helicopters and armored cars). There could be some fancy shootin' yet.

Texas Type No. 9

THE HOUSTON LAWYER

Well-bred old guard; clinches the big deals.

short, neat, conservative-length hair

smiling; just received invitation to join Tejas Club

rep tie with tiny gray map of Texas pattern by Pierre Cardin

white, pinpoint oxford clo button-down shirt by Gittman from Norton Ditto's Post Oak store

flecks of chili on lapel — from a quick hot dog lunch at James's Coney Island

Brooks Brothers two-piece navy pinstripe, single-breasted, tropical wool blend — wrinkled by combination of Houston's heat, humidity, air conditioning

pocket contents: keys to BMW; keys for Little Spread; keys to Houston Club locker

wallet contents: Exxon card; American Express card; gold life membership card UT Ex-Students Association;. tickets to UT–A&M Thanksgiving game (forty-yard line seats); Gittings photo of the wife and kids; secretary's home phone number; picture of twelve-point buck he shot last month

wedding band on left hand UT class ring on right hand, no stone

small-grained black lizard belt

traditional tongue-style silver buckle; inherited from Granddaddy, founder of the firm; engraved initials still faintly visible

monogrammed calfskin briefcase from Houston Trunk Co., contents: copy of Wall Street Journal; · sweatband for morning jog in Memorial Park; legal files for personal injury case; well-thumbed copy of Tommy Thompson's Blood and Money (Racehorse Haynes is his idol); jar of Pace's piquante sauce

90% cotton/10% nylon socks, darker blue than su

Cole-Haan's traditional black wing tips, well shin changes into black lizard boots from Stelzig's on Friday evenings when heading for the Little Spre

THE COUNTY SHERIFF

Easy-going country boy; made last arrest in 1953.

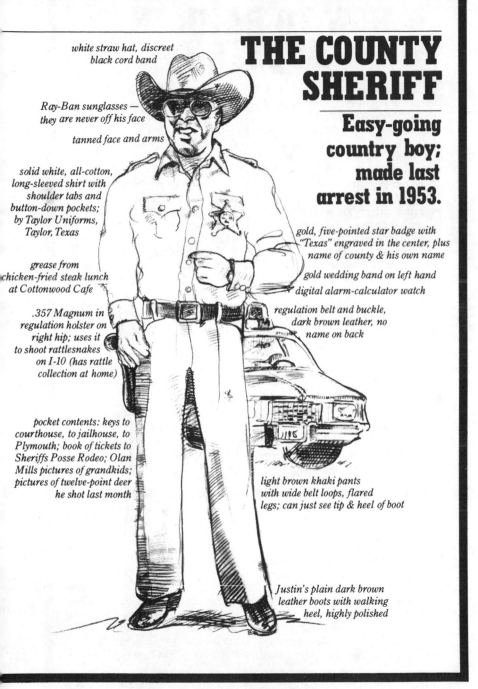

white straw hat, discreet black cord band

Ray-Ban sunglasses — they are never off his face

tanned face and arms

solid white, all-cotton, long-sleeved shirt with shoulder tabs and button-down pockets; by Taylor Uniforms, Taylor, Texas

grease from chicken-fried steak lunch at Cottonwood Cafe

.357 Magnum in regulation holster on right hip; uses it to shoot rattlesnakes on I-10 (has rattle collection at home)

pocket contents: keys to courthouse, to jailhouse, to Plymouth; book of tickets to Sheriffs Posse Rodeo; Olan Mills pictures of grandkids; pictures of twelve-point deer he shot last month

gold, five-pointed star badge with "Texas" engraved in the center, plus name of county & his own name

gold wedding band on left hand

digital alarm-calculator watch

regulation belt and buckle, dark brown leather, no name on back

light brown khaki pants with wide belt loops, flared legs; can just see tip & heel of boot

Justin's plain dark brown leather boots with walking heel, highly polished

HOW TO BANK IN HOUSTON

When you've finally amassed a sufficient sum of money to be counted among Texas's superrich, you'll need to know exactly where to bank. But more important is knowing *how*.

1. Never use wallet-sized checks with your name, address, and telephone number printed on them. All that should appear is your name — everyone already knows how to get in touch with you. The only checks to use are the large ones, torn from a hand-tooled, ledger-size book. Don't carry the book with you — that would be too showy. Just keep some checks folded in your wallet or stuffed casually into your purse. And never make any notation on the stub — the exact amount of money leaving your account is of little concern to you.

2. Even the wealthiest Houstonian needs a basic checking account, preferably at one of the biggest banks in town. Open your grassroots account at First City ... it's big and carries international clout.

3. Set up a trust fund with Texas Commerce Bank, because that's their specialty. A bank with "Texas" in the title is always a nice choice; good for dropping on out-of-staters.

4. You'll want two safety deposit boxes at two different locations. One of them must be at River Oaks Bank and Trust, to prove you're among the old-guard Houston banking set. All safety deposit box transactions should be saved for Monday mornings when the social activity is at its peak. Get a second box at Post Oak Bank. Trendy folks use this bank because it's convenient.

5. Having your own foundation is an unmistakable sign of having truly arrived, and the choice here has to be a traditional bank, such as River Oaks Bank and Trust. Of course, this account is used only to buy charity ball tickets or anything else that guarantees your check will be processed by your peers. What's the use of having a foundation if no one knows how extravagantly you spend your money?

6. For the ultimate in domestic empire-building, go to a small town like Sweetwater or Pecos and *buy* a nice little unincorporated bank. You'll want to change the bank's name to your own, and add something like "National Bank" on the end for an added touch of class. To combine practicality with prestige, buy a bank near your spread or close to an old, established oil field such as Spindletop.

7. If you want your empire to go international, you will also need an account in Grand Cayman named after yourself: "So-and-so Interests, N.A."

8. To further entrench yourself in international banking society, get an account with a European bank. The choice would be a Swiss bank for that ultrarich, numbered account.

9. For a joke account with checks that you can show off at the nineteenth hole at River Oaks Country Club, put a little money away with the "Cow Pasture Bank" in Rio Vista. Its real name is the First State Bank of Rio Vista, the only bank in the world with its own airstrip for "fly-in banking."

Chapter 6
TEXAS SIGHTS

THE ARMADILLO

Rivaling the longhorn as *the* Texas mascot is *Dasypus novemcinctus*, the nine-banded armadillo. This armor-plated cousin to the anteater has recently been seen decorating T-shirts, hat tacks, bumper stickers, gimme caps, and beer mugs; the makers of Christmas ornaments, cookie cutters, plush toys, and air fresheners have also cashed in on the dillo's cute but far-from-cuddly shape.

A rather dumb animal that hasn't changed much since prehistoric times, the dillo is loathed all over Texas by ranchers and gardeners, who often keep "dillo-killer poles" out back to discourage this compulsive digger from rooting up flower beds and burrowing dangerous holes in pastures. As "Hoover hogs," dillos made a tasty meal during the Depression; their meat tastes much like pork. Lately, Texas schoolchildren have been dressing in adorable armadillo costumes in an attempt to persuade the Texas Legislature to name the dillo the official state mammal.

ON THE ROAD

Taming the Wide Open Spaces

Going out of state for anything, including a vacation, smacks of desertion or outright treason in many Texas households. After all, there're plenty of things to see right in any Texas backyard—from a proud historical landmark (the Alamo) to a slightly less glorious monument (Paisano Pete). It is a Texan's duty to familiarize himself with his home state, and Texans accept this obligation with zeal and passion.

Most Americans can cover their home state in less than a week. In Texas, if you concentrate and work at it steadily, you can traverse your territory by about age thirty-seven. Fortunately, the state and federal governments have blessed the Lone Star state with more than 72,900 miles of highway. With all that road to travel, Texans have naturally taken to the automobile.

To take a Texas road trip, you must be prepared. For example, it would be unthinkable to go as far as the end of your driveway without first making certain you have enough Freon to keep the air conditioner running the entire trip. Also, absolutely everyone in Texas travels with a roadie (a drink for the road). Whether in a Styrofoam cup or a crystal bar glass, you must keep a steady supply of your favorite beverage on hand at all times. And you've got to have lots of food, more than you think you'll be able to eat. You'll still probably end up at Stuckey's for a pecan roll.

What follows are six tours of Texas that will help you familiarize yourself with the various regions (somewhat arbitrarily demarcated) of the Lone Star state. Of course, these trips do not encompass all there is to see in Texas; but they do highlight some of the more interesting and unusual sights the state has to offer. So saddle up and happy trails!

Tour No. 1

NORTH TEXAS

Famous for its "blue northers"—bitter cold fronts that disappear nearly as quickly as they move in. This Plains area has immense ranches, majestic cliffs, colorful canyons. You'll get a real feel for the life of the old-time cattleman as you drive past endless stretches of land fenced in by miles and miles of barbed wire. High 'n' dry, North Texas is best seen in the summer months. Bring a jacket.

WEATHERFORD

PETER PAN STATUE In Cherry Park playground is a small bronze statue of Peter Pan dedicated to Mary Martin, who created role on Broadway.

MARY MARTIN HOME Not open to public but house of famous actress can be viewed at 314 W. Oak St.

GRANBURY

GRANBURY OPERA HOUSE Built in 1886; restored in 1975. Twelve weeks of summer stock performances; other productions occasionally throughout rest of year. On the square.

FORT WORTH

MISS TEXAS PAGEANT Held every July, the place to see a bevy of Texas-born beauties.

KIMBELL ART MUSEUM Last building designed by the late Louis Kahn. Houses local philanthropist Kay Kimbell's collection of 18th-century portraits, Old Masters, Picassos. At 1101 Will Rogers Rd.

AMON CARTER WESTERN ART MUSEUM Built to honor one of city's most famous & controversial city fathers, this Philip Johnson-designed museum has superb collection of western art: Russells and Remingtons and fine Georgia O'Keeffes. At 3501 Camp Bowie Blvd.

KINCAID'S Fort Worthians flock here for best hamburgers in grocery store cum hamburger stand. Get in line at 4901 Camp Bowie Blvd.

THISTLE HILL Restored former cattle baron's mansion. Tours daily of romantic house listed in National Register of Historic Places. At 1509 Pennsylvania.

WATER GARDEN More than 4 terraced acres feature 5 fountains powered by 440-horsepower pumps pumping 19,000 gallons of water a minute. Adjacent to convention center. Spectacular waterworks.

THE STOCKYARDS Where you find the real cowboy. Trading in Livestock Exchanges still

OLD ABILENE TOWN Western-style amusement park depicting early Texas & Abilene frontier days. Last Chance Saloon, historical exhibits.

FORT GRIFFIN

FORT GRIFFIN STATE PARK Home of state-maintained herd of Texas longhorn cattle from which Bevo, the University of Texas mascot, is selected.

POST

LLANO ESTACADO TOURIST MARKER Marks eastern boundary of vast Llano Estacado or "Staked Plains" of Texas—the southernmost subdivision of Great Plains. Town is at foot of majestic Cap Rock.

OLD C. W. POST HOME Cereal manufacturer C. W. Post founded town in 1907 to demonstrate his economic ideas. Home is at 615 W. Main St.

SCENIC DRIVE F.M.-669 south toward Gail, reaches edge of the Llano Estacado.

goes on. Western-style merchants, such as M. L. Leddy & Ryon's, line Exchange Ave. on city's north side; saloons & restaurants capture feel of old West that never left Texas's most "cowboy" city.

ABILENE

FORT PHANTOM HILL Established to protect High Plains folk from Indians. Burned before finally abandoned. Intact ruins include guardhouse, powder magazine, & commissary. Ten miles north via F.M.-600.

NOCONA

NOCONA BOOT COMPANY Headquarters for well-known Texas boot company—the "Leathergoods Center of the Southwest." See display of boot-making tools from 1890s.

ALBANY

LEDBETTER PICKET HOUSE MUSEUM Dog-run cabin built of slender upright pickets. Fine example of unusual frontier ranch house. With period furnishings & locale. Open daily; Webb Park.

STAMFORD

MACKENZIE TRAIL MONUMENT Descendants of early Texas ranching families erected large, hand-carved marker honoring famous trail, what it meant to area pioneers in 1880s.

SNYDER

WHITE BUFFALO STATUE Recalls frontier days, honors a rare albino buffalo killed nearby. On courthouse square. Petting allowed.

TAHOKA

TAHOKA DAISY Lavender wild flower spreads lavishly over plains. First discovered at spring-fed Lake Tahoka.

LUBBOCK

CHRYSANTHEMUM CAPITAL OF THE WORLD Local residents are urged to plant these fall flowers. More than 40,000 mums on campus of Texas Tech, 40,000 more in city parks. October is peak season.

PRAIRIE DOG TOWN In MacKenzie State Park, colony for prairie dogs. Close-up view of frisky animals that once covered plains by the millions.

BUDDY HOLLY STATUE Life-size statue honors famous Lubbock-born singer killed in 1959 plane crash. Complete with his sport coat & guitar. At the Civic Center.

LEVELLAND

SOUTH PLAINS MUSEUM

Memorabilia of cattle kingdoms, horse-drawn agricultural implements, mounted big-game animals, local history. Open Tuesday through Saturday.

LITTLEFIELD

TALLEST WINDMILL

Originally constructed of wood in El Canyon de las Casas Amarillas (Canyon of the Yellow Houses) on XIT Ranch in 1887; height was 132 feet. Blew down in 1926. Replica is "only" 114 feet to axis of 12-foot sails. U.S.-84 at XIT Ave.

MULESHOE

NATIONAL MULE MEMORIAL

Life-size memorial honors mules that pulled covered wagons, broke pioneers' sod, hauled freight, helped build the railroad. Down-town. Giddy up.

WORLD CHAMPIONSHIP MULESHOE PITCHING CONTEST

Muleshoers celebrate 4th of July by hurling shoes at one another. Duck.

MULESHOE NATIONAL WILDLIFE REFUGE

Oldest refuge in Texas, established primarily as home for migratory waterfowl. Nation's largest concentration of sandhill cranes winter here annually. Open daylight hours.

HEREFORD

"TOWN WITHOUT A TOOTHACHE"

Natural fluorine & iodides in municipal water result in low incidence of dental decay. Plenty of "Look, Mom, no cavities" kids.

NATIONAL COWGIRL HALL OF FAME

The Deaf Smith County Library pays tribute to Texas women who contributed to development of state. Honors pioneer spirit of women everywhere. Paintings, sculpture.

CANYON

PALO DURO CANYON STATE PARK

Texas's largest state park. More than 15,000 acres of scenic landscape. Views of Red River, tabletop expanses of Texas High Plains. Walls plunge thousands of feet to canyon floor. Camping, horseback riding, miniature train, hiking facilities.

DUMAS

HELIUM

Two-thirds of nation's helium produced here. Tours available in several major industrial plants.

DALHART

EMPTY SADDLE MONUMENT

Designed by cowboy after a widow asked that statue of a horse bearing empty saddle be erected as tribute to her husband, a former XIT Ranch cowpoke. In City Park, U.S.-54 west.

AMARILLO

CADILLAC RANCH

Off I-40, local Amarillo good ol' boy Stanley Marsh 3 had the Ant Farm of Houston bury 10 fin-tailed Cadillacs in the ground. A favorite scavenger-hunt place for area church groups.

TASCOSA

BOOT HILL CEMETERY

When town was known as "cowboy capital of the 1880s," daily gunfights caused cemetery to fill up fast. Final resting place of some of Texas's most infamous citizens. Off U.S.-385.

CLAUDE

SCENIC DRIVE
One of most impressive drives in state. Take Texas-207 south toward Silverton. In nine-mile-wide Palo Duro Canyon, see Prairie Dog Town Fork of Red River. Another beautiful gorge, knife-edged butte, and rock strata visible in Tule Canyon.

PANHANDLE

SQUARE HOUSE MUSEUM
In historic Square House, charming museum displays early ranch implements & Indian artifacts. Antique chuck wagon parked outside, also reconstructed half-dugout typical of first shelters built by pioneer plainsmen in area.

SCENIC DRIVE
F.M.-293 west to Texas-136 north provides startling views of High Plains, Canadian River Valley, & Lake Meredith.

STEPHEN VILLE

COASTAL BERMUDA GRASS
Area is state's leading producer of popular range grass. Take a good look—this grass *is* greener.

SPEARMAN

ROLLING PLAINS MULE TRAIN ASSOCIATION
Area residents who maintain mule trains and covered wagons assemble several times a year for old-fashioned wagon trail rides across the plains. Local parades, overnight camp-outs, and week-long treks also. Plenty of plain fun.

LIPSCOMB

WILL ROGERS DAY
Noted humorist worked as cowboy on Little Robe Ranch outside town. Perfected his famous rope tricks used on stage. Last Saturday of August, town honors him with Western-style rodeo & barbecue.

BORGER

SCENIC DRIVE
Take 25-mile loop west & north to Stinnett, crossing rough, canyon-cut landscapes of Canadian River brakes, across dam impounding Lake Meredith. Texas-136 west, F.M.-1913 and F.M.-687 north. Hold your breath.

GLEN ROSE

DINOSAUR VALLEY STATE PARK
Best-preserved dinosaur tracks in Texas. First sauropod tracks in world were discovered here on banks of Paluxy River. Two gigantic plastic dinosaurs are caged inside a cyclone fence about a hundred yards from the tracks. Step lightly.

QUANAH

MEDICINE MOUNDS
Four unusual cone-shaped hills rise some 350 feet above surrounding plains. The Comanche Indians called them mounds, believed to be dwelling place of powerful spirits.

SHAMROCK

BLARNEY STONE WEST
Fragment of genuine Blarney Stone from Ireland's Blarney Castle mounted on pillar in Elmore Park. Kiss it for plenty o' luck.

VERNON

R. L. MORE, SR., BIRD EGGS COLLECTION
Collection started in 1888. Ten-thousand-egg exhibition features more than 750 kinds of eggs & 150 specimens of taxidermy.

CROWELL

McADAMS RANCH MUSEUM
Furniture and furnishings from five generations. Open Sunday afternoons, May–September. Ten miles west on U.S.-70.

Tour No. 2

EAST TEXAS

Where the great gushers got their start. Derricks and petrochemical complexes dot this piny woods area between Dallas and Houston. The state's most thickly settled region has vast rice and cotton farms, dogwood trails, and the deep and darkly mysterious Big Thicket. Flowering shrubs and trees abound, making spring the time for touring East Texas.

HOUSTON

ASTRODOMAIN $100-million complex includes Astrodome, Astrohall, & Astroarena. Calls itself Eighth Wonder of the World. First major league baseball stadium with a roof; first air-conditioned stadium in world. Home of Houston Astros & Houston Livestock Show and Rodeo.

TEXAS MEDICAL CENTER Most advanced complex of medical facility in U.S. Twenty-four institutions on 200 acres attract 10,000 visitors a day. Center stage for Dr. DeBakey vs. Dr. Cooley.

BAYOU BEND Former home of Miss Ima Hogg, philanthropist daughter of Texas's first native-born governor, James S. Hogg. Spanish Colonial 24-room structure houses a fine collection of American furniture & decorative arts. Two-hour tours by reservation only.

GALLERIA Modeled after famed *galleria* in Milan, the most elegant shopping center in Texas. Has indoor ice skating rink.

MARK ROTHKO CHAPEL Serene retreat on St. Thomas University campus houses last works of noted American abstract expressionist. Gift of DeMenil family. Open daily at no charge.

ASTROWORLD Over 100 shows, rides, attractions. Amusement park rides like Fender Bender, AstroNeedle, & Gunslinger attract long lines.

LBJ SPACE CENTER Headquarters of America's space program. See fabled moon rocks, Mission Control, Skylab, & Saturn booster. Free, self-guided tours daily.

SAN JACINTO MONUMENT A national landmark. Where Texas independence was won. The 570-foot structure with observation deck is topped by a 35-foot Lone Star weighing 220 tons.

SAN JACINTO INN Across from monument. Family-operated restaurant, one of Texas's oldest, famous for seafood & chicken dinners. Portions are as gargantuan as dining room. Best tablecloths — map of Texas is printed on them — in the state.

LIVINGSTON

ALABAMA-COUSHATTA INDIAN RESERVATION

Home of 300-year-old southern forest tribe. "Beyond the Sun" outdoor historical pageant presented nightly except Sunday, June–August. Daily tour of 4,000-acre reservation

features authentic Indian dances, food, arts, crafts. Camping facilities nearby. Open year round.

GALVESTON

THE STRAND

Once called "the Wall Street of the Southwest." Some

of finest examples of 19th-century cast-iron facades in America now front shops and restaurants.

THE BISHOP'S PALACE

Former home of bishop of Galveston-Houston diocese, elaborate 1886 landmark is only Texas building on American Institute of Architects' list of nation's 100 outstanding buildings.

GALVESTON ISLAND BEACH

Over 30 miles of sparkling clean sand on Gulf of Mexico. Stewart Beach *the* spot to sunbathe.

SEA-ARAMA MARINEWORLD

Food & game fish native to Texas Gulf Coast plus exotic tropical varieties on view daily. Performing sea lions & dolphins, too.

BOLIVAR FERRY

A diesel ferry operates between Galveston and Port Bolivar. Toll-free. Cars allowed.

FISHING PIERS

Free municipal jetties & rock groin piers for surf fishermen along Seawall Blvd.

ENNIS

NATIONAL POLKA FESTIVAL

Dancing in the streets. First weekend in May, Czech descendants gather in costume to do national dance of Czechoslovakia. Goes on into the night. Plenty of Czech food & drink.

BLUEBONNET TRAILS

Bluebonnets out in full glory last two weeks of April. Come look, but don't pick.

PORT ARTHUR

CAVOILCADE

Honors petroleum & petrochemical industry each October.

TEXAS-LOUISIANA CAJUN FESTIVAL

Crawfish & filé gumbo served up by exuberant Cajuns. A real *fais do do* every May.

RAINBOW BRIDGE

Highest bridge in South — 177 feet above Neches River — over a navigable stream.

CLEVELAND

HILLTOP HERB FARM

Dine smack dab in the middle of verdant greenhouse. Emphasis on natural herbs & fresh vegetables grown & cooked by Madalene Hill. Advance reservations & deposit necessary. Long waiting list.

HUNTSVILLE

SAM HOUSTON MEMORIAL PARK

Home & tomb of General Sam Houston, two-time president of Republic of Texas.

LUFKIN

SOUTHERN HUSH PUPPY OLYMPICS
Tons of deep-fried pups downed here every May.

WECHES

SAN FRANCISCO DE LOS TEJAS STATE HISTORIC PARK
Replica of first Spanish mission in East Texas stands on its former site.

RUSK

TEXAS STATE RAILROAD
All aboard the bright yellow, four-car Texas State Railroad for 3-hour, 50-mile chug through East Texas's pine forests. Old (1894) steam train goes 20 miles an hour round trip between Rusk & Palestine.

TYLER

TYLER ROSE FESTIVAL
One of state's great floral pageants. Five days each October honor Tyler's famed rosebushes. Rose garden tours show off more than 35,000 bushes, nearly 400 varieties.

BLACK BEAUTY RANCH
Bucolic retreat, purchased by Fund for Animals

(world's largest anticruelty society), is 200-acre ranch for abused equines. Where burros from Grand Canyon roundup were sent.

DE GUSHTABUS
Northwest of Tyler, unpack picnic basket under one of Texas Highway Department's oil derrick-style rest areas on I-20. Don't expect a gusher.

ATHENS

BLACK-EYED PEA JAMBOREE
Every July, pea pickers square dance, cook "reci-peas," & compete in pea-shelling contests. Drink a pea-tini—martini with black-eyed pea instead of olive.

BEAUMONT

SPINDLETOP MUSEUM
Pictures, documents, & artifacts from famous gusher.

GILMER

EAST TEXAS YAMBOREE
Salutes town's major crop each October. Lots of sweet potato pie eaten here.

CARTHAGE

REEVES MEMORIAL
Life-size statue of Jim Reeves, East Texas country & western singer, who died in 1964 plane crash.

GRAND PRAIRIE

TEXAS SPORTS HALL OF FAME
What a line-up! Willie Shoemaker's boots. Babe Zaharias's golf clubs. Bobby Morrow's gold medal.

JEFFERSON

JAY GOULD PRIVATE RAILROAD CAR
Atalanta, Gould's luxurious four-stateroom car, permanently derailed downtown. Open daily for inspection.

EXCELSIOR HOTEL
Oscar Wilde, Jay Gould, Ulysses S. Grant, Diamond Bessie, Rutherford B. Hayes all slept here. Has been in continuous operation since 1850. Filled with tiger-mahogany beds, marble-topped chests, sumptuous bathrooms—a bit of Texas's past opulence. Big plantation breakfasts.

CYPRESS QUEEN
Paddle-wheeler replica splashes down Big Cypress Bayou for 45-minute trips during summer. Complete with riverboat captain & guide.

KARNACK

BIRTHPLACE OF LADY BIRD JOHNSON
Former First Lady—born Claudia Taylor—spent her childhood here.

DENISON

BIRTHPLACE OF DWIGHT D. EISENHOWER
Thirty-fourth president of U.S. born in 2-story white frame house at 208 E. Day Street. Open daily.

HAGERMAN WILDLIFE REFUGE
Refuge for migratory waterfowl; 11,300-acre park houses some 280 bird species. On Big Mineral Arm of Lake Texoma. Open all year.

DALLAS

STATE FAIR OF TEXAS
Peerless week-long October exposition draws more than 3 million. Big Tex in complete cowboy regalia, including correct jeans, looms over festivities.

JOHN F. KENNEDY MEMORIALS
Polished granite marker at Main & Houston Streets designates spot of assassination on November 22, 1963. JFK Museum contains assassination stories from nation's newspapers, detailed model of city tracing motorcade route, films, narrations, mementos.

JOHN NEELY BRYAN'S CABIN
Home of Dallas's first settler. Bryan was city's savviest real-estate tycoon, selecting a high-value downtown plot for his one-room cabin that is now surrounded by skyscrapers. Between Main & Elm streets on Record.

CLYDE BARROW'S GRAVE
Appropriately located in a cemetery on the fringe of one of Dallas's toughest neighborhoods. Fans of Texas's outlaws flock to the Fort Worth Avenue site to read Clyde's tombstone: "Gone But Not Forgotten."

SWISS AVENUE
Major restorations going on in Big D revolve around these grand old early mansions.

WOODVILLE

BIG THICKET NATIONAL PRESERVE
Gateway to amazing array of subtropical flora & fauna covering more than 84,000 acres. Under control & protection of National Park Service. Ranger always on duty to answer questions.

ARLINGTON

SIX FLAGS OVER TEXAS
Huge recreational/entertainment park has six historically-themed sections. Relive flavor of Texas's past. Be sure to ride thrilling Log Flume & Judge Roy Scream.

QUITMAN

DOGWOOD FESTIVAL
Marked trails through woods afford views of beautiful white blossoms each April. More than 4 miles of this wildflower can be seen around picturesque Lake Lydia.

BONHAM

SAM RAYBURN LIBRARY
See exact duplicate of Speaker Rayburn's U.S. Capitol office, plus gavel he banged on historic occasions.

CORSICANA

CORSICANA FRUITCAKE
Stop by Collin Street Bakery and get your Texas pecan-laden cake early before Christmas rush.

MOUNT VERNON

SCENIC DRIVE
Take Texas-37 south to FM-21 through Franklin County's heavily wooded area. Especially popular in fall when autumn colors are vivid on gum and other hardwoods.

ATLANTA

ATLANTA FOREST FESTIVAL
Three days in October dedicated to woodlands of area and their products. Forest skills contests, products of East Texas timberlands on display.

DENTON

PILOT KNOB
Prominent 900-foot hill, once hideout of notorious 19th-century Texas outlaw Sam Bass.

IRVING

TEXAS STADIUM
Home on the range for famed Dallas Cowboys. From April to October group tours conducted of Stadium Club, private boxes, press box, playing field, & Cowboys' dressing room.

THE PICKUP TRUCK
The Humble Mobile Home

He drives; she rides. The kids and dog are in the back. The beer and food will be finished before they get there. The kids will be sleepy and the dog will throw up.

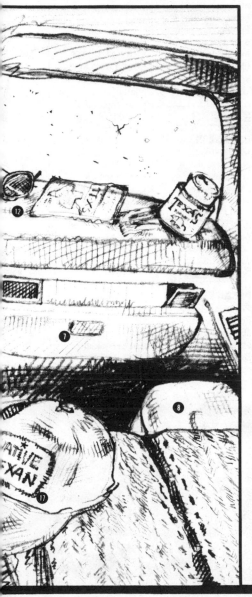

1. Texas state inspection sticker (about to expire).

2. Texas-shaped key ring.

3. Two half-empty Marlboro packs under visor.

4. Gas gauge. Indicates full: just filled up at Exxon station (got Black Gold trading stamps).

5. Air conditioner going full blast.

6. Radio tuned to KOKE going full blast.

7. Glove compartment contents: unused Dairy Queen napkins; packets of salt and pepper; matches; Oilers schedule; churchkey; maps; open package of Nabisco peanut-butter-and-cheese crackers (stale); unpaid speeding ticket; loose bobby pins; flashcubes; Kodak Instamatic.

8. Igloo cooler contents: Diet Dr. Pepper; cold fried chicken wrapped in foil; six-pack of Pearl beer; two bottles of Big Red; three bunches of green grapes.

9. Tubular hat rack installed on rear view mirror bracket; securely holds hat upside down.

10. Armadillo-shaped air freshener tied to mirror bracket.

11. Windshield: dusty; spattered with bugs; crack in right side caused by small flying rock.

12. On the dashboard: empty foam rubber roadie, says "Texas Turkey" over picture of armadillo; beef jerky still in cellophane wrapper; Texas Highway Department map, ripped and Scotch-taped; mirrored, aviator-style sunglasses; matches; half-eaten Payday candy bar, melted; tapes of Willie, Waylon, and Delbert.

13. Forty-channel Midland CB radio for keeping track of state police.

14. Roadie caddy contents: can of Pearl beer in a "Luv Ya Blue" roadie, half-empty; can of Diet Dr. Pepper not in a roadie, almost empty; package of unopened fried pigskins; box of Kleenex.

15. On the floor: matches; flashlight; two churchkeys; maps; empty Pearl beer cans; tackle box.

16. On the seat: saddle-blanket seat covers; dog hairs; Chee-tos crumbs; loose change, hoof pick.

17. Gimme cap; band is sweaty. "Native Texan" slogan essential when mingling with city folk.

Tour No. 3

CENTRAL TEXAS

LBJ land. The fabled Hill Country or "jewel of the state" as some Texans have been known to call it. Noted for its prestigious summer camps, hunter's ranches, fields of bluebonnets, the University of Texas, and the best of restored Texas houses. Lovely climate year round, but especially nice during the summer months.

BALLINGER

COWBOY & HIS HORSE STATUE
Local cowboy Charles Noyes was killed in a range mishap—this homage to him by Pompeo Coppini was commissioned by the Noyes family. Courthouse square at intersection of U.S.-83 & U.S.-67.

KILLEEN

FORT HOOD
Greatest concentration of armored power in nation; open to visitors. Main gate is on U.S.-190 one mile west of town. Jane Fonda picketed here in sixties.

SAN SABA

PECAN FESTIVAL
Pecan capital of Texas fetes its abundant groves each December. Bring a nutcracker.

COLEMAN

COLEMAN COUNTY MUSEUM
Large horse statue brought here in 1884 to display saddles. Open weekends.

NATIONAL CHAMPIONSHIP DOVE COOK-OFF
Big mourning dove hunting area—town hosts cook-off of prized birds. Cash prizes are awarded to best dove dish using 3 or more birds. Doves furnished by Coleman Chamber of Commerce if you let them know in advance. Recipes will be kept confidential and dishes are judged on flavor (40 points), appearance (40 points), uniqueness (20 points). Trophy awarded for most unique cook-site (one man came in

chuck wagon last year, another created Spanish setting).

BROWNWOOD

DOUGLAS MACARTHUR ACADEMY OF FREEDOM
Dedicated and endorsed by late general, study center on Howard Payne University campus displays personal souvenirs. Tours daily.

AUSTIN

MOUNT BONNELL
Overlooking Lake Austin with dramatic views of city and Hill Country, *the* make-out spot for local teens, UT fraternity & sorority folks. Also prime spot for watching the sun set. Careful of the rock ledge!

STATE CAPITOL
Pink granite building is largest state capitol — only slightly smaller than national capitol in Washington, D.C. Admission to 1888 structure is free.

GREEN PASTURES RESTAURANT
Lovely old Koock family home is longtime popular eating place. Many weddings held among peacocks and live oaks on

grounds. Still family-run, using many of Mary Faulk Koock's famous recipes, such as Van Cliburn biscuits, Lady Bird's chili, Nellie Connally's chutney. Gracious, antique-filled rooms are decorated in turn-of-century style.

MOON TOWERS
Since 1895 these 165-foot-tall structures have illuminated city with artificial "moonlight" effect. Listed in National Register of Historic Places. Only remaining light system of kind in world.

LYNDON BAINES JOHNSON LIBRARY
First presidential library built on a university campus; on 14 acres at University of Texas. UT paid for construction of massive building designed by Gordon Bunshaft of Skidmore, Owings & Merrill. Houses 36 million personal & official documents & presidential papers. Film of LBJ's career is on view. Tier after stunning tier of red buckram-bound document boxes visible through glass facade. Free to the public; open daily.

BARTON SPRINGS AT ZILKER PARK
Every Austinite & UT Longhorn's favorite swimmin' hole is this 1,000-foot, 68-degree pool. Open during summer months.

GOVERNOR'S MANSION
Austin's most elegant house. Constructed in 1855, mansion is across from capitol, still major residence of Texas governors.

O. HENRY HOME AND MUSEUM
Residence of William Sydney Porter, a.k.a. short story writer O. Henry. Desk, writing materials, other memorabilia on view daily.

HUNT

CAMP COUNTRY
Along meandering Guadalupe River are prestigious summer camps like Mystic, Stewart, La Junta, Heart o' the Hills, & Waldemar.

LA GRANGE CHICKEN RANCH

Gone but not forgotten: Texas's most famous ranch—next to the King-sized one. It never was a poultry farm, but at one time had plenty of cute chicks. Closed down in 1973 by Marvin Zindler, a Houston TV consumer advocate, the ranch has been successfully renovated into a hit musical, a best-selling record album, and a Hollywood movie. It has earned a lot of chicken feed for Texans Larry King (Putnam), Pete Masterson (Angleton), Carole Hall (Abilene), and Tommy Tune (Houston), who collaborated on bringing the legendary story to Broadway as *The Best Little Whorehouse in Texas*.

MADISONVILLE

YESTERYEAR
Recreated frontier town. Bank, saloon, blacksmith shop, general store, cobbler shop faithfully redone. Homemade lemonade ice cream in summertime. Open daily in summer; weekends in winter.

BRENHAM

MAIFEST For over 100 years annual fair has been held on second weekend in May. Entire town joins in old-fashioned country fair-fest.

MEXIA

TEHUACANA HILLS
Once farmland for peaceful Tehuacana Indian tribe destroyed by invading Comanches. Highest land area between Houston & Dallas.

COLLEGE STATION

TEXAS WORLD SPEEDWAY
One of nation's best racing facilities. Two-mile oval speedway, three-mile grand prix course. Attracts top names in racing world, seats 26,000.

GIDDINGS

SERBIN COMMUNITY
Six miles south of oil-booming town on F.M.-2239 is old Wendish church (Wends were an early German people). Unusual seating arrangement—men occupy balcony, women & children downstairs. Ball on steeple's weather vane engraved with history of Wendish, their church.

SAN MARCOS

AQUARENA SPRINGS
On Spring Lake, where huge springs are source of San Marcos River. Submarine theater features underwater shows. Also glass-bottom boats, old mill, aerial tram. Don't miss swimming pigs. Open year-round.

WONDER WORLD
Earthquake-formed cavern discovered in 1893. Cave tours every 15 minutes.

REPUBLIC OF TEXAS CHILYMPIAD
Chili cooking contest held in September to select chef to represent Lone Star state in World Championship Chili Cookoff at Terlingua.

TEXAS WATER SAFARI
Eight days each June one of the world's toughest canoe races takes place on clear, cold, spring-fed San Marcos River. Very splashy.

ROUND ROCK

INN AT BUSHY CREEK
Restored 1850 landmark now a charming restaurant. *The* place to go for Sunday dinner. Antique decor. Reservations essential.

ROUND ROCK CEMETERY
Most famous resident here is notorious outlaw Sam Bass, who was ambushed & shot by Texas Rangers in 1878 during local bank holdup.

LULING

WATERMELON THUMP
Always the last weekend in July, this annual event pays tribute to the area's major crop. You thump a watermelon to test for ripeness by flicking third finger against melon—a hollow sound says ripe.

LOCKHART

BATTLE OF PLUM CREEK
On second weekend in May, locals reenact Battle of Plum Creek, an Indian battle that took place hereabouts on August 12, 1840. Outdoor drama presented in city park.

GRUENE

GRUENE HALL
Texas's oldest dance hall in recently restored town (pronounced "green") on banks of Guadalupe River north of New Braunfels. Gruene is an old German cotton town now listed on the National Register of Historic Places.

GRUENE RAFT TRIPS
Gruene River Company at 1496 Gruene Loop Road arranges guides or rent-your-own rafts for trips down rushing Guadalupe River. Will also plan float trips down lower canyons of Rio Grande in Big Bend National Park.

ROUND TOP

HENKEL SQUARE
One of last remaining picturesque towns in Texas. Thanks to Miss Ima Hogg & Mrs. Charles Bybee, two great philanthropists, 19th-century German-influenced town has been faithfully restored. See real dog-run houses, chinked-wall stout houses, clapboard churches, stenciled ceilings, board & batten cottages, superb simple furniture of early Texas. Open daily, candlelight tours by arrangement.

HENKEL SQUARE COTTAGES
Live like early settlers — at least for one night. Several quaint restored cottages with period furniture available for limited number of visitors. For reservations write *P.O. Box 28, Round Top 78954*

BRADY

TEXAS MUZZLE-LOADING RIFLE ASSOCIATION
Headquarters for group that meets 3 times a year. "Frost on the Cactus" shoot is held every February, others in June, October.

FREDERICKS BURG

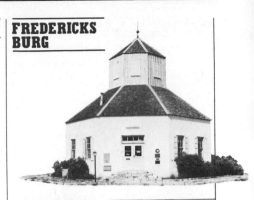

VEREINS KIRCHE
Reconstructed eight-sided structure known as coffee mill church, first public building in the city; served as a school, meeting hall, church.

LADY BIRD JOHNSON PARK
190-acre municipal park named for former First Lady has small lake, camping facilities, and hiking trails.

ADMIRAL NIMITZ CENTER
Located in historic Nimitz Hotel, constructed by grandfather of native son Admiral Chester W. Nimitz, commander in chief of Pacific fleet during World War II, center features naval exhibits, war relics.

BALANCED ROCK
Perched on incredibly small base is huge, easily accessible boulder. A favorite spot for snapshots and picnics.

SUNDAY HOUSES
Early German settlers built these tiny houses to use only on weekends. They journeyed into town from nearby farms & ranches for marketing, church. Many houses have been restored, historical markers granted. Not open to the public but visible from street.

BASTROP

"LOST PINES" OF TEXAS
In 3,550 rolling acres of Bastrop State Park are strange, misplaced "lost pines" — an isolated area of East Texas in which pine trees have inexplicably grown.

LOCK'S DRUG STORE
Nineteenth-century drugstore, doctor's office at 1003 Main Street with all furnishings, equipment preserved. Plus old-fashioned ice cream parlor still serving goodies.

SALADO

GRACE JONES
Chic, former New York model-Air Force test pilot opened exclusive fashion shop in 1961. Has been dressing crème de la crème of Texas ladies in Halston, Geoffrey Beene, Michael Vollbracht ever since. Legendary for her personal attention and service. Air strip near the Austin limestone shop is where South Texas ranchers' wives land in Cessna crop-dusting planes and where Houston/Dallas clients arrive in helicopters.

TEMPLE

SCOTT-WHITE
CLINIC Famed hospital sits on hill overlooking town. Founded by local Texas doctors who had studied at Mayo Clinic, it is internationally known for medical facilities and services.

BLANCO

SCENIC DRIVE
Follow dramatic ridge known as Devil's Backbone by taking R.M.-32 from U.S.-281 south of Blanco toward Wimberley.

JOHNSON CITY

LYNDON BAINES JOHNSON NATIONAL HISTORIC SITE
Boyhood hometown, house of LBJ. Johnson family, early pioneers to area, settled town. Open daily.

CONCAN

GARNER STATE
PARK On freezing cold Frio River, park named for former vice-president of U.S., John Nance Garner, raised near here. Popular park with Texas teen agers.

SCENIC DRIVE
See exceptional scenery along Frio Rio Canyon by taking routes U.S.-83, F.M.-1050.

NEW BRAUNFELS

LANDA PARK
Exceptionally lovely city park on crystal- clear Comal River. Good picnic spot; boating, swimming in spring-fed pool.

COMAL COTTON
MILLS Where Texas mothers buy dark cottons for back-to-school clothes. Mill open daily.

WURSTFEST One
of most beloved Texas fetes. Held every November, 10-day event is state's biggest beer bust. Features traditional German bands, dancing groups, singing societies, a "sausage dog" show, costumes, lots of hangovers. Best of the wurst.

CAMP WARNECKE
Popular resort for generations. Since the twenties, Texas kids have been riding inner tubes down chilly Comal River rapids here. Screen-porched cottages on water's edge. Open from Easter till two weekends after Labor Day.

WACO

TEXAS RANGER MUSEUM AND HALL OF FAME
Honors Texas's most famous arm of the law. Fort Fisher is now headquarters for Company F Rangers. Established in 1837, fort is on I-35 near Lake Brazos. Arresting exhibitions!

ARMSTRONG BROWNING
LIBRARY World's largest collection of Robert & Elizabeth Browning works, memoirs. On Baylor University campus.

OLD SUSPENSION BRIDGE
Nation's largest single span suspension bridge when completed in 1870; still in use across Brazos River.

HIGHLAND GAMES
On bonny banks o' the Bosque River, annual mid-May gathering features Scottish games, music, dances, contests. On McLennan Community College campus.

BRAZOS QUEEN
View Lake Brazos from replica of 18th-century riverboat. Excursions daily; Saturday night dinner cruise. Reservations required.

STONEWALL

LYNDON BAINES JOHNSON NATIONAL HISTORIC SITE
See famed LBJ Ranch, Herefords. See late president's birthplace, grave in family cemetery. Free bus tours daily.

STONEWALL PEACH FESTIVAL
Peach capital of Texas honors native fruit each June with 2-day celebration featuring plenty of fresh peaches & fresh peach ice cream.

LUCKENBACH

TEXAS'S TINIEST TOWN.
Luckenbach —population 3— was center stage for late Hondo Crouch, who owned part of it. Now site of annual Luckenbach World's Fair (each June) run by Guich Koock. Town has wonderful Texas decor, memorabilia, architecture. Takes only a minute to see it all.

BOERNE

OLD KENDALL INN
Former stagecoach inn built in 1859 still takes guests. Catered to frontier celebrities, lawmen, cattle drivers, army officers. If these walls could talk . . .

CLIFTON

NORSE SETTLEMENT
Norwegian capital of Texas. Groups of Norwegians were brought to area in 1850s by Cleng Peerson, known as "father of Norse immigration to America." Peerson's grave located in Lutheran churchyard northwest of town. Every November, giant smorgasbord held at church—women wear the traditional Norwegian *drakt* costume.

WASHINGTON

WASHINGTON-ON-THE-BRAZOS STATE PARK
May be most historic spot in all Texas. In 1822 a ferry operated here across Brazos River; in 1836 provisional government of Texas was formed here and Texas Declaration of Independence & Constitution written; in 1842 briefly capital of Texas. Park's star-shaped museum chronicles all in detail.

BANDERA

DUDE RANCH CENTER
Ranch life as it actually was. Center of dude ranch country. Over a dozen accredited dude ranches with corrals, airstrips, trail rides, cookouts dot Hill Country. Don't overlook hitching posts still in use downtown.

KERRVILLE

ROAMING DEER
Caution: white-tailed deer so numerous motorists are warned to watch out for them on highways around area, especially at night.

INGRAM

HILL COUNTY ARTS FOUNDATION
Summer theater & art programs held daily June-August. Theater sits on banks of Guadalupe River.

JUNCTION

HILL COUNTRY BILLY SALE
Annual event in August with prize Angora goats featured in auction ring.

SCENIC DRIVE
Southwest along U.S.-377 as it follows Llano River. Overlook about 20 miles south.

Tour No. 4

WEST TEXAS

The Wild West section of the state. So isolated you can drive for miles in some parts before seeing any life form more complicated than a horny toad. Never travel here during the summer if you can help it (the wintertime can also be harsh); the crisp air of spring and fall's blooming cactuses, however, are not to be missed. Salt tablets and a canvas water bag for the car radiator are almost mandatory.

TERLINGUA

WORLD'S CHAMPIONSHIP CHILI COOKOFF
Every November thousands of Texans and non-Texans fly into this former ghost town and start firing up their bowls of red.

MERCURY MINE
See where millions of dollars' worth of quicksilver was mined in 1890s. Rock hounds & cactus fans can have their pick, too.

CHISOS MOUNTAINS LODGE
Open year-round, the only place to stay other than the park's camp facilities. More than a mile above sea level, a magnificent view of the vast park.

BIG BEN

BIG BEND NATIONAL PARK
More than 1,000 square miles on the Big Bend of Rio Grande. Includes Chihuahuan Desert, Santa Elena canyons, Chisos Mountains. Over 350 bird species, 1,100 plants, & varied desert wildlife have been identified, more than at any other national park. Rare Colima warblers' only U.S. nests are here.

PRESIDIO Prides itself as "hottest spot in nation." It is.

EL CAMINO DEL RIO HIGHWAY
While enjoying spectacular scenery along famed "River Road," stop at tepee shelters provided by the Texas State Highway Department. Perfect spot for shade and a sandwich.

EL CAMINO DEL RIO DRIVE
Spectacular drive starts here on F.M.-170. Follows twisting Rio Grande into canyons of Chinati Mountains.

STRAWBERRY CACTUS Keep eye out for—but hands off—tall succulent topped with red fruitlike blossoms growing profusely in these parts.

WOODWARD AGATE RANCH

Collect world-famous Texas red plume & pompon rough agate for 35 cents a pound on ranch's 4,000 acres. Ranch experts grade stones for you. Lapidary shop offers selected specimens.

FORT DAVIS

MCDONALD OBSERVATORY On 6,791-foot Mount Locke, UT facility houses nation's third largest reflector (107 inches). Look through telescope on last Wednesday of every month—arrangements must be made in writing.

DAVIS MOUNTAINS STATE PARK Camping facilities are in sloping basin of these dramatic mountains. Also a multilevel hotel Indian Lodge.

SIERRA BLANCA

YUCCA FORESTS Drive along flat ranching areas edged by Quitman Mountains and gasp at giant yuccas growing 15 to 20 feet high. Best in March & April when stalks topped with huge white blossoms.

BRACKETT VILLE

ALAMO VILLAGE Movie set where John Wayne filmed *The Alamo*. Now family recreation center operated by the Shahan Angus Ranch, site includes stage depot, saddle shop, & jailhouse. Stagecoach rides during summer months.

LAJITAS

RIO GRANDE FLOAT TRIPS One- to three-day raft trips through canyons of Big Bend availabe from the Lajitas Trading Post. All trips made with professional guide. Also wilderness mountain pack trips.

DEL RIO

VAL VERDE WINERY Oldest bonded winery in Texas. A family enterprise in its fourth generation, the winery welcomes visitors daily.

MERINO SHEEP AND ANGORA GOATS Area touts itself as "Wool and Mohair Capital of the World." Thousands of sheep, lambs, goats on nearby ranches.

LANGTRY

JUDGE ROY BEAN CENTER Rustic saloon, courtroom, & billiard hall of famous, controversial "Law West of the Pecos" Bean.

MARATHON

BLACK GAP WILDLIFE MANAGEMENT AREA Over 100,000 acres devoted to studying native wildlife ofarea. Visitors can see bobcat, javelina, coyote, & pronghorn antelope. Camping facilities.

GAGE HOTEL

ALPINE

RIO GRANDE CANYON FIELD TRIPS Chihuahuan Desert Research Institute conducts special field seminars on rafts going down Rio Grande.

EL PASO

SOUTHWESTERN SUN CARNIVAL

This city gets more days of sunshine than any other in U.S.—from December 20 to January 1 city celebrates its magnificent climate.

TIGUA INDIAN RESERVATION

Oldest ethnic community presently in Texas. Tour Ysleta del Sur Pueblo & see Tigua descendants create pottery, beadwork, silver crafts; bake bread in beehive ovens. Tribal dances on weekends.

OLD MISSIONS. El Paso has several gracious Spanish missions, older than better-known California ones. Chapels still in daily use. Tour San Elizario Presidio, Nuestra Señora del Carmen, Ysleta, Guadalupe, & Nuestra Señora de la Concepción del Socorro.

SCENIC DRIVE

Take winding Loop 375 (Trans-Mountain Road) to climb through Smugglers Gap & Mount Franklin. Road provides panoramic view of city, 2 countries, 3 states. Most romantic at night.

RANGER PEAK TRAMWAY

Aerial cable car provides exciting view of El Paso, White Sands National Park in New Mexico, & Mexico. Starts at noon; last ride 8 P.M.

MCKELLIGON CANYON PARK

During summer months, stage productions include pageant with priests, Indians, horse-mounted conquistadors in the amphitheater.

PINE SPRINGS

GUADALUPE MOUNTAINS NATIONAL PARK

Park with elevation ranging from 3,650 to 8,751 feet is at summit of Guadalupe Peak, highest point in Texas. Along with deep canyons and rare mixture of animal life & plants, four of state's highest peaks are here.

PECOS

CANTALOUPES

Grown in sun-drenched fields irrigated from vast underground water sources, Pecos cantaloupes are to Texas as lobsters are to Maine. Recommended source: Foster's stand on I-20.

FORT STOCKTON

DINOSAUR PARK

Preserved footprints of prehistoric animals are attraction in county park. Step on it!

GREY MULE SALOON

One of first Texas honky tonks has been restored at Callaghan & Main Streets.

PAISANO PETE

"World's largest roadrunner"—a 20-foot-long, 11-foot-high statue erected downtown to honor local, fast-moving bird. Don't try to catch Pete.

MONAHANS

SANDHILLS STATE PARK

Sahara Desert of Texas. Over 4,000 wind-sculpted acres. Huge sandpile is a big favorite with little kids & sand surfers alike.

ODESSA

JACKRABBIT STATUE

"World's largest jackrabbit," ten-foot bunny sits downtown & is a favorite photo spot. The real things hop around outside town. Watch out, they *are* big.

GLOBE OF THE GREAT SOUTHWEST
Authentic replica of original Shakespeare theater. Only group in Southwest offering year-round classics with professional actors.

MIDLAND

PERMIAN BASIN PETROLEUM MUSEUM AND HALL OF FAME
Lots of black gold lore. Traces history of petroleum—its discovery, production, & formation in famed Permian Basin.

CRANE

FREEZE-OFF CELEBRATION
July 4 celebration features homemade ice cream judging & selling. Plenty of big drips gather.

MCCAMEY

OLD FIFTH STREET
False fronts of stores along town's old main street recall early boom days—general store, assay office, bakery, etc.

SCENIC DRIVE
Take U.S.-67 east to U.S.-385 northwest across King Mountains for extraordinary views of oil wells, ranch land, & a 3,000-foot mesa.

IRAAN

FANTASYLAND
Huge statues of Alley Oop, comic strip caveman, created by hometown boy Vince T. Hamlin. Also Oola & dinosaur Dinny, who is 65 feet long, 16 feet tall, weighs 80,000 pounds. Best snapshot—atop Oop's 20-foot hat.

BIG LAKE

SANTA RITA NO. 1
Well plus large oil pool around it is one reason why University of Texas is so damn rich. UT system owns most of grazing land in Big Lake. Hook 'em.

ROBERT LEE

HAYRICK GHOST TOWN
Northeast of town in Kickapoo Mountains on hayrick-shaped hill are crumbling remains of abandoned town, once county seat.

SAN ANGELO

SAN ANGELO ROPING FESTIVAL
Cowboy roping competition in November; two-day event. Lotsa lassos.

FORT CONCHO
Among best preserved of Texas frontier military forts. Eighteen original (1860s) buildings still standing and in use. Open daily.

MERTZON

SHERWOOD COURTHOUSE
Example of early Texas courthouse still stands in Sherwood, one mile north of town.

ELDORADO

EL DORADO WOOLEN MILLS
Only woolen mill in Southwest weaving fabrics from virgin wool and mohair produced on nearby ranches. Sales showroom sells thick, woolly stadium blankets & upholstery fabrics.

SONORA

THE CAVERNS OF SONORA
Past president of National Speleological Society proclaimed these caves "the most beautiful in the world."

ROCKSPRINGS

ANGORA GOAT BREEDERS ASSOCIATION MUSEUM
See how your favorite sweater or blanket came to be. Early history of Angora goat-raising industry on record here. Only registry office for industry in U.S.

Tour No. 5

SOUTH TEXAS

Coastal, semitropical, this section features fine beaches, serious hunting and fishing spots, old missions. Where breakfast grapefruit and assorted vegetables are grown for the nation's tables. "Snowbirds" flock down from the north each winter in their Winnebagos—the South really shines from Thanksgiving till Easter.

BAY CITY

RICE FESTIVAL Honors area's major industry. An Outstanding Rice Farmer of the Year chosen; rice luncheon. Two days every October.

VICTORIA

TEXAS ZOO Zoo devoted exclusively to species native to Texas. Animals displayed in their natural environments.

NAVE MUSEUM Named for Royston Nave, Texas artist who made a name for himself in New

York art circles in 1920s. Painted extensively in and around Victoria. Greco- Roman hall built by his widow in 1931 houses Naves's paintings. Open Wednesday–Sunday.

INDIANOLA

GHOST TOWN Texas's best-known ghost town. Wiped off map by Sept. 17, 1875 hurricane. Rebuilt. Another severe storm struck 11 years later and again literally blew it away.

LA SALLE STATUE Only person left standing in town. Rose granite statue of Rene Robert Cavelier, Sieur de La Salle. French explorer was first foreigner to leave boot-prints in sands of Indianola.

FANNIN

FANNIN BATTLEGROUND Monument marks site where Col. James W. Fannin, Jr., and his men surrendered to Mexican army after battle of Coleto Creek on March 20, 1836. Picnic facilities.

GOLIAD

MISSIONS Goliad is one of Texas's oldest municipalities, inhabited long before recorded history. Spanish built missions when they arrived. See Nuestra Señora del Espiritu Santo de Zuñiga in Goliad State Park; ruins of Mission Señora del Rosario, founded in 1754 by missionaries.

REFUGIO

FIESTA FAELA

Each June Spanish and Irish descendants in this town fling themselves into joint festival with food, drink, crafts from their respective countries.

BALLYGARRETT

Outstanding old mansion listed in National Architectural Registry. Named for town in County Wexford, Ireland, from which many colonists came to Refugio in 1833. Restored house has been turned into a gift shop.

STATE CHAMPIONSHIP FROG JUMPING CONTEST

Held every July 4. Takes big leap to get to event.

SINTON

WELDER WILDLIFE FOUNDATION

Largest privately endowed wildlife refuge in world. Gift from late rancher Bob Welder, portions of acreage are on Welder Ranch, established from a Spanish land grant. Tour groups admitted each Thursday at 3 P.M., except holidays.

ARANSAS PASS

SHRIMPOREE AND SHRIMP STATUE

Salutes huge Gulf of Mexico industry with shrimp-boil luncheon, colorful blessing of fleet. Don't miss 19-foot shrimp statue. In May.

FISHERMAN'S PARADISE

Town advertised as "where they bite every day." Countless bait & tackle shops supply anglers' needs. Many wharves, piers, jetties for catching redfish, sand trout, sheepshead, flounder, drum, croakers. Group boats for hire for bay, deep-sea fishing.

ROCKPORT

"BIG TREE" An immense (422 inches in circumference, 44 feet high, 89-foot crown) live oak tree, largest in Texas; estimated to be 2,000 years old.

SANDIA

KNOLLE JERSEY FARM

World's largest Jersey herd corralled. And you thought Texas had only beef cattle on the hoof.

PORT ARANSAS

TARPON INN

Landmark hotel & restaurant was built in 1855. Wide, open porches overlook Corpus Christi ship channel. Twenty-six rooms. Dining room seats 100—serves Gulf shrimp, red snapper, kingfish, flounder bought daily off local fishing boats.

MUSTANG ISLAND STATE PARK

Five miles of Gulf beach. Features sand dunes, sea oats, picnic arbors, nature trails, beach morning glory, bird-watching.

CORPUS CHRISTI

BUCCANEER DAYS

Local pirates, pirate maids annually capture city hall, take mayor for dunk in nearby Corpus Christi Bay. Ten days of pageantry in late April.

PADRE ISLAND NATIONAL SEASHORE

One of longest natural seashores in U.S.

Texas's seacoast playground. Narrow island stretches from Corpus Christi south almost to Mexico.

KINGSVILLE-RAYMONDSVILLE

Fill 'er up if driving between these two towns on Highway 77. No gas stations for over 73 miles in heartland of vast King Ranch.

HARLINGEN

CONFEDERATE AIR FORCE FLYING MUSEUM

Impressive array of World War II planes from U.S., Britain, Japan, Germany. Collection includes German Messerschmitt, British Supermarine Spitfires, American F8F Bearcat & P-47 Thunderbolt. Flying demonstrations staged at well-attended CAF air show every October.

SAN BENITO

"RESACA CITY" Noted for gracious residential areas on edges of beautiful *resacas* —quiet lakes that were formerly channels of Rio Grande.

PORT ISABEL

PORT ISABEL LIGHTHOUSE STATE PARK Built in 1853, in use until 1905. Climb spiral staircase for fine view of Laguna Madre, South Padre Island.

QUEEN ISABELLA STATE FISHING PIER Abandoned causeway offers exceptional angling opportunities. Fish-cleaning tables, attractor lights. Fishing fee valid for 24-hour period.

BROWNSVILLE

PORT OF BROWNSVILLE Only U.S. seaport within railroad switching distance of two nations.

PALMITO HILL Final land engagement of Civil War fought at nearby Palmito Ranch.

MERCEDES

PALM AND CITRUS GROVES Lush, irrigated area of Lower Rio Grande Valley known as state's winter garden. See huge palm trees, lush groves of grapefruit, orange trees. Famed fruit for sale at roadside stands.

ALAMO

LIVE STEAM MUSEUM Many types of steam engines, pumps — all in running order — that have generated power since 1880s. Engines on display range from 140-ton World War II Liberty Ship power plant to miniature that can be held in hand. Open Tuesday–Saturday, November–April.

MISSION

LOS EBANOS FERRY Only existing hand-operated ferry on U.S.–Mexican border. Crosses Rio Grande from clump of ebony trees (*los ebanos*).

LA LOMITA CHAPEL Tiny chapel (12 by 25 feet) hidden away in Texas mesquite trees was built by Oblate Fathers in 1849.

RIO GRANDE CITY

OUR LADY OF LOURDES GROTTO Replica of healing shrine in France. Contains statue of St. Bernadette, peasant girl who was visited by Virgin Mary near the French town.

LAREDO

REPUBLIC OF RIO GRANDE BUILDING Whitewashed adobe building with 2-foot-thick walls has had 7 flags fly over it. Now a museum, houses lots of Rio Grande Republic (1839–41) memorabilia.

COTULLA

WELHAUSEN ELEMENTARY SCHOOL Modest red brick schoolhouse is site of LBJ's first (1928) teaching assignment.

CARRIZO SPRINGS

WORLD CHAMPIONSHIP SLINGSHOT TOURNAMENT Sponsored by Dimmit County 4-H Club, annual event features male & female contestants firing slingshots at targets at range of 33 feet.

CRYSTAL CITY

POPEYE STATUE Town famous for outstanding spinach crop erected salute to cartoon sailor in city square.

UVALDE

GARNER MEMORIAL MUSEUM Former home of John "Cactus Jack" Garner, vice-president of U.S. under F.D.R. Open daily.

HONDO

WORLD CHAMPIONSHIP CORN SHUCKING CONTEST Every July 4. Ah, shucks.

DINOSAUR TRACKS Preserved in stone, easily visible tracks probably made by Trachodons, duck-billed herbivores about 40 feet long. In Hondo Creek riverbed.

CASTROVILLE

ST. LOUIS DAY HOMECOMING Held in August on banks of Medina River. Village, settled by French-Germans in 1844, hosts 5-ton beef barbecue with mouthwatering Alsace-style sausages.

SAN ANTONIO

THE ALAMO
Mission San Antonio de Valero, "Cradle of Texas Liberty," is on Alamo Plaza. Open daily.

BUCKHORN HALL OF HORNS
One of world's finest animal horn collections. Horns, memorabilia from trappers, traders, hunters, cowboys.

HEMISFAIR PLAZA
Site of 1968 World's Fair; 750-foot Tower of the Americas offers 2 sky-high dining levels plus observation deck with panoramic views of Alamo City.

MENGER HOTEL
Opened doors in 1859. Wealthy south Texas ranchers keep suites so their wives can shop at Frost's. In Roosevelt Bar, T.R. recruited notorious Rough Riders. Ask for Roosevelt Special, relive San Juan Hill. Taft, McKinley, Eisenhower, LBJ, Nixon all slept here.

KING WILLIAM DISTRICT
State's first historic district. Lovely street of mansions originally settled by German merchants in late 19th century. Walking tour availabe from Conservation Society.

LA VILLITA
Mexican village with romantic, narrow streets, shaded patios, adobe houses.

RIVER WALK
The Venice of Texas. Paseo del Rio built by WPA in 1939–40. In heart of city, 21 blocks meander along San Antonio River.

PEARSALL

PEANUT STATUE
Honoring area's most important crop — more than 44 million pounds of peanuts marketed here annually — is giant cement goober.

FLORESVILLE

CANARY ISLANDERS CEMETERY
Established sometime prior to 1732 by islanders who formed first organized civil settlement in Texas at San Fernando de Bexar, now San Antonio. Several old Texas families can trace their lineage from these colonists.

PANNA MARIA
Said to be oldest Polish settlement in America. Established December 1854 by Polish Catholics, town's name means "Virgin Mary."

POTEET

STRAWBERRY MONUMENT AND WATER TOWER
"Strawberry capital of Texas" created world's tallest strawberry — actually 130-foot water tower painted to resemble fruit. On Texas-16.

SEGUIN

PRE-TEXAS REVOLUTION BUILDINGS
Designated by historical markers. Texas Ranger station built in 1823, Magnolia Hotel in 1824, Juan Seguin post office built in 1823 by Mexican government.

SHINER

SPOETZEL BREWERY
Maker of "big beer from littlest brewery" gives tours of Shiner plant Monday–Thursday. Have a longneck on the house.

HALLETTS VILLE

STATE CHAMPIONSHIP DOMINO TOURNEY
On fourth Sunday in January watch really good Texas domino players "down" those spinners & draw from the "graveyard."

THE UNPLEASANTNESS AT THE ALAMO

Only Texans could turn defeat into a legend — and a song, and a tourist attraction, and a major motion picture.

In 1836, 188 rebellious white settlers took over the Alamo — a mission church serving as a Mexican cavalry outpost — and managed to hold off Santa Ana's 5,000 soldiers for 13 days. On March 6, the fort was overrun and its defenders all killed, including Davy Crockett and Jim Bowie. Forty-six days later, Sam Houston drove the Mexicans out of Texas for good at the Battle of San Jacinto.

The Daughters of the Republic religiously maintain the Alamo in all of its original glory (no air-conditioning, for authenticity's sake). But even they couldn't prevent the features of John Wayne, Laurence Harvey, and Richard Widmark from appearing on the huge painting, "The Battle of the Alamo," that hangs within its walls.

Special Tour

THE BORDER TOWN BINGE

Six border towns dot the 1,800-mile stretch of the Rio Grande dividing Texas and Mexico— Texans go to them all the time, anytime, for any reason. Although purists claim border towns are not exactly Mexican, they are Mexican enough to provide the fun-filled experience known as the Border Town Binge. Saying, "Let's go to the border" to a Texan brings to mind thoughts of one grande party, of going to a place where you can let your hair down and do a lot without spending a whole heck of a lot of money. It is a vacation never limited to any one season. Senior citizen groups make the trek as often as UT students. Everyone gets their fair share of Tecate, margaritas, and frog legs. Bienvenido!

● **EL PASO/CIUDAD JUAREZ** Where sun "has failed to shine only 31 days in the last 16 years." Ciudad Juarez is Mexico's largest border city. Located in mountain pass (from which name El Paso comes). Superb climate, dramatic scenery, & best shopping make Juarez most popular border town. Lots of army personnel plus tons of tourists give it a twenty-four-hour party atmosphere. Traditional *mercados* (markets) plus government-sponsored Pronaf (*Programa Nacional Fronterizo*) shopping center across from Cordova Bridge. Famous Juarez Race Track (dog racing), nightclubs, original Julio's Cafe Corona where crowds line up nightly for *filet ranchero* (steak with chiles).

● **DEL RIO/CIUDAD ACUÑA** Called "Queen City of Rio Grande," Del Rio is only recognized port of entry from Texas into Mexico between San Antonio and El Paso. *Fiesta de Amistad* (Festival of Friendship) held four days each October when Del Rio and Ciudad Acuña jointly celebrate international friendship with Good Neighbor Parade, *charredda* (rodeo). Ciudad Acuña shops feature handmade silver, decorative wrought iron, woven goods, & legendary Mrs. Crosby's— oldest, most famous border town meeting place. Bullfights & La Macarena for *cabrito* (barbecued goat), floor shows, dancing.

● EAGLE PASS/PIEDRAS NEGRAS

First U.S. settlement on Rio Grande. Now noted winter garden of Texas. Sportsmen come here to fish for Rio Grande catfish, hunters for upland game & white-tailed deer. Celebrates — jointly with Piedras Negras — eagerly awaited George Washington International Fiesta three days annually in February. Piedras Negras has bullfights at intervals throughout summer. Restaurants, nightclubs, including the sensational Moderna (at 407 Allende) with a real forties interior. Good mercados, too.

● LAREDO/NUEVO LAREDO

Laredo tops other Texas cities in number (7) of national flags flown over it. Crowds gather every February 13 to celebrate George Washington's Birthday — four-day event that's been held since 1898. Honors George Washington as first Western Hemisphere leader to free New World country from European dominance. Fireworks, dances, an impressive parade & coronation make you feel you're at Mount Vernon — with Latin beat. Nuevo Laredo is home for two Border Town institutions: Marti's & Cadillac Bar. Known as Bendel's of the Border, Marti's carries impressive line of men's, women's, children's apparel made in Mexico. Museum quality Pedro Friedberg chairs, carved furniture, *mas importante* paper *flores*. Cadillac Bar's air-conditioned dining room, fried frog legs, margaritas, spunky service have turned it into giant Texas club. Rumor has it Cadillac birthed Ramos gin fizz. Local mercados have fine selection of Mexican jewelry, precious metalworks. Nightclubs often feature name headliners from Mexico City.

● McALLEN/REYNOSA

Subtropical-climate city in Lower Rio Grande Valley is noted for vast citrus groves, large number of "snowbirds" who hibernate here all winter. Shares International Museum with Reynosa, featuring arts, crafts, historical memorabilia from both countries. Charming, quiet Reynosa has plenty of handcrafted goods in traditional mercado off plaza. Sunday afternoon bullfights. Everyone eventually winds up at Sam's. For over 50 years, this restaurant two short blocks from Mexican customs has drawn Hollywood types, LBJ, John Connally, hunters from all over world in search of great game dinner. Packed during whitewing season. Sunday midday meal is big event. Jorge & Pepe Elias run the hunting lodge-like restaurant.

● BROWNSVILLE/MATAMOROS

Brownsville is Texas's southernmost city; international seaport, railroad interchange point. Dates from colonial days of imperial Spain. Jointly celebrates Fiesta Internacional with Matamoros three days in September, honoring Mexican independence. Also Charro Days, a spectacular four-day-long pre-Lenten fiesta. Pageant features Mexican riders — *los charros* — and lots of the glittering, swirly national costumes of Mexico. Matamoros is wealthy cotton center for Mexico. Excellent woven goods can be found in local mercados. Bargains on pottery, too. Nightclubs and bullfights.

Mercado musts.

MERCADO MADNESS

Border town shops and mercados are filled with a variety of items at attractive prices—in other words, bargains. You must haggle with the merchants—and bartering is *mucho* easier if you know some Spanish, although every shopkeeper and mercado vendor understands English. There are no fixed prices in border towns—"I saw the same thing across the street for less" is one sure way of dropping the price on something you can't live without. You should not, however, buy everything that's *hecho en Mexico*. Some suggested things to buy—and not to buy—on the Border Town Binge:

BUY

Tortilla accessories. Covers, presses.

Serapes. Ones made in Saltillo are best; wool (*lano*) only, no synthetics or neon bright colors, please.

Clothing. Embroidered sundresses from Oaxaca, huaraches (best have "Goodyear" stamped on rubber tire soles), wedding shirts and jackets.

Crepe paper piñatas. For children's next birthday party. Also stock up on small Mexican-made objects (toys, whistles, games, jewelry) to fill piñata with.

Perfume. All well-known brands dutyfree. Good buys on Dior and Chanel. Maja is a best-seller.

Paper flowers. Stiff bouquets in brightly-colored Mexican crepe paper, stuck in vases in UT dorms and in homes all over Texas; adds permanent blooming color.

Kitchenware. Bright blue-and-white enamel spatterware bowls, cups, pots, dishes, utensils, etc.

Liquor. Real buys on cases of Mexican *cerveza*, bottles of tequila or mescal. Gets cheaper the closer you get to international bridges.

Chairs. Classic *equilaques* style with split cedar bases and rounded rawhide coverings—the chair found on many Texas porches or patios. Small, floral-painted lacquered chairs with raffia seats for children.

DON'T BUY

Oil paintings on black velvet. Especially with bullfight scenes or trio portraits of JFK, RFK, and Martin Luther King.

Spanish fly. Loses its potency the closer it gets to Texas; seems a better idea than it is.

Machetes. Bloodthirsty mottoes etched on these giant blades don't increase quality of tools.

Mounted longhorns. Texas longhorns supercede Mexican ones.

Goatskin rugs. Badly patched designs. They usually shed too much, too often.

Ojos de Dio. "Eyes of God." The story goes that one of these over a doorway or bed will warn off evil spirits. Previous owners haven't been all that satisfied.

Large, sequined sombreros. Best on the walls of Tex-Mex restaurants. They *are* works of art but you will wear yours once to a costume party and never again—so heavily encrusted with shiny sequins it gives *mucho* headache.

Jumping beans. Border town merchants swear there are critters inside making these things hop all over your palm; more like a ball bearing inside a plastic capsule.

Onyx chess and backgammon sets. Weigh a ton and are much too slippery and bulky for any serious playing.

Chapter 7

KICKER CULTURE

THE BEER BELLY

Not so much a sign of prosperity as an indication of how many cold ones a Texan has drunk. Found more on the male of the species, it is acquired in honky tonks, beer joints, and ice houses, and worked on daily. The genuine Texas Beer Belly is a good four inches of solid flab rolled over the top of the belt buckle, which can no longer be seen. A definite let-it-all-hang-out look. The boys are so proud of 'em. The girls like to pat 'em.

DRINKIN', DANCIN', & DOIN' IT

The Honky Tonk Mystique

Kicker culture got its start during the last century, in those weekly tribal gatherings of the lonesome cowhands (*kicker* is Texan for cowboy — you kick up a

A kicker and his belly.

lot of cow patties when you're out on the range). Come Friday night, after a week of campfire food and back-breaking work, the kickers would straighten out their smile pockets, brush off their boots, strap on their Colts and ride into town to the kicker palace, where they promptly blew their week's pay. It was home.

It still is. Of course, kickers are more likely now to spend their days drilling for oil or punching computers. But pay is good and honky-tonk nights are the only way to spend it — in fact, kicker culture is basically good old conspicuous consumption, prairie style. When the money is not being shelled out on the next round, it goes for a brand-new pickup (it's replaced the horse), the biggest hat, the tallest pair of boots. If you took every man and woman in every kicker palace at store-bought face value, you'd think the actual cowboy population in Texas had increased a hundredfold since the last drive to Abilene.

So practice your swagger and belly up to the bar.

KICKER PALACE PROTOCOL

You've come straight from work, maneuvered your pickup into a space in the glutted parking lot and landed a table near the band. Still you need more help. While you sit there with your first beer of the night, study these dos and don'ts for correct honky-tonking.

DOs

1. Keep your hat on inside. Whether you're a country or city cowboy, an exposed head is considered naive or downright ignorant. You will not find a dance partner.

2. Belly up to the bar. The spot for watching the angels parade by on their way to brushing their hair and redoing their makeup. Devils are found leaning up against cigarette machines and jukeboxes.

3. Drink as much as you can. Beer loosens up muscles for dancing. You may leave your beer on the table when you get up to dance. (Longnecks do get stolen, but as a rule, the waitress will leave alone all but the empties.)

4. Talk to a devil or angel when the band takes a break. This is the time to hustle.

5. Sit out breaks until the band returns. Think of what you want to request. Save your dancing energy for the band's return.

6. Write down your song request on a paper napkin and hand it quietly to a member of the band.

7. Hang out and become a regular. Know everyone's first name and you'll be afforded more privileges — a table near the band and check-cashing privileges on payday.

8. Have fun. If you can't, then go home to Johnny Carson.

DON'Ts

1. Wear a hat inside if you are a lady. This is not a costume party or the rodeo. You will defeat your purpose. Brim collisions are a hazard, and you want to get close to your cowboy when dancing.

2. Circulate around the outer perimeter of the club. This is couples' tables area. Stay out if single.

3. Stack your cans or bottles into some kind of complex design. The waitress has enough to do — don't make her unravel any Gordian knots. Never spend time counting the longnecks that have been downed at your table.

4. Talk while the band is playing. You can't possibly communicate much when the kickers are yelling "Bullshit."

5. Dance between the band's breaks unless the jukebox has a glut of Bob Wills tunes. (This is when older folks shine on the dance floor.)

6. Interrupt the band while they are playing or go up to them at the break when they are trying to enjoy their longnecks and angels.

7. Slip up and stop going five times a week. You must go regularly. Kicker regulars go honky-tonking every time the doors open at their favorite palace.

8. Get burned up, go outside, and start a brawl.

THE BIRTHPLACE OF THE BEER BELLY

Or, the Land of "*Tell Her I Ain't Here, Boys*"

Kicker palaces are the real country clubs of Texas, the places where Texans go lookin' for love and trouble. A heaven on earth for all the honky tonk devils and angels who hang out raising hell and getting drunk and the birthplace of the beer belly, a lot of weekly paychecks are blown in kicker palaces buying endless rounds of longnecks. Cowboys try to dazzle cowgirls with tall tales and fancy footwork, the bull gets spread so thick a shovel comes in handy, the parking lot is guaranteed action central if enough isn't going on inside. There are three basic kicker palace forms—the honky tonk, the ice house, and the beer joint. But in all three macho conduct and rowdy behavior are much in vogue.

Honky Tonks. Cavernous, ramshackle spots on the side of superhighways, their parking lots feature plenty of pickups with gun racks. Of course, the honky tonk has changed some since early sa-loon days. Women are no longer dance hall girls; they are custom-ers who have come to do the two-step. The spittoons have been replaced by plastic ashtrays on the bar. The piano player has given way to the jukebox or a live band people sometimes want to shoot. And the traditional swing-ing doors have been replaced by a cover charge and a hand stamp. However, simplicity remains the interior-decorating principle—breakable lamps and furniture, wall-to-wall carpeting, back-gammon boards, $200,000 sound systems or disc jockeys are not in evidence. Honky tonks are rough-and-ready and *must* have a live band or a jukebox with sensational selections.

Beer joints. Rougher and steamier than honky tonks. There is seldom, if ever, a live band. With plenty of neon beer signs for decoration, draft beer and fresh popcorn, they are also more colorfully named. The Six-Pack Lounge, Joe's Dump, Blo-N-Go, Here It Is, and Dewdrop Inn are typical. The jukebox should be very loud. A pool table is standard, and maybe some customers are playing dominoes or other bar games. Ladies who hang out in beer joints are not angels, but the men are clearly devils.

Ice houses. Although they may vary from town to town, expect a place where you can buy ice and beer. Happy hours are extremely popular and can start as early as 9:00 A.M. to accommodate the neighborhood shift workers. Basically a low-key men's club, strangers aren't always welcomed and women never come alone. This is a male-dominated outpost. Converted filling stations make great ice houses.

SATURDAY NIGHT SPECIAL

Unfortunate but true —when good ol' boys and girls go bad in Texas, they usually do it with a Saturday Night Special. This is not a packaged tour, but a cheap pistol of either .20 or .25 calibers that can be hidden in boots or the front of a pearl-snapped shirt.

Most outbursts take place in the home (crimes of passion are still the number one reason the SNS gets whipped out), in honky tonks, in parking lots, in ice houses, at football games. Fights start over women. Over insults. Over the pool table. Some guy touched another guy's hat. Someone danced with his angel one too many times. Short-order cooks sometimes get the SNS treatment for oversalting the soup. And quite a few shootings take place over a parking space.

Several sure-fire things that burn Texans up: calling The University of Texas "Texas University," referring

Gets loaded on Saturday night.

to the Dallas-Fort Worth area as "Fort Worth-Dallas," and spelling Neiman-Marcus "Nieman-Marcus." So watch your language and don't forget to duck. This legacy of frontier justice has meant that a lot of good and bad Texans leave the state with a bang.

EL TORO, THE MECHANICAL BULL

Originally designed to train riders for rodeo competition, El Toro is plenty of bull. The six-hundred-pound machine, which spins and bucks at various speeds, is made at Gilley's Bronco Shop in Pasadena. Ever since *Urban Cowboy* was released, the mechanical bull has been shipped worldwide. It is now as popular with fun lovers as it is with the rodeo crowd.

There is no secret to riding El Toro well. Men tend to muscle-up a bit too much while women and children relax more. (John Travolta may have ridden the bull well in the movie but Debra Winger was better.) The most important thing to remember before mounting up is to know your speed limit. The bull has three speeds that go from thirty bucking motions a minute up to ninety. So El Toro can go as slow as a rocking chair or a lot faster than a real bull. You may specify your speed, but keep an eye out for the operator of the bull. The machine is only as safe as its operator. Other El Toro riding tips:

1. Keep hat on.
2. Cut down on the number of longnecks consumed. You need a clear head and good vision to buck the bull.
3. No running shoes or Top-Siders; wear kicker boots to protect your feet.
4. No Bermuda shorts or bikinis; skin can be chafed by the bull's PBC rubber hide. Wear jeans — cords and polyesters don't give good traction.
5. Keep heels down, toes up — just like riding a horse.
6. No heavy chains or medallions around your neck — you could get slapped in the face with this jewelry. Take rings off, too; they can dig into fingers when hanging on to the horn for dear life.
7. Always wear the riding glove provided by the club or bring your own Leo Camarillo fingerless glove.
8. Go with the motion of the bull, hold legs tight, lean back, throw your left hand (assuming you are right-handed) in the air.
9. If you want to be thrown onto the cushions or mattresses, try to come off to the right as the bull spins left. Throw left leg over, duck head, and somersault onto the pads. Don't ever just jump off El Toro.

Nightclub bronc.

Texas Type No. 10

HONKY TONK DEVIL

A two-steppin' two-timer.

armadillo, longneck bottle hat pins

pale from being inside refinery all day

gold chain with longhorn charm around neck

Stetson's "Rustler" with Shotgun crease; fighting-cock feather band; toothpicks stuck in band

bruise under right eye from trying to break up brawl best friend was in

smiling; just got lucky

pinch of Skoal between cheek and gum

Panhandle Slim's loud plaid shirt with pearl snaps, straining open

embossed cowhide belt with white buckstitching; name hand-stamped on back

brass initial buckle made by younger brother in high school shop class

Leo Camarillo fingerless glove for riding the bull

back pocket contents: stale longneck; Ace bandage for sprains from mechanical bull; bandana

Larry Mahan jeans, still dark blue (haven't been washed regularly)

leather vest — attempt to hide beer belly

three inches of beer belly hanging over belt — too many longnecks

front pocket contents: keys to ¾-ton pickup; ticket stubs from last week's Oilers game; shred of Skoal

bowed legs from riding mechanical bull at least times a night

bits of broken longneck

plain black Nocona boots, modest stitching; no traces of manure (hasn't been near a four-footed animal in years); scuffed and cracked from having been driven over by pickup to break them in

HONKY TONK ANGEL

Will stand by her man.

Resistol's "Stampede" with High Sierra crease; multicolored band: white feather plume on side

"Let's Rodeo" and Lone Star flag hat pins

smiling; best friend just won the Dolly Parton look-alike contest

long blond hair, lots of it, one tiny braid down side

lots of makeup

face sweaty from dancing

CLUB

purse contents: keys to mobile home; Cosmopolitan's astrology guide; pink plastic hairbrush; hot pink lipstick; sunglasses with initials in lens corner; Sears credit card; gum wrappers; Maybelline eyebrow pencil; blue and green eyeshadows

Anna Zapp's checked gingham shirt with pearl snaps and contrasting piped yoke

rings on both hands, one from an old boyfriend, another from best friend since ninth grade; gold chain with gold-plated boot charm, diamond chip on the spur's rowel; pierced ears with tiny armadillo-shaped gold studs

left thumb permanently crooked from holding on to devil's belt loops when slow dancing

nails bitten down from watchin' devil ride bull

hand-tooled tan leather belt with white buckstitching; name burned in back

red-and-white enameled Gilley's buckle

Willie Nelson jeans, skin tight and washed until faded, tucked inside boot tops

Acme high-top boots, contrasting two-tone stitching on toes; soles worn from doing the Cotton-Eyed Joe

STRUTTIN' & STOMPIN'

How to Kick Up Your Heels & Let Down Your Hair

Dancing allows Texans to get a real kick out of a good time. Long before the Lone Star state joined the Union, cowboys and cowgirls were lettin' off steam on the dance floor, where *most* of the kicking in kicker palaces takes place. The dances are relatively simple ones that combine a flat-footed glide with some heel and toe movement. Smoothness and staying in step with your partner are all-important.

But dancing in Texas has as much to do with attitude as it does with learning a bunch of steps. For once, excess is out. While the cowboy and cowgirl dance, their faces are almost expressionless — no grinning or mouthing of lyrics on the floor. And the upper body is very still and relaxed. All the movement is concentrated in the legs and feet. Kicking and gliding are the major elements, done in a very composed, controlled manner.

Touching your partner is encouraged — during the two-step, women will hook their left thumbs around the belt loops of their partner's jeans, and men take a gentle hold of their partner's hair and pull it back with their right hands. (This practice alone has resulted in generations of Texas women being unwilling to cut their hair short.) Of course, cowboy macho prevails — men always lead, and women follow.

Dances you'll find on any Texas dance floor are the Texas two-step and the Cotton-Eyed Joe. Everyone has learned these two basics, and they remain the all-time favorites. The best dancers in Texas are those whose parents dragged them to Dewey Grooms's Longhorn Ballroom in Dallas, those who summered at Garner State Park and danced with the goat ropers from nearby ranches to "Blackland Farmer," and those Hill Country camp counselors who, after tucking the little campers into bed, headed down the road to the legendary Crider's.

HONOR YOUR PARTNER

Do si do-ers.

Since the early settlers danced under the stars to celebrate a successful roundup, a wedding, or just a good time, Texans have been big on square dancing.

A couples' dance with a wide variety of steps, square dances have a lot of underarm swings, promenades, simple swings, and sashays. There are seventy-five basic calls, or dance instructions, and a real do-si-do-er must learn all of them. Honor your partner, allemande left, grand right and left, and do paso are some of the steps to learn and practice. Be able to slip the clutch, box the gnat, scoot back, fan the top, and shoot the star. The most important person on the square-dance floor is the caller. Listen hard—the caller gets a real kick out of messing dancers up. The caller of callers is Cal Golden.

Texas square dancers belong to clubs with cute names—Stompin' Saints, Prairie Promenadiers, Bluebonnet Squares—and they meet as many as five or six times a week. Square dancing gives women dancers a chance to wear a lot of stiff, organdy petticoats, pettipants, and full-skirted outfits, which are color-coordinated with her partner's shirt and pants. Men keep a towel or bandana in back pocket. Square dancing is fast-moving and everyone gets hot and sweaty. There's always some "yellowrocking" going on—an unauthorized step that allows the men to get a free hug on the ladies.

LONE STAR MUSIC
Tuning into Texas Sounds

Like a giant patchwork quilt, Texas music is a pieced-together portrait of the Lone Star state and its people. It is a lively mix influenced by the variety and backgrounds of all the folks who have come to Texas over the years. To help you get acquainted, here's a handle on the kinds of music Texans make and listen to.

TEXAS COUNTRY. The Lone Star brand of C&W, this is music that has come to be known as Outlaw Country. Less orchestrated, with fewer string backgrounds than the Nashville brand, the songs are what every cowboy wants to say, and what every cowgirl wants to hear—simple, direct, and to the point. You can actually hear the lyrics, and there's a nice smooth beat that kickers love to dance to. More a kind of feeling than anything else, it's music to make you feel good, make you laugh, make you cry—and make a Texas honky tonk open early and close late.

PROGRESSIVE COUNTRY. Close in sound to Texas country, but with more of a rock and blues influence. The song content is often more complex than straight country, but the music still twangs. Hip truckers and city kickers listen to progressive country; it's very popular on college campuses. The foremost proponents of this near-outlaw sound are Emmy Lou Harris, Willis Alan Ramsey, and Rodney Crowell. A favorite progressive country tune: "Ain't Living Long Like This."

BLACK COUNTRY. Bits and pieces of jazz, gospel, and blues come together with horns, piano, and guitar. Mance Lipscomb, Lightnin' Hopkins, and Leadbelly are the singers whose albums you'll want to collect. And don't forget native-born Scott Joplin and his ragtime tunes. The best clubs are in Austin, Houston,

Bob Wills: Ahhaaa!

and Dallas, where new talent appears frequently.

CAJUN. The Cajuns, or Louisiana French (a great many of whom live in Texas's southeast Golden Triangle area) love to get together on a Saturday and party in a big way. "Fais do do" they call their frantic fun-times. The music they like to sing, dance, and drink to is a wild bayou beat featuring an accordion, a banjo, a fiddle, and an organ. "Big Mammou" and "Jolé Blon" followed by "Talk that Trash, Drink that Mash," and "Diggy Diggy Lo" are the all-time favorites. Link Davis, Doug Kershaw, and Harry Choates are the preferred Cajun singers. Best listened to while eating fried catfish, dirty rice, or filé gumbo—all washed down with sour mash, of course.

COUNTRY POP. Fence-straddling music. A more homogenized version of country, featuring "crossover" songs, this is easy-listening-meets-Nashville. Country pop has made superstars out of lot of native Texans like Mac Davis and Kenny Rogers. Purists, of course, don't cotton to this type of music. Great for highway cruising, with one arm around the cowboy or girl of your choice.

TEXAN-MEXICAN. Introduced by the early *vaqueros* who strummed a small Spanish-made guitar out on the range. Other instruments were later added, producing a pulsating, colorful beat. Mariachis, cumbia, and conjuntos (a lively form of salsa) are heard throughout south Texas and near the border. Trio San Antonio and Flaco Jaminez are the stars of the ice houses. Best accompanied by a bowl of menudo or some barbacoa.

WESTERN SWING. The original Texas sound that got started when Bob Wills left his barber chair in Turkey, Texas. Backed by his Texas Playboys band, Wills sang his own brand of country—an eclectic blend of Dixieland jazz, blues, and hillbilly. It's country and western with good old-time fiddling,

THE REQUIRED RECORD COLLECTION

Here is a list of the twenty-one record albums that every kicker must own and play constantly.

1. Asleep at the Wheel, *Asleep At The Wheel* (Epic Records)
2. Guy Clark, *Texas Cooking* (RCA)
3. Ry Cooder, *Borderline* (Reprise)
4. Rodney Crowell, *Ain't Living Long Like This* (Warner Records)
5. Dottsy, *The Sweetest Thing* (RCA)
6. Joe Ely, *Musta Notta Gotta Lotta* (MCA)
7. Kinky Friedman, *Lasso from El Paso* (Epic Records)
8. Lefty Frizzell, *Lefty Frizzell's Greatest Hits* (Columbia)
9. Larry Gatlin, *The Pilgrim* (Monument Records)
10. Buddy Holly, anything Buddy ever recorded, especially with The Crickets
11. George Jones, *Golden Hits of George Jones* (Starday Records)
12. Kris Kristofferson, *Silver Tongued Devil and I* (Capricorn)
13. Delbert McClinton, *The Jealous Kind* (Capitol)
14. Willie Nelson, anything he ever recorded
15. Doug Sahm, *Best of the Sir Douglas Quintet* (Tacoma Records)
16. Isaac Peyton Sweat, *Cotton-Eyed Joe/Schottische/Jole Blon* (Bellaire)
17. Kenneth Threadgill, *Yesterday & Today* (Kerrville Music Found.)
18. Townes Van Zandt, *Townes Van Zandt* (Tomato Records)
19. Jerry Jeff Walker, *Viva Terlingua* (MCA)
20. Don Williams, *I Believe in You* (MCA)
21. Bob Wills and his Texas Playboys, anything they ever recorded

breakdowns, and waltzes. The Wills style has been carried on by disciple Merle Haggard, popular recording group Asleep at the Wheel, and by dance hall bands across the state. Superior dance music, it is best heard in old-timey honky tonks with a nice big dance floor.

TEXAS TROUBADOURS
A Select Hall of Fame

The hardest and fastest rule of induction to the Texas Music Hall of Fame is being Texan by birthright. Having recognized the good sense to *select* Texas as a permanent residence (Glen Campbell, Van Cliburn, Charley Pride) is insufficient grounds for membership: one's parents should have thought ahead.

The range of music industry success stories to be found within the state's borders is a tribute to Texans' tolerance for variety . . . or perhaps to their love of pointing out yet one more thing at which they are the biggest and the best.

GENE AUTRY. *Tioga.* Most successful singing-cowboy film star. Oklahoma named a town after him. Owns a string of radio and television stations — and the California Angels baseball team. Big hits in late thirties: "Yellow Rose of Texas," "Tumbling Tumbleweeds."

JOE KING CARRASCO. *Dumas.* Foremost proponent of "nuevo wavo," or Tex-Mex punk. Born Joe Teutsch, renamed himself after the late San Antonio heroin don Fred Carrasco. Big hits: "Houston El-Mover" and "Federales, Bring My Baby Back."

MAC DAVIS. *Lubbock.* Most of his hits are pop music with a vague country flavor: "Stop and Smell the Roses," "Baby, Don't Get Hooked on Me." Probably known better for his numerous "Tonight Show" appearances and film role as playboy quarterback in *North Dallas Forty.*

JIMMY DEAN. *Plainview.* Though he is now known to Texans primarily for his folksy sausage commercials on TV, he had a big hit with "Big Bad John" in the early sixties.

FREDDY FENDER. *San Benito.* Born Baldermar Huerta. Tex-Mex star with hits "Wasted Days and Wasted Nights" and "Before the Next Teardrop Falls." Managed to cut some records while serving a three-year prison sentence for marijuana possession in early sixties. Has a distinctive aspirated, pained, staccato voice.

KINKY FRIEDMAN. *Rio Duckworth.* Known for his outrageous attire as much as his outrageous music. Former leader of the Texas Jewboys. Performs regularly at the Lone Star Cafe in New York City. Favorite Kinky tunes are "Lasso from El Paso" and "Get Your Biscuits in the Oven and Your Buns in Bed."

LEFTY FRIZZELL. *Corsicana.* Got his name from his early days as a left-handed boxer. Probably best known for his 1950 recording of "If You've Got the Money I've Got the Time."

LARRY GATLIN. *Odessa.* Rooted in gospel music, establishment country singer. 1976 Grammy Award winner with "Broken Lady," member of the Grand Ole Opry. Had a hit with "All the Gold in California."

BUDDY HOLLY. *Lubbock.* Untimely death took away a great talent. One of the major influences on rock 'n' roll music. From Elvis to the Beatles, most major artists have recorded Buddy Holly tunes: "Peggy Sue," "That'll Be the Day," "Maybe, Baby." Many new wave artists have adopted the Buddy Holly look with skinny-legged trousers and big, black-rimmed glasses.

WAYLON JENNINGS. *Littlefield.* Gritty-voiced "outlaw" singer of Texas country style. Yet another musician associated with Buddy Holly. When Holly's plane crashed in '59, it was

Waylon who had given up his seat to "The Big Bopper." Big hits with "Mamas, Don't Let Your Babies Grow Up to be Cowboys" and "Honky-Tonk Heroes."

GEORGE JONES. *Saratoga.* Thought to have the best voice in country music today. Notorious for his stormy marriage to Tammy Wynette and his serious drinking problems. The "Rolls-Royce" of country singers has had huge successes with "The Race is On" and "He Stopped Loving Her Today."

JANIS JOPLIN. *Port Arthur.* Attended UT briefly where she performed at Threadgill's. The top female rock performer of the sixties. Died at age twenty-seven, presumably of a drug overdose. *Cheap Thrills* her most noted album.

KRIS KRISTOFFERSON. *Brownsville.* Rhodes scholar turned superstar singer, heartthrob, and movie star. Big hits with "Me and Bobby McGee" and "Help Me Make It Through the Night." More recently has turned to a career in films appearing in *Alice Doesn't Live Here Anymore, Convoy,* and the box office disaster *Heaven's Gate.*

TRINI LOPEZ. *Dallas.* First successful Tex-Mex singer. In recent years has gotten out of the recording studio and into the kitchen: he now owns a chain of Tex-Mex food restaurants. Hit: "If I Had a Hammer."

ROY ORBISON. *Vernon.* Rockabilly roots, always wears sunglasses when he performs even though he isn't blind. Unusual voice with lots of vibrato and growl, as in his big hit "Pretty Woman." Beset with tragedy throughout his life (a 1968 motorcycle accident killed his wife, months later his two children died in a fire).

BUCK OWENS. *Sherman.* Regular on "Hee Haw." Big hits included "I've Got a Tiger by the Tail" and "Rollin' in My Sweet Baby's Arms."

TEX RITTER. *Murvaul.* Starred in films as a singing cowboy in the Gene Autry tradition. His unusual accent made him popular with tunes like "Jingle, Jangle, Jingle" and "I Dreamed of a Hillbilly Heaven." Political ambitions culminated in a failed bid for the U.S. Senate in 1970. He died three years later in a jailhouse while arranging bail for one of his musicians.

JOHNNY RODRIGUEZ. *Sabinal.* Got pushed into country music by a Texas Ranger who had arrested him for goat thievery. A real ladies' man, records a bland variety of Mexican music. First hit "Pass Me By"; more recent success with "North of the Border."

KENNY ROGERS. *Conroe.* First success came during psychedelic era of music with First Edition hit "Just Dropped In (To See What Condition My Condition Was In)." Turned his hippie image into Hollywood cornpone and has continued to make millions from his slick country tunes: "Lucille," "Something's Burning."

DOUG SAHM. *San Antonio.* Influenced today's "nuevo wavo" sound. First became known for his mid-sixties' hit "She's About a Mover" with the Sir Douglas Quintet. Organist Archie Moore considered major influence on rock 'n' roll sound. Now moving toward the "outlaw" country sound in Austin.

ERNEST TUBB. *Crisp.* Pioneer of country music, helped launch careers of Patsy Cline and Loretta Lynn at the Grand Ole Opry. Big hits: "Waltz Across Texas" and "Walking the Floor Over You."

TANYA TUCKER. *Seminole.* Musical Lolita. Currently in the gossip columns for her on-again, off-again romance with Glen Campbell. Has been singing country hits since she was fourteen. Best known for "Delta Dawn."

BOB WILLS. *Kosse.* Pioneer of western swing with his band the Texas Playboys. Built Longhorn Ballroom in Dallas. Popular throughout thirties and forties. Punctuated his songs with his trademark "Ahhha!" hollers. Wills standards: "San Antonio Rose," "Faded Love."

THE WILLIE CULT

Willie Nelson: the collected works.

The outlaw. The nonconformist. The picker poet who did it his way. Willie Nelson sums up the frontier spirit in music. The July 4 picnic, the jams with South Texas musicians, the appearances at Gilley's have given him a loyal and loving following.

Born in Abbott, near Waco, Willie Nelson is Texas's favorite singing son. He began his musical career at age ten playing rhythm guitar in a local Bohemian polka band. There were lean years as a disc jockey, a saddle-maker, and a salesman of Bibles, encyclopedias, and vacuum cleaners. In the mid-sixties, Willie left for Nashville to try his luck at breaking into the music world. There he penned a lot of songs that made other singers famous. He signed on with the Grand Ole Opry, won some awards, recorded a lot of albums but was basically fed up with the politics of becoming a star.

Refusing to go along with their clean-cut show business approach to music, Willie moved back to Texas. His first post-Nashville performances were at Austin's Armadillo World Headquarters where his concerts became legendary. His rich baritone voice, the winning smile, his deceptively simple lyrics captivated audiences and critics. Willie not only made people listen, he made them care.

Nashville pricked up its ears again, recognized the undeniably strong Willie Nelson cult, and in 1973, inducted him into the Music City's Hall of Fame. Four platinum albums later — "Red-Headed Stranger," "The Outlaws," "Willie and Waylon," and "Stardust" — Willie was awarded the Country Music Association's top honor, Entertainer of the Year.

Willie still goes his own way. Movies and Las Vegas have not changed his style. Long hair braided in two pigtails, bib overalls with no shirt, and always the bandana, he's doing his best singing in years.

STEPPIN' OUT
The Best of the Barrooms, Dance Halls, & Honky Tonks

When steppin' out in Texas you must put your best boot-clad feet in the right direction. Kickers all over Texas have their special watering holes, music saloons, and hoedown halls. Here are some genuine suggestions for places to stop on the kicker culture trail.

AMARILLO

The Jersey Lilly. *Third and Buchanan, 806/372-0047.* Real good live music played here nightly, but don't get lost when wandering through the mazelike overhead balconies.

ANTHONY

Anthony Gap. *113 North Main Street, 915/886-9954.* One of the most original honky tonks in west Texas, a real oasis for Western-music lovers. A fifteen-minute drive from El Paso.

AUSTIN

The Soap Creek Saloon. *11306 North Lamar, 512/835-0509.* A variety of music nightly, plus room enough for 350 drinkers, dancers, and all-around partyin' folk.

The Dry Creek Cafe. *Mount Bonnell Road, 512/453-9244.* Overlooks Lake Austin. Go at dusk and watch a spectacular sunset while downing a cold long neck. A very romantic kicker spot.

Silver Dollar North. *9200 Burnett, 512/837-1824.* Largest ballroom dance hall in the capital city. Decor is tin dance hall style. Traditional schottische and Cotton-Eyed Joe danced here nightly. The place has a huge UT following.

Alamo Lounge. *400 West Sixth and Guadalupe, 512/472-0033.* Full of colorful Austin folk listening to live music from some of the city's best performers. No cover charge.

CORPUS CHRISTI

Doc Holliday's. *5820 South Staples, 512/993-0528.* A real popular club with a huge dance floor for two-steppin' and line dancing. Tip a cool longneck with cowboys, roughnecks, and sailors just off the boat.

DALLAS

The Longhorn Ballroom. *216 Corinth at Industrial, 214/428-3128.* Built by Bob Wills in 1950, this Dallas dance palace is now run by Dewey Grooms, a country and western singer/band leader. Features a roller rink-size floor bracketed by pillars in the shape of cactuses. Big-name acts on weekends and free dance lessons given any time.

Diamond Jim. *5601 Greenville, 214/691-2411.* One of Big D's hottest C&W clubs. Dancing with your Stetson on is still the thing to do. Everybody from bronc-riders to businessmen seen here. Check out the three-for-one happy hour. Always more action after sundown.

Gilley's

The Bayou City Bea

Gilley's
PASADENA
TEXAS

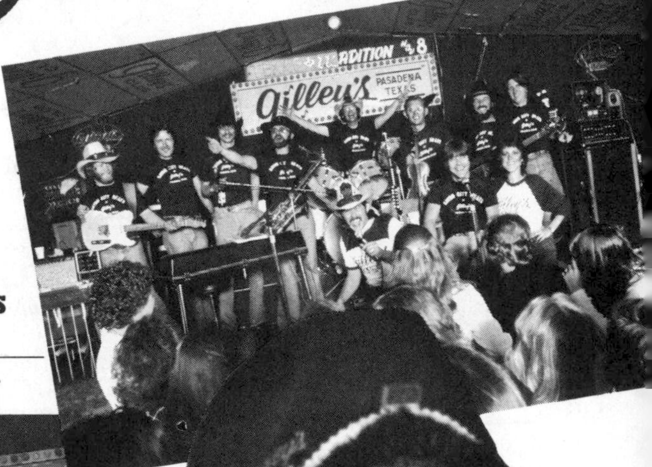

4500 Spencer Highway
Pasadena, Texas
713/941-7990

Open seven days a week.
Last bar call 2:00 A.M.

PASADENA
TEXAS

Johnny Lee: lookin' for love.

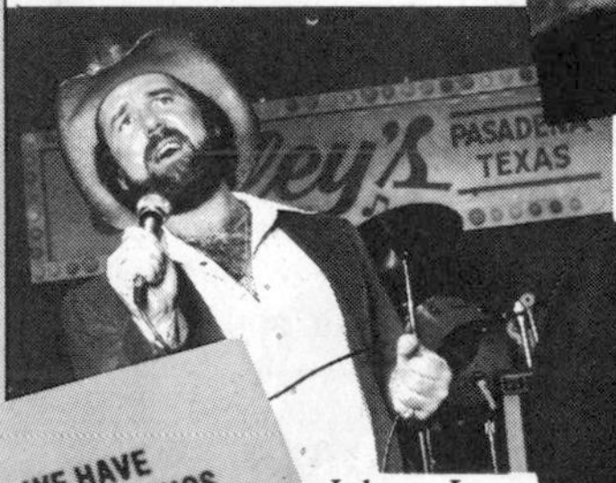

WE HAVE
STEAKS, NACHOS
PIZZA, POOR BOYS AND
BAR-B-Q, MIXED DRINKS
BEER AND WINE
—o—
MICKEY GILLEY AND
JOHNNY LEE ARE AT
GILLEYS
NEW YEAR'S EVE
RIDE THE BULL,
BRING THE KIDS

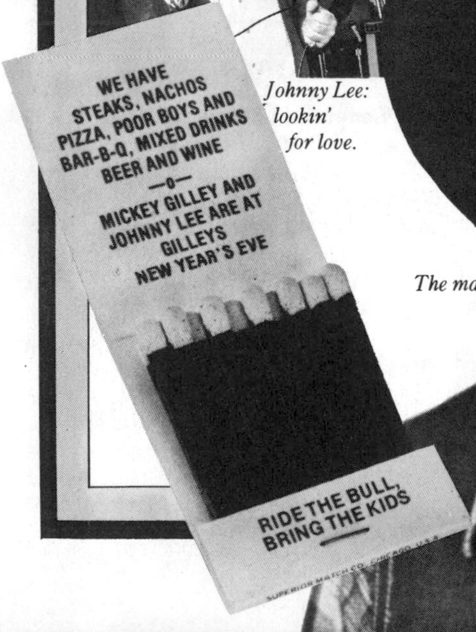

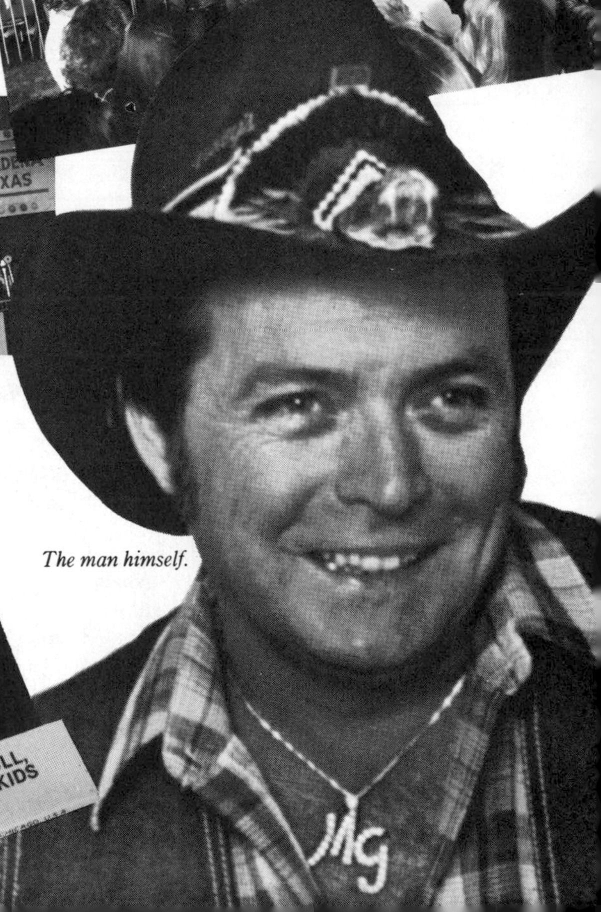

The man himself.

The most famous honky tonk in the world. Was a landmark way before "that movie" was ever made. Gilley's is the catalyst for the current boom in kicker palaces across the country and for the new generation of C&W fans. Located in a small oil refinery town outside Houston, Gilley's features about five thousand real and urban cowboys and cowgirls who crowd the huge, hangar-size club seven nights a week.

Willie, Waylon, Merle, and other name acts play the club, but the big draw is the club's namesake, Mickey Gilley, if he's in town these days. Gilley, who for years had been singing and playing piano in a succession of Texas clubs up and down Spencer Highway, constantly being upstaged by his cousin, Jerry Lee Lewis, has finally come into his own. After twenty-seven years of honky-tonking, Gilley was awarded the Academy of Country Music's Entertainer of the Year award and he and his Urban Cowboy band won a Grammy for Best Country Instrumental for "Orange Blossom Special/Hoedown." He now hosts a radio show, "Live from Gilley's," syndicated in three hundred national markets. He plays Lake Tahoe and Las Vegas, flies a twin engine 340-Cessna, owns nothing but cowboy boots, and is a national spokesman for the Schlitz Brewing Company, even though he sells his own Gilley's beer at the club. Standard Gilley hits include "Room Full of Roses," "Stand By Me," and "A Headache Tomorrow or a Heartache Tonight."

Even though *Urban Cowboy* has done a lot for the club — and Gilley and co-owner Sherwood Cryer as well — some say the place hasn't been the same since fame arrived. A big concession stand now sells hundreds of products stamped with the red-and-white Gilley's logo: postcards, T-shirts, key chains, beer trays, hat tacks, beach towels, hurricane glasses, bandanas — plus a line of jeans, a *Gilley's* magazine, and an international fan club.

GILLEYRATS

Regulars at Gilley's are known as Gilleyrats. These are kickers who live nearby; many are shift workers at one of the oilfields or construction sites. They are not tourists or people who have seen *Urban Cowboy* three times. All are on a first-name basis with Mickey and Sherwood, spend every waking minute of their free time at the club, and dance with more than average expertise. The most well-known Gilleyrat is Gator Conley, an expert kicker who advised John Travolta on the correct way to two-step around the floor. Gator can always be recognized by his all-black outfits, small cigar, and the line of ladies waiting to dance with him.

Gator Conley: the dancin' devil.

EDINBURGH

The Split Rail Saloon. *1615 West University, 512/383-6151.* A South Texas Valley favorite with ranch hands and foremen from the nearby King Ranch and Pan American University coeds. There's always a lively local country and western band to dance to.

EL PASO

The Caravan East. *8750 Gateway East, 915/593-7340.* A favorite club of ranch hands and truckers alike. Name road shows booked regularly, often at the last minute, providing many evenings of surprise entertainment. Dress up a bit and check your hat at the door.

FORT WORTH

The White Elephant Saloon. *106 East Exchange Avenue, 817/624-1887.* On the site of many a famous gunfight in the stockyards area. Plenty of drinkin', dancin', and great country music. Beer garden overlooks Marine Creek.

Billy Bob's. *2520 North Commerce, 817/625-6491.* Owner Billy Bob Barnett just built this place as a "monument to the real cowboy." Features an arena stocked with live bulls and excuse phone booths where, for $1.25, you can get the appropriate background noise (airport, gas station, office) for that call to your loved one.

The Stage Coach Ballroom. *2516 East Belknap, 817/831-2261.* A cavernous kicker palace for locals who love to go out two-steppin' and sippin'.

GRUENE

Gruene Hall. *Main Street, 512/625-9013.* Oldest operating honky tonk in Texas, just outside New Braunfels. Opened in 1878, Gruene (pronounced "Green") Hall still has the traditional pool table, beer garden, old bar, and huge wooden dance floor. A required stopover for the weekend rafters and tourists coming to or from nearby Comal River.

HOUSTON

Moe & Joe's. *102 Portland, 713/443-1832.* Owned by Moe Bandy and Joe Stamply. Tuesday night is anti-inflation night — down all the bar-brand firewater you can hold for half price. For the truly brave, there is a bucking armadillo.

Kay's Lounge. *2324 Bissonnet, 713/528-9858.* The intellectual's honky tonk. This West University beer joint is a city landmark for nearly a quarter of a century. Try to grab the huge Texas-shaped table.

The Winchester Club. *5714 Bissonnet, 713/667-7994.* One of the last kicker joints left in the Bayou City. Outstanding live music. Be prepared for a red-hot evening. You'll find plenty of action here.

LUBBOCK

Cold Water Country. *7301 South University, 806/745-5749.* Wednesday nights' Crash & Burn packs 'em in (tequilla 25¢, Lone Star 35¢.) A real crush of Texas Tech students every weekend.

NEDERLAND

Texas Swing. *2700 Twin City Highway, 713/722-5868.* Skating rink-size combination of a twenty-four-hour restaurant, western shop, and bar. Look up when dancin' and see the biggest wagon wheel in Texas overhead.

SAN ANTONIO

The Farmer's Daughter. *542 Northwest White Road, 512/333-7391.* A dance hall in the old Texas tradition, a big hit for over thirty years. Nearly every name performer has played here.

SAN MARCOS

The Cheyenne Social Club. *Thirty-fifth Street and Roberts, 512/392-1635.* One of central Texas's true Western dance halls. Even if you don't dance you're always welcome to sit, listen to the music, and watch the locals sashay around the floor.

Chapter 8
DUDIN' UP

FIVE EASY PIECES

The Western Wardrobe & How to Wear It

The American look. The look that won the West. The look that says independent, rugged, rowdy, and really tall. Every time you don your cowboy duds you put on the fantasy; you become the long, lean, dusty cowboy just off the range, the high plainsman searching for a new frontier. You're John Wayne in *Stagecoach*, Elizabeth Taylor in *Giant*—those men and women with grit, determination, and an endless thirst for adventure.

Dressing in cowboy duds also shows good horse sense—this is the look that's built to last. Originally work clothes, now a fashion statement, it is based on practicality, durability, and a sexiness born of the romance of the Wild West. In style whenever you wear them, the clothes themselves will never die. Good, sturdy fabrics combined with simple, solid construction mean easy-to-wear, easy-to-take-care-of, easy-to-look-good-in clothes. The basic outfit is five easy pieces—a pair of boots, a hat, a shirt, a pair of jeans, and a belt with a buckle. Learn to put these pieces together, and the Maverick Mystique is yours.

★

THE TALL TEXAN EXPLAINED

Being tall is expected of Texans—it's part of their psychophysiological heritage. There's even a single's club in Houston called the Towering Texan Club—women must be five feet ten inches, men cannot be one centimeter less than six feet two inches (they hold a Miss Towering Texan beauty pageant every year). How did it get this way? Are Texans really taller, or is it all a highly successful PR campaign? Well, Texans certainly *seem* taller, thanks to an additional five to nine inches from the Western Look. Figure that a hat with a six-foot RCA crease and a pair of boots with three-inch roper heels make anyone—Texan or not—seem larger than life. That's one of the real nice things about cowboy clothes—not only do you feel bigger, you *are* bigger.

WALKIN' TALL
The Anatomy of the Boot

Cowboys in Texas dress from the ground up. Although cowboy boots are all-occasion, all-purpose shoes, it's a good idea to buy two pairs—one for the pasture and one for the dance floor. But before you head into the nearest boot shop, understand the options that you will face. Well-made cowboy boots should last you a long time, so they might as well be a pair you like.

HEELS. The four most common heel styles are riding, walking, block, and dogger. The riding heel is classic but extreme—narrow, high, and severely undershot, it looks the most "cowboy," but may not be the easiest to walk in. The walking heel is wider, lower, and less underslung—you won't walk as tall, but you may get a lot farther. Block and dogger heels are lower still. Somewhat broader, not underslung, they don't convey the image as quickly, but you may find them more comfortable.

TOES. Pointed, rounded, or squared. The sharply pointed "toothpick" style favored by the genuine cowboy (because of the ease with which it fits into a stirrup) is not as popular these days, but for authenticity it's still number one. The more moderate rounded toe is the choice for the novice wearer. The blunt, square toe goes back a ways, too, and has always been particularly favored by ranchers.

TOPS. How high should your boots be? High enough to keep the rattlesnakes out. From just over the ankle to just below the knee, the range of heights allows for the whims of the fashion-conscious female patron of Cutter Bill's to the more function-conscious Texas sheriff. The top may have a V shape, straight stovepipe, fancy scallop, or deep V, but must have stitched-on pull straps.

LEATHERS. Originally horsehide or mule skin, boot leathers now range from the classic calfskin to lizard, eel, water buffalo, and crocodile. For kicking around cow patties, the basic boot is best. The more exotic, more expensive leathers are harder to take care of, and won't hold up as well under punishment, but for sheer showmanship they can't be beat.

DESIGN. From the simple multi-stitching of the classic cowboy boot to overlays and inlays of colors and contrasting leathers. The design on the calf area may be coordinated with a matching design on the toe or not. The piping on the inner and outer seams may be subtle or dramatic, depending on the bootmaker's whim. Just remember: in general, the more elaborate the design, the more expensive the boot.

FIT. When you buy them the boots should fit easily, with a slight sliding at the heel. Snug, but not tight. Your toes should touch but not push against the inner wall of the boot—the biggest mistake you can make is buying boots that are too short. They may need to be broken in a bit, but a good pair of boots, after a week or two of wearing, should be quite comfortable. As you give the final pull of the strap to get your heel in place you should hear a slight snapping sound—the sign of a good fit.

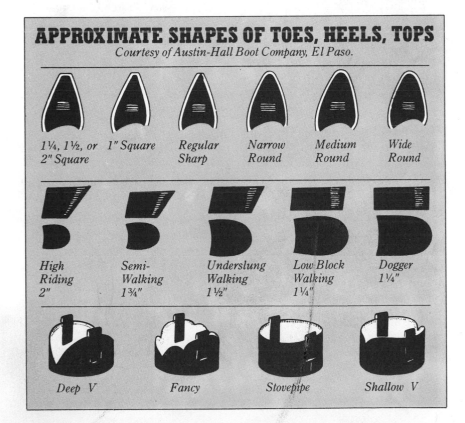

APPROXIMATE SHAPES OF TOES, HEELS, TOPS
Courtesy of Austin-Hall Boot Company, El Paso.

1¼, 1½, or 2" Square	*1" Square*	*Regular Sharp*	*Narrow Round*	*Medium Round*	*Wide Round*

High Riding 2"	*Semi-Walking 1¾"*	*Underslung Walking 1½"*	*Low Block Walking 1¼"*	*Dogger 1¼"*

Deep V	*Fancy*	*Stovepipe*	*Shallow V*

THE LAST LITTLE BOOT MAKERS IN TEXAS

A highly endangered species, Texas custom boot makers are much in demand and plagued with back orders. Many won't take on new clients without references from previous customers. Because of this, some Texans guard the name of their boot maker as jealously as they do the number of their Swiss bank account. Others are willing to sell their waiting list position for more than the price of the boots they were going to buy. Be prepared to lay out big bucks at one of these not-so-secret custom boot shops for boots that should last a lifetime.

CHARLIE DUNN. *Texas Traditions, 2222C College Avenue, Austin 78704. 512/443-4447.*

Black-bereted Charlie Dunn, the octogenarian dean of Texas boot makers, retires periodically, but customers who know his reputation always force him back to his Austin bench. Dunn is the favorite made-to-measure man of Texas celebrities—Jerry Jeff Walker once wrote a song about Dunn. Known for being a meticulous fitter, Dunn makes exquisite inlays on his boots of longhorns, oil derricks, bluebonnets, and marijuana plants.

ROBERT GRISSON. *Leopold Boot Shop, P.O. Box 401572, Garland.*

Protégé of longtime Texas boot maker Henry Leopold, Grisson builds five pairs of boots a week. He'll do exotics as well as basic leathers. Leopold, who only takes previous customers now, calls young Grisson "a natural boot maker."

LITTLE'S BOOT COMPANY. *110 Division, San Antonio 78214. 512/923-2221.*

When the famed Lucchese stopped making custom boots, David Little took over a lot of their made-to-measure business. From a third-generation family of boot makers in Texas, Little specializes in making the traditional "Old West" style boot with the underslung heel and the needle toe. His best-selling custom boot is made in small-grained horn-back lizard.

TEX ROBINS BOOT SHOP. *115 West Eighth Street, Coleman 76834. 915/625-5556.*

Although Tex often works in exotic leathers, for his rancher and professional cowboy clients his classic, best-selling custom boot is crafted of heavy calfskin. Will remake a boot if it doesn't fit the first time.

PAUL WHEELER BOOT COMPANY. *4115 Willowbend, Houston 77025. 713/665-0224.*

Wheeler, his wife, and two sons make fancy boots with panoramic landscapes, multicolored stitchings, and flying eagle inlays. Has an unusual selection of exotic leathers such as python and ostrich.

THE BASIC BOOT

This is the one all other styles of boots derive from. It is a direct descendant of the Spanish riding boot the conquistadors brought to Mexico. Good, well-made cowboy boots have all these qualities—and pulling on a pair of boots that are not the real thing seems a waste of time. The jeans can be too tight, the shirt can have too much embroidery, the tie slide can even have a tiny bit of turquoise on it—but show up in a lousy pair of boots and you'll never see the action side of Gilley's again. And remember, a certain benign neglect is part of the look. An occasional application of saddle soap and neat's-foot oil is fine, but don't overdo it. The highly polished, carefully looked-after boot is for county lawmen and champion-belt-wearing rodeo stars. Period.

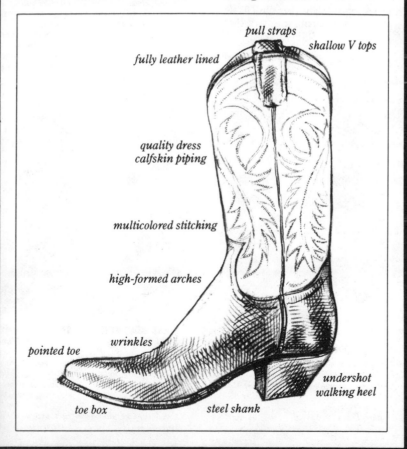

pull straps

shallow V tops

fully leather lined

quality dress calfskin piping

multicolored stitching

high-formed arches

wrinkles

pointed toe

toe box

steel shank

undershot walking heel

BOOTS

The he availability of colors, styles, and leathers these days boggles the traditional boot buyer's mind. In the past ten years, boot design has thundered into the modern era—boots can now be purchased in a huge variety of styles, allowing the crossover cowboy and cowgirl to match their boots to their evening wear. Old habits die hard—genuine Texans still prefer the more subtle colors and styles—but the current range in selection is luring many of them into a ride on the wild side.

STUDIO BOOT.
Justin's classic boot was developed just for Hollywood westerns. This high-topper was designed to almost any foot–movie star's or movie extra's.

BLANCO BOOT.
Smooth-skinned, snow white boar-skins are perfect get-me-to-the-church-on-time boots–or for the cowgirl who wants to marry in the corral or pasture. Justin for To Boot.

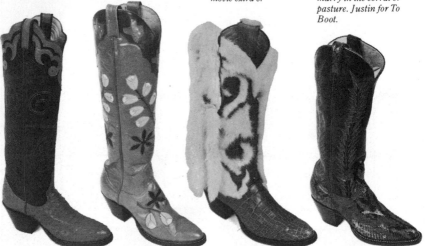

BEANSTALK BOOT.
Rodeo-bright boot is full-quill ostrich in two shades of green with an extremely high scalloped calfskin top, scrollwork overlays, and twin cording inlays. Larry Mahan for To Boot.

BLUEBONNET BOOT.
Keep the state's beloved bluebonnets on your toes and blooming up the high tops of these tall Larry Mahan-for-Cutter Bill boots. Tan calfskin with multicolored flower overlays.

MAKE MINE MINK BOOT. *Sure to be noticed in any crowd are these gray Malaysian crocodile boots with white mink scrolled inlays. From the Larry Mahan Collection for Cutter Bill.*

SNAKE CHARMER BOOT. *Larry Mahan's red python boots with extreme high black calfskin tops. With riding heel, flame stitching, and python pulls, these would go swell with a basic black dress.*

THE MULESKINNER BOOT. *Justin's indestructible mule-skin boot is for the real shitkicker. A 1,600-pound Brahman can walk across the toes of this ultra-simple design and never make a dent.*

COWHIDE BOOT. *Striking hair-on-calf boots have a medium round toe; deeply scalloped, 12-inch tops; matched natural skins. Mercedes Boot Company for M.L. Leddy & Sons.*

PINTO BOOT. *These stark, black-and-white hair-on-calf boots have old-timey short tops and stylized longhorn motif. Silver conchos hold down the large mule-ear pulls. From Larry Mahan.*

URBAN COWBOY BOOT. *Ladies' version of the boot worn by John Travolta in "that movie." Tony Lama's two-tone calfskin features a brown leather top, beige leather vamp, brown lizard wing tips.*

GRAND ENTRY BOOT. *These snappy, ruby red patent leather boots are a favorite with rodeo girl calf ropers and grand entry riders. Has riding heel and feather-stitched tops. Tony Lama.*

OLD-TIMERS BOOT. *Justin's favorite style from the thirties. Features a two-tone combination of white kid leather and brown lizard; short, 11-inch tops; riding heel.*

DRESS BOOT. *Nocona's matched eel-skins make a fine Sunday-go-to-meetin' boot. The vamp and top feature matched skins on the diagonal. A nice low walking heel.*

WILDCATTER BOOT. *Your well may or may not have come in, but you can always look the part. Large-grained crocodile with rust-colored calfskin tops. Mercedes Boot Company for Cutter Bill.*

JEANS

Y ou have just laid out a lot of bucks to have Charlie Dunn inlay custom boots with your Little Spread cattle brand. Now go out and buy a pair of jeans to cover them up. Essential, timeless, universally revered, jeans are a must in every Western wardrobe. And fit, cut, and the right manufacturer are just as important as the pants themselves. You went to the trouble of getting your own name hand-tooled onto a Tex-Tan leather belt, so you don't need Gloria Vanderbilt's or Sergio Valente's back there, too. Needless to say, custom tailoring is out of the question—if the ones in the store don't fit right, try rounding up a few head of cattle first. Cowboys—real cowboys— do not wear designer jeans. Levi's, Lees, and Wranglers are all there is. Or used to be. Now that Texans like Cutter Bill and Willie are putting out their own brands of jeans, exceptions to the old rule are being made. So if you've got to display something for the rearview, let it be made in Texas.

HOME-MADE STYLE. *Texas mamas' favorite pastime — making a blue jean skirt from a beloved pair of old jeans, which are cut apart and patched with more denim to create an A-line skirt. Handwork is a personal option. This Texan stitched cactus, the map of the State, a steer, the sun and a Luling watermelon on hers.*

PRAIRIE PERFECT. *Liz Claiborne's flouncy denim prairie skirt. Has smooth-banded, back-button waist and deep ruffle. Everything stitched with all-important burnt orange thread. Dress it up by adding a starched white petticoat to peek out below the hem.*

CHAP HAPPY. *Chaplike jeans perfect for mounting a broncing bull. Designed by rodeo star Larry Mahan. The red flannel-lined chap buttons with solid brass down the sides of the legs. "Every pair is bull proof" says back pocket label.*

THE MAN BEHIND THE PANTS

T here really was a guy named Levi. A German immigrant, Levi Strauss headed west during the Gold Rush in 1853, taking with him a supply of dry goods. Upon arrival, Levi immediately saw the miners' need for a good, sturdy pair of work pants. He and a tailor friend designed some pants and cut them from some canvas fabric Levi had brought with him. It wasn't long before the word spread east to cowboys on the trail—pants that could take the punishment had been found. Later made from a tough fabric loomed in France that came to be known as denim (from *serge de Nimes* after the French town), Levi's jeans have become synonymous the world over with cowboys, frontier life, and the American style of casual, functional—and somehow very sexy—clothes.

BACKSIDE.
Leave a little room here — you want to be able to swing up into the saddle, or at least onto a barstool.

WAIST.
Always belted, the jeans should rest comfortably on hips rather than high on the waist.

RIVETS.
Copper riveting was introduced by Levi Strauss in the 1870s for extra security at points of stress. The perfect match of decorative and functional.

FIT.
From the beginning of jeandom, cowboys have been jumping into water troughs for the perfect fit. That may not be necessary, but the snug-but-not-tight look is muy importante.

STITCHING.
Introduced with jeans themselves, orange stitching (no, not for UT) says your jeans mean business.

LEG.
Only the toe and heel of boot should be visible — any more and folks may think you're expecting a flood. Boot cut or straight legs are best. Never tuck legs of jeans into boots.

HEM.
Back hem should touch pavement — ideally it will be frayed enough to indicate plenty of time put in at the corral.

CUFFS.
Never.

THE WESTERN SHIRT

The original cowboy shirt was designed—plain and simple—as a work shirt. It was not until the Wild West shows that satin and fringes and embroidered yokes came into being. Then came western movies, Roy Rogers and Dale Evans, the opening night of the Houston Livestock Show and Rodeo. The elaborate Western outfit was here to stay. But from a no-fringe, no-flash basic to a Ryon's made-to-order, certain ground rules of design are always in effect.

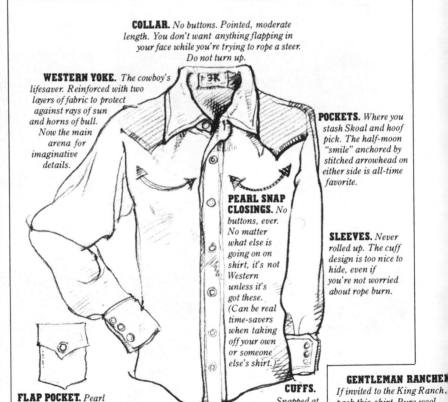

COLLAR. *No buttons. Pointed, moderate length. You don't want anything flapping in your face while you're trying to rope a steer. Do not turn up.*

WESTERN YOKE. *The cowboy's lifesaver. Reinforced with two layers of fabric to protect against rays of sun and horns of bull. Now the main arena for imaginative details.*

POCKETS. *Where you stash Skoal and hoof pick. The half-moon "smile" anchored by stitched arrowhead on either side is all-time favorite.*

PEARL SNAP CLOSINGS. *No buttons, ever. No matter what else is going on on shirt, it's not Western unless it's got these. (Can be real time-savers when taking off your own or someone else's shirt.)*

SLEEVES. *Never rolled up. The cuff design is too nice to hide, even if you're not worried about rope burn.*

FLAP POCKET. *Pearl snap keeps Sheriff's Posse Rodeo tickets from flying across the Rio Grande.*

CUT. *Full cut to allow moving around in. Long to prevent pulling out of jeans. Shirt is always worn tucked in.*

CUFFS. *Snapped at all times.*

GENTLEMAN RANCHER. *If invited to the King Ranch, pack this shirt. Pure wool gabardine, tricolored, with black bodice, red yoke and cuffs, blue piping. An exclusive design from Manuel of North Hollywood.*

WESTERN SWING.
Tailored antique gabardine shirt from H Bar C. Two-tone combination of light and dark green, yoke and smile pockets piped with white cotton cording. The kind of shirt Bob Wills wore.

SINGING COWBOY.
Tex Ritter rides again in H Bar C's traditional-cut pale blue shirt with dark blue zigzag yoke, rhinestone rosettes. The shirt to wear when you cut your first C&W album.

STADIUM SHIRT.
Straightforward, simple. Dark green cotton with unusually deep, scalloped yoke. Lots of piping. Tailored enough to wear under a pigskin blazer. From Mad Man.

BULL RIDER. *For the novice rodeo rider, Wrangler's blue chambray and plaid-yoked shirt. Just enough flash provided by gold Lurex threads running through the yoke.*

HONKY-TONKER. *A lot of dash, a little flash. Oeste's two-tone satin shirt would certainly catch the eye of your favorite angel or devil. Features a crazy scallop yoke, rattlesnake stitching.*

COWPOKE. *Levi's shirt for the working cowboy. Navy blue gingham checks with white pearl snaps on the front placket and flap pockets. Cowpokes add an adjustable bolo tie when they dude up.*

AMERICAN BEAUTY. *Stage West's antique cotton shirt graced with American beauty roses pinned down with a rack of longhorns! Note asymmetrical flap pocket with off-center pearl snaps.*

BANDANA SHIRT.
Tacey Tajan of Houston's shirt created from a variety of old and new bandanas. Heavily fringed around yoke and cuffs. Distinctive brass gun cartridge snaps.

CITY SLICKER KICKER. *Classic cowboy shirt styling meets pure cotton oxford cloth — wear it under a suit to the office. With full placket cuff detail and fancy gull-wing yoke. Norman for Cutter Bill.*

CALICO COWGIRL.
Calico print charmer has enough frontier fantasy to put a girl back home on the range. Piped in hot pink cord across the shoulders, around print yoke. From Anna Zapp Designs.

RODEO PLAID. *You'll be riding high in this antique from the forties. In custom-made red-and-black cotton, it has a tiny collar, patched yoke, and rare, diamond-shaped black pearl snaps.*

SIDEKICKS

Accessories are as close as the cowboy comes to funk and flash on the prairie. Always a stickler for quality, the cowboy's fashion sidekicks are of fine leather and beaten silver, for which he has a passion. Excessive display of silver is, however, considered unattractive as well as downright dumb—you do not want to be a walking advertisement to the gambler who just lost it all the next table over. Judiciously worn, these accessories are perfect for putting a little fun—and sometimes protection—into your Western Look wardrobe.

HAT PINS. *More than exotic feathers adorn "the cowboy's beach umbrella" in today's Wild West. Hat pins (or tacks) in bright enamels now dress up these crowning glories. Available at Western stores (Stelzig's has a vast selection) and through cattle- or horse-breeding associations. On this chapeau: the armadillo, Bevo, map of Texas, and Lone Star longneck.*

BOLO TIES. *Cowboy's tie. Just the thing to spruce up Western-style shirt. Motif slide might be favorite cattle or horse breed. (Turquoise slide is dead giveaway that cowboy hails from Arizona or New Mexico.) Durable, inexpensive—every Western-wear store has a revolving rack of them.*

BUCKLES. *Top, a touch of Texas pride near your beer belly. Authentic replica of Texas state seal, antique-finish solid brass. Exclusive at Cutter Bill. Bottom, Vogt's elegant sterling silver buckle has tip and keepers edged with gold rope design.*

HATBAND. *Vogt's hand-tooled leather belt-style band; adjustable, with embossed Mexican silver buckle, tip, and keeper. Spiffs up a Stetson.*

SPURS. *You must have Vogt's sterling silver spurs with 18-karat gold overlays on your Muleskinner boots for next branding season. One-inch band, offset shanks, multispoked rowels.*

GLOVES. Left. *Leo Camarillo's tan Algerian goatskin glove. Strongly reinforced in the palm, this glove protects the hand from rope burn. Right. Natural deerskin gloves in saddle tan. Hidden seams conform to individual hand shape for extra comfort. Don Loper for Cutter Bill.*

COLLAR TIPS. *To Boot's sterling silver filigree tips turn plain shirt into a dazzler. Popular with wildcatters, cattle auctioneers.*

BOOT TIPS & HEEL GUARDS. *Will protect and gussie up boots. Heel guards feature longhorn motif, tips are shiny nickel with hand-engraved design. Regular tips fit up to ¾-inch toe, wide fit up to 1 ¼-inch. Kauffman's.*

BELTS. Left, *genuine cowboy belt. Tex Tan's top-grain cowhide deeply embossed with oak leaves and acorns; plain in back for stamping name.* Right, *The Belt Factory's hand-tooled, hand-painted cowhide belt; antique Western scenes, tongue-style buckle.*

SHIN GUARDS. *Protects knees and shins while slaloming around close-set barrels. Martha Josey's autograph design is molded of lightweight vinyl foam. These guards have wide elastic straps and Velcro fasteners to keep them comfortably in place.*

ROSIN BAG. *One-pound lump of Tex Tan's black rosin. Rodeo cowboys apply it to the palm of their riding gloves to help maintain good grip on handle of the bareback rig. Comes in red waterproof drawstring bag.*

THE BANDANA

O ne of the few bits of color on the lone prairies, the bright red bandana was one of the cowboy's most indispensable accessories. As utilitarian as it is good looking, this square of pure cotton has long been associated with sweat and hard work. These days it comes in a myriad of colors, but a red one with a black and white paisley motif is still the most common. Construction workers, Japanese sushi chefs, and *Elle* magazine models have taken this durable look far from the range, giving it a new prominence on foreheads everywhere. But then the bandana was always more than just something for a cowboy to sneeze into. He had a whole slew of uses for this trusty cloth companion. Here are some genuine ways to tie one on.

SCARF. *A la Tex and Texana and the genuine cowboy. Can be knotted right at the throat or moved around for a variety of looks.*

BACK POCKET. *Give a longneck some company. Male square dancers must have one for the vigorous sashays they do. The place to start a rowdy game of tag.*

BABY DIAPER. *All out of Pampers? In an emergency, cover the baby's bottom and tie around the stomach. Can also cover the Pamper to give the toddler style — and extra protection.*

RUNAWAY LUGGAGE. *An instant suitcase for the short-distance traveler. Wrap your lunch and mad money up and tie around a long pole. Gives you a good head start.*

FRONT POCKET. *Pick a pocket, smile or otherwise, and fill it with this cheerful spot of decorative color.*

BABUSHKA. *Wear when cleaning house; for hiding curlers, looking cute. (For women only.)*

BELT. *Haven't won a trophy belt and buckle yet? Here's an instant, attention-getting way of keeping your jeans up. Tie two together and knot.*

FOREHEAD. *The Willie way. Willie Nelson is seen with bandana—folded and tied around his head—in Hollywood, Las Vegas, and Austin.*

PRESENT-WRAPPER. *Birthday and Christmas presents take on a whole new look when gift-wrapped in this manner. All you have to add is the ribbon.*

ON THE HATBAND. *Fold into a narrow strip and wind around the crown of your RCA-creased Stetson. Knot it at the back.*

HANDKERCHIEF. *The perfect repository for a sneeze. The nose knows no finer friend.*

DOG COLLAR. *Make a colorful canine collar by tying one around Fido's neck. Absorbs doggie perspiration. Vaccination and identification tags can be slipped on too.*

NAPKIN. *Tie one biblike or lay across lap when chowing down. The red color is perfect for disguising chili grease and BBQ stains.*

DISTRESS SIGNAL. *Should the car break down on your way to a Longhorn game, run one up the radio antenna. You won't be missed.*

COWBOY MASK. *A popular style among Panhandle wheat workers. Tie in back of head and pull up over nose when riding on a dusty road or crop-dusting the Little or Big Spread. Do not wear this style when entering a bank to cash a check.*

TEXAS EASTER BONNETS

The cowboy's pillow, fly swatter, horsewhip, drinking cup, and campfire bellows. John B. Stetson introduced the basic design in the 1850s with his "Boss of the Plains." Made of felt, which held its shape better than wool, from which hats were previously made, it had a wide brim to protect the eyes from sun and dust, and a high crown to keep the top of the head cool. A basic wardrobe ingredient, the hat should rarely be off the head.

DUDE STETSON.
Stetson's "Overlander" made of 3XXX black felt with hemp and plaited leather band. Makes you mean and ornery the instant it's on your head.

PANAMA STRAW.
For genuine Texas cowboys. Wear it every day, including holidays. Lightweight, white Panama straw, made in Mexico for Ravin Hat Company, features narrow black cord band, cluster of exotic feathers, and cutting-horse crease. Favorite hat of the King Ranch Kineños, who do not add the feathers.

COWGIRL FANCY.
Hot pink felt cowgirl hat. Perfect for wearing when carrying the flags in rodeo's grand entry. An antique Buckaroos brand from legendary Arnim & Lane Dry Goods Store in Flatonia.

OILMAN'S SPECIAL.
Guaranteed to make you look like you have a piece of the Austin Chalk and can swap kickback stories over lunch at the Petroleum Club in Midland. A silver mist 3XXX beaver with silk band and boomtown crease. From Miller Brothers.

COWBOY STRAW.
This high-crowned jute hat is seen frequently on rustlers when they get caught red-handed with a heifer. Overall woven pattern, three-cord black band, and Canadian crease —named for the Canadian River in the Panhandle, a popular rustling spot.

JOE BOB STETSON.
The one to wear into the honky tonk, to hang on your pickup truck's gun rack. Stetson's tan felt with wide embroidered band and clump of black maribou feathers.

RODEO STETSON.
The rodeo cowboy's top hat. Stetson's "Winner" in cognac 4XXXX beaver with plaited suede band and quail feathers. Has RCA-approved crease.

THE CATTLEMAN.
The classic Stetson. Worn by LBJ at the ranch — and at the White House. Also worn by cattlemen whose Santa Gertrudises are sold at Western Heritage Sales. In pure imported beaver with a two-cord matching silk band and cattleman's crease.

CUSTOM-MADE.
Manny Gammage's Texas Hatters. 2058 South Lamar Blvd. Austin 78704. 512/444-9485. *John Connally and Willie Nelson both wear Manny's hats. This family-run organization with over half a century of experience in custom hat-making is the home of the Hi-Roller and Texas Queen style. Hand creasing is an art here. Manny will personally make any style a cowboy or cowgirl desires.*

THE RIGHT CREASE

is all-important. A whack of the hand in the middle of the hat will not do. For those who wish to stray from the standard creases shown below, it is possible to get custom creasing at a good Western shop.

CALGARY

RODEO COWBOY

CATTLEMAN

OPEN CROWN

BULLRIDER

HIGH SIERRA

Name card to guard against your Resistol being "accidentally" picked up when you hang it on the longhorn hat racks at Brick's Bar-B-Q in Fredericksburg.

THE GENUINE TEXAS HAT.
Seen everywhere, on everybody. Resistol's classic Brisa Panama with a 6" crown. In natural white with two cord black band, precreased Roper. The cowboy chapeau for Texas hat tack display.

Like Hell It's Yours
This Hat Belongs To
Rosemary Kent
BUT YOU CAN GET ONE LIKE IT FROM
AMERICAN SHOE AND SADDLE REPAIR, INC.
402 E. Travis Avenue, Dayton, Texas
COURTESY: AMERICAN HAT CO.

BARONESS.
The cattleman's daughter wears Stetson's "Stampede," a sorrel-colored felt and 4XXXX beaver cowgirl chapeau. Has self-plaited band and Bronco crease. Makes you look every inch the lady who can stand plenty of bull.

DRESSING UP WESTERN

THE RANCHER *dudes up with a black velvet, western-cut blazer worn over a pima cotton, tucked, cavalry-styled bib tuxedo shirt. Holding up a new pair of jeans is his antique silver concho belt. Silver collar tips, a tall beaver hat, and boa constrictor boots accessorize his struttin' stuff.*

THE CITY SCHOOLMARM *slicks herself up in M.L. Leddy's tailored, western-styled ranch suit: front-slit straight skirt with matching blazer edged in leather arrowheads. Worn with a striped, oxford cloth western shirt, antique hot pink cowgirl hat, and two-tone boots.*

THE LADY RANCHER *gussies up in Cutter Bill's khaki prairie skirt with a rodeo-bright red western shirt piped in khaki. Worn with short-top boots studded with silver nails, a high-roller hat, and LaCrasia Creation's red leather fringed gloves.*

For going out on the town or to a party at your boss's Big Spread the Western Look's five easy pieces can be mixed with plenty of flash and dash. Slip a hand-tooled hatband around your Stetson or pull on a pair of exotic-skin boots. Put a starched, lacy petticoat under a prairie skirt or a big, bold bolo tie over a Lurex-threaded cowgirl shirt. Dressin' up western means puttin' on the dog—and the cow and the horse—and then some.

THE DANCE HALL GIRL *shimmies in a fringed black suede outfit from M.L. Leddy. The black mid-calf wrap skirt has a deeply fringed hem and matching suede western-cut shirt with turquoise suede scalloped yoke. Her steppin'-out boots are python high-toppers.*

THE WILDCATTER *strides out in a white cowboy shirt tied up with an antique cattle-motif tie. Over his oldest jeans he pulls a Remy calfskin jacket with hair-on-calf yoke and shoulders. Full-quill ostrich boots put him in high cotton.*

WHERE TO BUY THE WESTERN LOOK

Where a genuine Texan buys his or her Western duds is mighty personal. As important to a Texas town as its BBQ and Tex-Mex restaurants, Western-wear stores are so numerous that everyone has his or her favorite. Texans aren't closemouthed about where they get their clothing; they just want the goods to be good and the surroundings authentic.

ANDERSON SHOE & SADDLE REPAIR SHOP. *102 East Texas Avenue, Baytown.* Bill Anderson, a noted horseman himself, carries an excellent assortment of horse tack plus a full line of brand-name jeans, shirts, and boots. Big variety of bolo ties and hat pins. The best selection of Panama hats. The place to bring your boots or saddle for major overhaul or minor repair.

CUTTER BILL WESTERN WORLD. *5647 Westheimer, Houston.* The original store started by Houston businessman-rancher Rex Cauble, who named the store after his favorite cutting horse. Caters to the River Oaks cowgirl and cowboy. Bluebonnet boots, coyote-collared leather jackets, Western-style mink coats, bareback horse pads, barbed wire Christmas wreaths, hair-on-calf cowhide luggage. Special corner for expensive boot shines.

CUTTER BILL WESTERN WORLD. *5818 LBJ Freeway, Dallas.* Big D's version of the popular Houston store. Home of cowboy chic. Crocodile blazers, solid brass dominoes, beaded Pocahontas dresses, and Spanish show bits for the horse. A hangout for the Highland Park and SMU crowd.

FEFERMAN'S. *2108 Paramount, Amarillo.* Been around since 1926. Stocks a huge selection of brand-name boots. Plenty of Resistols and Stetsons. The store to get the best outerwear for Panhandle winters. Where Stanley Marsh 3 shops.

HI-YO SILVER WESTERN WEAR. *Horizon and I-10, El Paso.* Located in a truck stop on the major highway to New Mexico. Open twenty-four hours a day. The workingman's cowboy clothing store. Carries H-Bar-C and Panhandle Slim shirts; Lee, Levi's, and Wrangler jeans; Miller hats. Good line of medium-priced boots. They redeem Gold Bond stamps.

JUSTIN BOOT COMPANY FACTORY OUTLET. *301 South Jennings, Fort Worth.* Bargain boot buys at one-third off the regular price. Most have only minor flaws. Not all sizes, styles available. Very popular among the TCU crowd.

KALLISON'S WESTERN WEAR. *124 South Flores, San Antonio.* "Where the working cowboy buys his duds" since 1899. Texas farmers and ranchers. Sells bull-riding supplies, horse tack and blankets, deer blinds and feeders, and a complete line of brand-name hats, boots, shirts, and jeans. But what everyone comes for is the Old-Timer's Boogared Jacket. A reddish denim jacket, it's water- and brush-resistant and never wears out.

LARIAT RANCH WEAR SHOP. *1610 South Congress, Austin.* Owned by Dee Collier, a well-known retired saddlemaker. Carries strictly cowboy clothes; no fancy stuff here. Stocks boots by Hondo, Acme, Rios, and Nocona. UT students head here in droves for the Longhorn cowboy shirt with burnt orange yoke and bulls stitched on each flap pocket. Also known for expert hat creasing.

M. L. LEDDY & SONS. *2455 North Main, Fort Worth.* Three stores in Texas, including Midland and San Angelo. Since 1922 Leddy's has sold superb custom-made boots, saddles, and chaps. Other unusual Texas-type items: hand-tooled ice buckets, bar glasses with well-known cattle brands, quill ostrich attaché cases, and a 14-karat gold-plated model of an oil derrick and pump jack. Golf soles put on any pair of cowboy boots.

RYON'S. *2601 North Main at Stockyards, Fort Worth.* Calls itself "The Nation's Finest Western Wear Store." Specializes in custom-made saddles, hand-carved breast harnesses, personalized spurs and horse pads, practice steer heads. Where the rodeo girl has rodeo clothes custom-made.

SAENZ WESTERN WEAR. *300 North Washington Street, Beeville.* A favorite with South Texas valley farmers and ranchers. Stocks good selection of batwing chaps, rodeo hats, Leo Camarillo ropes and gloves, and Dallas cologne. Posts announcements of local calf futurities and does custom cattle brand monogramming.

SHEPLERS. *6001 Middle Fiskville Road, Austin.* Austin branch of this huge national chain of Western stores. Features over an acre of selling space. More than 75,000 pairs of jeans and 14,000 pairs of boots. A complete tack and saddle department. Brand-name Western wear for the entire family. Lucchese boots.

STELZIG'S. *410 Louisiana, Houston.* One of the oldest cowboy stores in the country. The favorite with old guard Houston area ranchers. Downtown in the historic Old Market Square. Run by five generations of Stelzigs. Custom-made saddles, terrific bumper stickers for the pickup, cute (and genuine) cowgirl sales staff, and the best hat blockers/creasers. Look for the famous rearing stallion on top of the store.

THE WESTERN SHOP. *520 Granite Avenue, Fredericksburg.* Complete line of brand-name shirts, boots, and hats. Hand-tooled belts (they'll stamp your name on back), farm and ranch supplies. LBJ shopped here.

WILLIAMS WESTERN TAILORS. *1104 N.W. Twenty-eighth Street, Fort Worth.* Fine handmade Western shirts are this store's specialty. You can pick out your fabric and even try your hand at designing your own shirt. They'll monogram your cattle brand or ranch name. Be warned: there's often a three month wait for these custom beauties. Ernest Tubb has his showy Western-style suits made here.

MAIL-ORDER CATALOGS

CUTTER BILL WESTERN WORLD. *5818 LBJ Freeway, Dallas 75240.* The Neiman-Marcus of Western wear stores puts out a stunning, beautifully photographed catalog that's geared to the high-fashion customer and not the serious cowboy or girl. Has good selection of pint-size Western wear. Issued once a year, features a guide on how to order custom-made chaps and a hat-sizing chart on its order blank. Gift certificates available. Honors all major credit cards. For faster, easier ordering call toll free number 800/527-5333, Monday through Saturday. (Texas residents can call collect 214/980-4244.)

M. L. LEDDY & SONS. *2455 North Main, Fort Worth 76106.* The "Texas Gold Edition" catalog is handsome, well-designed, and displays its custom-made boots and saddles against authentic ranch locations. Fine selection of nosebands, reins, and headstalls, but probably not a good idea to order these by mail unless you're positive of your horse's sizes and needs. Issued once a year, the catalog has an extensive order blank with charts for choice of hat crease styles and a place on which to draw the outline of your foot when ordering boots. Gift certificates come with either a tiny plastic Stetson or boot. Leddy's has its own charge card (with barbed-wire motif) and honors all major credit cards.

RYON'S. *P.O. Box 4280, Fort Worth 76106.* The catalog from "the nation's finest western store" is highly informative and visually pleasing. Most of its stock is for the serious cowboy and cowgirl. Has the best rodeo outfits and chaps to custom-order but limited in name-brand clothing. Two catalogs (fall-winter and spring-summer) are issued. Order blank has a footprint outline, a chart of boot toe, heel, and top styles, and how-to guides for ordering custom-made belts and chaps. Takes all major credit cards. For orders outside Texas call 800/433-2119. (In Texas call 817/625-2391.)

DRESSING TEX-MEX

Mexico's proximity to Texas does more than influence food and interior decoration. This south-of-the-border neighbor exerts strong pressure on a Texan's closet. Offering a vibrant, folkloric alternative to dressing like a cowboy or cowgirl, the Tex-Mex look is perfect for the patio or a chalupa party. Wear the Tex-Mex look during San Antonio's annual Fiesta, at George Washington's birthday celebration in Laredo, at Cinco de Mayo parties, and to Ninfa's for supper. Olé.

LA SEÑORA *wears an antique, circular skirt made in Mexico featuring landscape scenes liberally covered with bright sequins. With it an off-the-shoulder Isla de Mujeres hand-embroidered blouse, Mexican boots, a Veracruz-style silk shawl.*

LA MUCHACHA *has on a children's version of the classic hand-embroidered sundress from Oaxaca belted with a beaded "Texas" belt. Over her shoulder a genuine armadillo bolsa.*

LA MUJER *wears the sleeveless embroidered sundress from Oaxaca and carries a woven straw sac-bag to keep her pesos in. At her huarached feet is the* muy importante *plaid plastic Mexican shopping bag stuffed with* mercado *finds.*

EL HOMBRE *has on black denim jeans, a white cotton Mexican wedding shirt, a bolo tie with Mexican onyx slide, a calfskin jacket with hand-tooled en Mexico yokes and silver concho buttons, and Mexican boots. On his head is* the necesario *vaquero's hat in Mexican Panama straw.*

WHERE TO SHOP FOR THE TEX-MEX LOOK

CASA INTERNATIONAL. *4614 Montrose, Houston.* Open by appointment only. Rosa and Raoul have a "closed clientele list," so go with someone who has been there before. Complete line of embroidered dresses and shirts, straw purses, huaraches, and Mexican silver jewelry.

CHARLES LEWIS CO. *2301 Hancock Drive, Austin.* This gallery/shop carries those Oaxaca children's dresses so popular with UT sorority girls, who are some of their best clients. Also has a small line of the much more costly dresses by famed Sabina Sanchez, embellished with exquisite, elegant hand embroidery. Carries an unusual selection of Mexican folk art, weavings, and antique furniture.

DOS GRINGOS. *1610 Hickory, Houston.* Colorful shop run by Barbara Staley, wife of popular Texas artist Earl Staley. Carries large stock of Mexican folk art, pottery, furniture, embroidered Oaxaca sundresses, and Staley's Mexico-inspired weather vanes.

EL BUZON. *Highway 27 at the fork in Ingram, seven miles west of Kerrville.* Popular among the summer camp crowd and the Houston set, this Hill Country specialty shop carries jewelry and some one-of-a-kind, authentic Mexican dresses. They will even dress wedding parties in special light cotton Mexican gowns. Lady Bird Johnson and her daughters have shopped here.

EL MERCADO. *514 Commerce Street, San Antonio.* The closest thing to a real border town market. Located in the recently renovated Market Square — formerly the produce area of the city — this large building re-creates an authentic *mercado* with thirty-two small shops set up in stalls. Imported Mexican curios, straw bags and purses, clothing, onyx items, leather goods, and wrought iron decorative items.

LIRIO'S. *84 Highland Park Shopping Village, Dallas.* High-class, authentic, handmade Mexican clothing. The sort of casually elegant dresses you would buy to wear to a Tex-Mex debutante party. The Mexican Preppy look is big here; Highland Park High School girls favor the simply embroidered, straight, unbelted San Antonino dresses with cap sleeves. Huaraches with hand-painted designs are sold here as are some Mexican artifacts, Christmas decorations, and woven baskets. Larry Hagman, Paul Newman, Barbara Bel Geddes (Miss Ellie on "Dallas"), and Betty Ford have all shopped here.

MARTI'S. *Guerrero and Victoria Streets, Nuevo Laredo, Mexico.* Two blocks from the international bridge across from Laredo. Texans consider this elegantly appointed store to be the Neiman's of border town emporiums. True to its motto: "A museum with everything for sale." Much in demand are the Pedro Friedberg hand-carved furniture and one-of-a-kind Mexican jewelry pieces.

NAPOLEON'S. *206 Produce Row, San Antonio.* This elegant shop features Mexican imports, including a fine selection of folk art, mirrors, and black Oaxaca pottery. It also stocks embroidered sundresses, Mexican wedding shirts, Girasol dresses designed by Mexico City's Gonzalo Bauer, authentic Mexican folk costumes, and papier-mâché animals and vegetables.

PILAR. *3814 South Alameda, Corpus Christi.* Emphasis on Mexican folk art, with some clothing. Pilar carries Oaxaca dresses and blouses; hand-loomed, earth-tone rugs made by Mexico's Zapotec Indians; and various kinds of pottery and stoneware. Especially popular are the blue-gray Jorge Wilmot pots and the Heron Martinez Mendoza terra-cotta candelabras.

Chapter 9
LOVE &
LARD

RULES FOR EATIN' TEXAS STYLE

Work up a hunger.

Put a lot of food on your plate the first time 'round; cover plate completely.

Be polite—don't talk and chew at the same time, keep one hand in lap.

Have fly swatter constantly at hand.

Wash down food with frequent gulps of liquid, preferably beer.

Practice boarding-house reach—an occasional forkful off someone else's plate is expected.

Use toothpicks halfway through meal.

Show appreciation for what you're eating—compliment the cook, ask for recipes, belch.

Go back for seconds—cover plate completely.

THE CHISHOLM TRAIL TRADITION

Cowboy Grub
& the Art of Chowing Down

It all began as cowboy grub. When the boys were driving longhorns to the Kansas City and Abilene stockyards they needed stick-to-the-ribs food for the long haul. But in 1866, when Captain Charles Goodnight invented the chuck wagon, cattle-drive food was lifted from the level of mere chow to that of a cultural tradition. The original goal of feeding lusty men after a grueling day on the trail—along with the romance of cooking and eating outdoors—remains the foundation of the Texas approach to food.

Forget al dente vegetables. Texas food is home-cooking with a vengeance—heavy, fattening, plentiful. Cholesterol levels often reach the danger zone—it is considered impolite to refuse a second helping. This "love on a plate and lard in the skillet" school of cooking is not even close to *nouvelle cuisine*—if you can see your plate at the beginning of a meal, you simply haven't taken enough. The cowboy's respect for a stomachful of good, hot vittles prevails. Dinner table conversation never drifts into the particulars of the newest diet craze; calories are not discussed.

The timing of meals reflects the frontier way of life. Dinner at eight is a meaningless phrase to the Texan who had breakfast at six in the morning and supper at five in the afternoon. Besides, *dinner* is the word for the midday meal—lunch is what Texas ladies and their mothers or girlfriends do in Neiman's Zodiac Room or Sakowitz's Sky Terrace. Brunch just doesn't fit in anywhere at all.

FROM CHUCK WAGON TO COCINA
The Big Foods

T he Big Food Three—barbecue, Tex-Mex, and chicken-fried steak—are Texas's most distinquished contribution to American cuisine. All are basic, unpretentious, and cheap. The genuine Texan knows his way around all three. And if you're going to make the Lone Star lifestyle your own you've got to be able to tell them apart, and enjoy their distinct pleasures. Kick the quiche-and-spinach salad habit by learning what's cooking in God's Big Acre.

BARBECUE

It has been said that Texas is a place where they barbecue everything except ice cream. Derived from the Spanish word *barbacoa* for the grill on which meat is roasted, barbecue is as a verb a way of preparing meat; as a noun the social event centered around eating it (millionaire ranchers and oilmen are forever introducing their daughters to Texas society via a barbecue at the Big Spread). In the cities and along the highways, smoky, delicious-smelling

⭐ 12 TEXAS JUNK FOODS

Things big, creamy, spicy, or crumbly are preferred. None of the below listed is considered a full meal, just something to tide you over until the next scheduled chow-down.

1. Peanuts in Dr. Pepper
2. Beef jerky
3. Frozen Snickers
4. Moon pies

Moon Pie.

5. Corn dogs
6. Cream gravy poured over white bread, dotted with catsup, and cut into pieces
7. Frito pie (chili and Fritos)
8. Pickled pigs' feet
9. Corn bread crumbled into a glass of buttermilk and eaten with an iced tea spoon
10. Jalapeño-stuffed olives
11. Hot dip made with Ro-tel tomatoes and Velveeta cheese (must at slumber parties)
12. Hot okra pickles

barbecue establishments abound. BBQ (as it is called on roadside signs) is to Texans what pasta is to Italians—the national badge of culinary honor.

TEX-MEX

Tex-Mex is seldom prepared at home unless you have live-in Mexican help, but the genuine Texan does eat Tex-Mex at least once a week. Every town has at least one Tex-Mex restaurant, and in big cities every third restaurant listing in the phone book is an El or La Something-or-other. The Texas refrigerator should, however, always be stocked with Pace's hot sauce or homemade salsa cruda—if only to make the after-work beer-and-nachos taste even better.

CHICKEN-FRIED STEAK

A Depression-era holdover, chicken-fried steak reigns supreme as *the* Texas noontime meal. Eaten as often as barbecue and Tex-Mex, it should never be referred to by any abbreviation such as CFS. An inexpensive cut of beef deep fried like chicken, it is to be found in every small-town cafe and restaurant across the state. But—for all its popularity at truck stops on the Interstate—the best chicken-fried steak is still what a Texas mama makes at home.

TEXAS COOKS HALL OF FAME

HELEN CORBITT Director of Neiman-Marcus restaurants, creator of low-calorie menu for The Greenhouse. Famous for her poppy seed dressing, ice cream molded into flowerpots, and "Texas caviar" (pickled black-eyed peas). Responsible for putting blue sugar in the N-M Zodiac Room.

WALTER JETTON LBJ's personal barbecuer, called the King of Barbecue; was forever dragging his chuck wagon and chowhounds down to the LBJ ranch to barbecue for world dignitaries.

MARY FAULK KOOCK Founder of Green Pastures Restaurant in Austin; close friend of LBJ family and Texas governors. A big help with culinary projects during the Texas HemisFair. Serves the biscuits Van Cliburn can't stop eating. Clever party hostess, planner.

NINFA LAURENZO Turned her Houston tortilla factory into a Mexican food empire. Responsible for inventing and marketing "tacos al carbon." Dared to use Italian seasonings with her Tex-Mex dishes.

FRANK X. TOLBERT Known as the "Godfather of Chili" in Texas. Co-founded the Terlingua World's Championship Chili Cookoff; has own chili parlor in Dallas. His cookbook is considered the chili Bible.

JOSEPH "CAP" WARREN Chuck wagon boss for fifty years at Waggoner Ranch. Fed hundreds of hungry cowboys daily; carried his Dutch oven and frying pans in a cowhide sling under rear axle. Wearing an apron made of two flour sacks, his specialties were fried steak and sourdough biscuits.

ZEPHYR WRIGHT LBJ's personal cook at the White House and at the LBJ Ranch. Developed Pedernales River Chili. Famous for her White House hash and for trying to keep LBJ on a diet.

Texas Menu No. 1

BARBECUE

Barbecue is meat grilled over an open fire with some kind of spicy, tomato-based marinade or sauce that is applied often during the cooking. Beef brisket is the barbecuer's first choice, followed by chicken, sausage, cabrito, and beef short ribs, as well as the leaner pork ribs.

Barbecue is never served rare or medium. Real Texas-style barbecue has a tender, moist texture that never needs a knife. Slow, slow cooking over a steady heat is the required procedure. BBQ leftovers are chopped up and used for sandwiches, making for an excellent lunchtime special in BBQ restaurants.

brown wrapping paper, butcher paper, or paper plate

stacks of raw white onion slices

extra sauce

slabs of beef covered with BBQ sauce

GENUINE TEXAS BARBECUE SAUCE RECIPE

The perfect Texas BBQ sauce? Everyone in Texas who barbecues—and we don't mean with a hibachi or a Little Smokey—possesses his or her own personalized, often fiercely guarded recipe. The Genuine Texas Barbecue Sauce can be used as both a basting sauce and a barbecue sauce. When Texans barbecue, they swab the sauce over the cooking meat with a clean, white rag wrapped around the top of a stick or strong twig.

1 small onion, minced
1 clove garlic
½ cup butter
1½ teaspoons prepared mustard
1½ teaspoons salt
2 tablespoons chili powder
2 cans tomato soup
6 tablespoons lemon juice or vinegar
½ cup water

Over medium heat, cook onion and garlic in butter in a skillet just until tender and golden brown. Transfer mixture to a large stew pot. Add all the remaining ingredients. Bring to a boil and simmer 5 minutes or until thick. Pour sauce over hot barbecue, chicken, or ham, or use to baste while cooking.

longneck beer

coleslaw

jalapeño peppers, whole

potato salad

sliced white bread, fresh from its plastic sack

plastic knife and fork

BBQ FOR 200

Big-time barbecues are centerpieces of Texas social life. For a century and a half they've been the Texan's dinner party. Lots to eat, more than lots to drink. Cowboy attire is a must (jeans are great for wiping BBQ-sauced hands on). After most of the food is gone, music—live or recorded—is put on and the dancing begins, largely in an attempt to work off the mucho calories recently acquired—and to work up a new thirst for the second beer-drinking shift. To properly style your Genuine Texas Barbecue, the following instructions are provided.

1. Rent fake grass from the local funeral home or buy some AstroTurf for a ranch look. A tent is a festive touch.
2. Start your fire the night before. Use a hardwood for its long-burning qualities.
3. Ice down the beers—longnecks, of course—in a big washtub. Be sure and tie a church key (opener) to each of the tub handles with a long string. Beer must be kept icy cold.
4. Make enough iced tea to fill an Igloo cooler. Put a block of ice in cooler first. Sugar and slices of lemon on the side.
5. Soak pinto beans the night before to get sand out. The day of the barbecue, cook them in a big, black iron pot. Tie a bandana around the handle for extra color. You might toss in a few slices of jalapeño for snappy flavor. Cook all day, slowly. Keep adding water so the beans won't stick to pot.
6. Make towering stacks of Bermuda onion slices, sour pickles, and more jalapeños.
7. Also on the menu: huge bowls of potato salad and coleslaw—homemade,

GENUINE TEXAS BBQ CATERERS

Cowboy grub can be catered Texas-style within the state. The cook and his cowboys will set up an authentic chuck wagon, complete with a fire pit for barbecue and big tubs full of pinto beans. Some of the best in BBQ catering:

ERNIE'S PIT BARBECUE. *P.O. Box 585, Greenville, 214/455-4730.* "Ernie Knows How" is his slogan.

GOODE COMPANY BARBECUE. *5109 Kirby Drive, Houston, 713/522-2530.* Jim Goode and his crew will bring the meat, the beans, the beer, and the music—anytime, anywhere—and serve it up right. Jim guarantees good barbecue and a party you won't forget.

CLIFFORD TEINERT. *Box 1398, Albany, 915/762-2493 or 762-3641.* A former winner of the International Cowboy Cookoff; has cut back from his Texas Trails Chuckwagon operation to smaller parties.

JOE ALLEN PIT BBQ. *1233 South Treadaway, Abilene, 915/672-6082.* Bought some of Teinert's chuck wagon equipment. Local restaurant popular with noontime crowd.

PERINI RANCH CATERING. *P.O. Box 728, Buffalo Gap, 915/572-3339.* An old Texas ranching family, does large and small parties, also has some of Teinert's equipment.

of course, with lots of mayo and more peppers.
8. Put out bowls for extra BBQ sauce, everyone will want to dip in.
9. Have plenty of paper napkins,

HOW TO MAKE A "TEXAS HIBACHI"

Although some people still barbecue meat in real pits dug in the ground, many are turning to the Texas hibachi. Sturdy, dependable, and portable, it is fairly easy (with a reasonable knowledge of metal working) to make from a fifty-five-gallon oil drum. Because oil drums are difficult to clean, you may want to try a drum used to ship tomato paste, detergent, or some other nonpetroleum-based product. If correctly cared for, your hibachi will last twenty years.

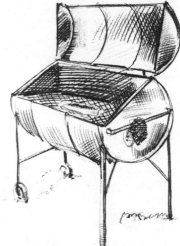

1. *Clean drum thoroughly with soap and water.*

2. *Lay drum on its side. Saw off top one-third of drum lengthwise, as shown. Top will be lid, remaining two-thirds the bottom.*

3. *Smooth cut edges with file, saw, or blowtorch. Torching will leave smoother, more finished edge.*

4. *Attach handle, preferably wooden, to lid. It can either be welded, screwed, or bolted on.*

5. *Along one of flat ends of bottom section, cut five-inch-square opening. Reattach square with hinges. This "trap door" serves as damper, also as*

opening through which charcoal or wood may be added.

6. *Attach set of legs to bottom, using one-inch-wide angle irons about 30" long. Angle irons can be bought from steel supply stores. Legs may either be welded or bolted on. Lawn mower wheels may be attached to legs for mobility.*

7. *Install chimney on lid, using a standard plumbing-size "pipe elbow." Pipe is attached to top of lid by cutting a hole in lid to pipe diameter. Pipe has a threaded end so that it can be screwed directly into hole.*

8. *Attach two swing hinges to bottom. Attach lid*

to hibachi bottom via hinges so that chimney is at opposite end of trapdoor.

9. *Line bottom with firebricks, then fill cracks between bricks with sand. Charcoal (or mesquite logs) go on top of bricks.*

10. *Place a crosshatched grill over bottom section. Grill can be purchased from steel supply stores. It should be expanded metal, 21" by 32".*

11. *Paint your hibachi with a high-heat-resistant aluminum paint to prevent rusting. Paint is available from auto supply stores. Regular paint should not be used, since it will burn off.*

12. *Use pit constantly.*

plates, cups, plus bandanas for festive color and double duty as napkins. Nobody washes dishes after a barbecue in Texas.

10. Make Texas toast—at the last minute, toss on the grill thick hunks of white bread brushed with melted butter. Toast until crisp.

11. Dessert—homemade berry cobbler with homemade ice cream.

Texas Menu No. 2
TEX-MEX

Mexicans do not consider this food related to their national heritage. Real Mexican food is light and filled with subtle tastes — Tex-Mex is heavier, greasier, more filling. It is also delicious. Generally all the same reddish brown color, Tex-Mex relies heavily on chili, which gets poured over almost everything on the plate. Cheesy and spicy-hot, it must be inexpensive or it's not real Tex-Mex.

pats of butter

guacamole

stack of steamed, soft tortillas

platter of nachos

NINFA'S RED SAUCE (SALSA CRUDA)

4 medium, ripe tomatoes, quartered
3 cloves garlic, finely chopped
4 sprigs coriander
1 teaspoon salt
2 chiles de arbol (small, dried chiles)
1 or 2 fresh or canned jalapeño peppers

Boil tomatoes in medium saucepan with garlic about 15 minutes. Remove and place in blender. Add coriander, salt, chiles de arbol, and jalapeños. Blend for 2 minutes. Serve accompanied by toasted tortilla chips.

basket of freshly made tortilla chips

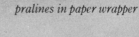

pralines in paper wrapper

chili con queso, refried beans and rice

Red, Hot, & Alarming
CHILI

A true Texas invention. San Antonio is the founding city of chili, home of the chili "queens" of the late 1880s who sold their chili from carts in the town square until health officials closed them down in the 1940s. Early Texas chili did not contain tomatoes—only meat and peppers simmered down to a stewlike concoction. Officially known as chili con carne—it is also known as "bowl of red," "bowl of fire," and "soup of the devil"—genuine chili is flavorful, spicy, meaty, and hot enough to raise the roof of your mouth.

Texas-style chili should have grease in it (although LBJ always insisted that his cook skim the grease off his chili before eating it). The chili should be eaten plain, never garnished with sour cream or cheddar cheese, but it is okay to put in crumbled Saltines. Hamburger meat is not recommended—coarsely ground meat holds the flavor much better. Besides appearing in most Tex-Mex dishes like enchiladas or huevos rancheros, chili is poured on hamburgers, foot-long hot dogs, and Frito pie. A lot of chili is served in Texas schools and prisons.

glass of milk

bowl of chili
grease floating on top

jalapeño
pepper on
side

Saltines

REACTIONS TO TEXAS CHILI

nose runs
eyes water
sinus cavities open
lips blister
cheeks flush
sweat breaks out on brow
roof of mouth ignites
heart pumps rapidly
throat sears
breathing comes hard

Note: Texans deny that any of the above happens to them when they eat chili.

MAIL ORDER CHILI AND CHILI MIXES

CAROL SHELBY'S ORIGINAL TEXAS BRAND CHILI PREPARATION Makes two quarts of what Shelby calls "world's best" chili. Includes the genuine corn masa flour plus chili spices in brown bag. (Shelby Texas Chili, *P.O. Box 45303, Los Angeles, Calif. 90045*)

D. L. JARDINE'S TEXAS CHILI SPICES Each box includes a bag of blended chili spices, a bag of masa flour, and a bag of crushed red peppers, as well as recipes for "Chuckwagon Chili" and a host of other favorites. (D. L. Jardine's Texas Chili Spices, *P.O. Box 10110, Austin 78766*)

NEIMAN-MARCUS'S RED RIVER CHILI Sold in frozen bricks. Can be delivered anywhere in the United States. Available at all N-M stores in and out of Texas.

WICK FOWLER'S 2-ALARM CHILI Seven packets containing nine ingredients for making chili. Anywhere from False Alarm Chili to Four Alarm Chili is possible with this mix. It was developed by the late Wick Fowler, an Austin newspaperman, who used this mix in the World's Championship Chili Cook-off at Terlingua. Sold singly or by the dozen. (Caliente Chili, Inc., *P.O. Drawer 5340, Austin 78763*)

LOST TEXAN SURVIVAL KIT Contains jars of jalapeño peppers, tortilla mix, chili mix, a "deed to the ranch," a Texas flag, and more. Available in two sizes. (The Wooden Star, *4344 Westheimer at Mid Lane, Houston 77027*)

PECOS RIVER CHILI All the spices come in a silver foil packet. (County Fair, Inc., *P.O. Box 202, Greenville 75401*)

PECOS RIVER SPICE COMPANY Jane Butel's personally mixed spices for Mexican foods and chili. Sold in big tins and little packets of mild, hot and chili caribe spices. If you're planning a Tex-Mex party try Pecos River's *Super Chile Fire Bucket* — it contains 11 packets of spices and seasonings (enough for 50 servings of chili, or 6 meals of tacos, burritos, enchiladas or tamales), as well as a 24-page recipe booklet. It all comes in a steel lithographed bucket that can be used to serve chips, hold forks and spoons, or just for decoration. (Pecos River Spice Company, *P.O. Box 680, New York, NY 10021*)

PEDERNALES RIVER CHILI

Named after the river (pronounced "Purrd'n-Alice") which runs in front of the LBJ Ranch, this chili was prepared by LBJ's cook, Zephyr Wright. It was a popular dish served at both the White House and at the ranch. There was always some chili on board Air Force One when flying back to Washington from Texas. Eat it the way LBJ did, accompanied by saltines and a glass of milk.

4 pounds beef, coarsely ground
1 large onion, finely chopped
2 cloves garlic, finely chopped
1 teaspoon ground oregano
1 teaspoon cumin seed
6 teaspoons chili powder (more if desired)
2 16-ounce cans tomatoes
2 cups hot water
Salt to taste

In a heavy stewpot, brown the meat (in its own fat) until it loses its pink color. Add onions and garlic and cook until onion is translucent. Add remaining ingredients, bring to a boil, lower heat and simmer for an hour, covered. Skim off the grease. *Serves 8.*

WHERE TO EAT GENUINE TEXAS CHILI

FRANK X. TOLBERT'S ORIGINAL CHILI PARLOR *3802 Cedar Springs, Dallas.* The godfather of Texas chili's own home base.

CHILI'S RESTAURANTS. Any of the chain in Dallas, Houston, San Antonio. An "honest bowl of red" and terrific margaritas.

THE TEXAS CHILI PARLOR *1409 Lavaca, Austin.* Claims to serve the "best bowl of red" in the state. Recipe developed by "Peter T. Westmoreland, Maverick." Serves X, XX, and XXX chili—restaurant insists that customers sign a release when ordering XXX chili.

MINI LEXICON NO. 3
TEX-MEX FOOD

Texans slip in and out of Spanish when talking about or ordering Tex-Mex food. For instance, tacos are always called tacos but refried beans are seldom called frijoles refritos. It is important to know what it is you are ordering or eating:

arroz Rice. Tex-Mex rice is reddish-brown in color and served slightly gummy.

burrito Flour tortilla folded around spicy beef or chicken filling and covered with chili, cheese, and onions. Two or three to an order.

cabrito Kid. Used for barbecuing in Southwest Texas.

carne Meat. Most often spiced up with peppers.

cerveza Beer. For the preferred Mexican beers see *What to Drink—Beer, page 215.*

chili A spicy stewlike dish containing chili peppers, tomatoes, and meat.

chiles Hot to mild peppers used in Tex-Mex foods and chile con carne.

chile con queso Literally, "chile with cheese," but actually a flat tortilla covered with melted, diplike cheese.

chile rellenos Large poblano peppers stuffed with spicy meat-and-raisin mixture.

cilantro Fresh coriander. Also called Chinese parsley. Appears chopped in salsa cruda.

comino Cumin, a spice used primarily in making chili and tamales.

enchilada Steamed soft tortilla filled with refried beans, beef or chicken, covered with chili and cheese and onions and rolled up.

flautas Tightly rolled tortillas, stuffed with spicy beef or chicken filling, that are deep-fat fried. Called Mexican cigars, delicious dipped in guacamole or hot sauce.

frijoles Beans (pintos, preferably) cooked with water, salt pork, and onions. Beans remain semi-firm.

frijoles refritos More commonly known as refried beans; cooked beans fried in lard until they resemble mashed potatoes. Served hot or cold; causes a condition called "clouds over Mexico."

guacamole Really ripe avocados mashed into a salad with tomatoes, chiles, and chopped onions; also a topping for tacos, tostados, or nachos.

huevos Eggs.

huevos rancheros Eggs covered with chili; big breakfast favorite for genuine Texas cowboys.

leche What milk is called when drunk with chili as LBJ did.

limones Small, hard limes. Used for making margaritas, and served with Tecate beer, tequila, or Mescal straight up. Not to be confused with lemons.

menudo A hearty soup made from tripe; rumored to be a great remedy for hangovers. A lot of menudo is served in the wee hours in San Antonio at Mi Tierra and at Cisco's Bakery in Austin.

masa harina Mexican cornmeal. Used for making tortillas and tamales, and for thickening chili.

nachos Triangular-shaped tortilla chips covered with refried beans and cheese, and dotted with a circular slice of jalapeño pepper; the classic hors d'oeuvre in Texas.

oregano The marjoram that grows wild in Texas.

poblano The large bell-like pepper used in making chiles rellenos.

pollo Chicken. Shredded into enchiladas or topping for tostados and tacos.

queso Cheese. Longhorn cheese or Monterey Jack tops enchiladas, tacos, tostados, and nachos.

salsa cruda Spicy hot red-colored sauce more important than salt and pepper on the Tex-Mex table. Made from chopped chiles, cilantro, garlic, onions, and tomatoes. Tortilla chips are dunked into this sauce until the main courses arrive. Addictive, but test first to make sure it's fresh—if it bubbles when you stir it, send it back to the *cocina* (kitchen).

taco Actually means "wad" or "mouthful." It is a tortilla folded in the middle and deep-fat fried into a U-shape; filled with ground, spicy meat; topped with shredded iceberg lettuce and fresh chopped tomatoes. Can also be topped with salsa cruda and guacamole.

tacos al carbon Thin strips of charcoal-grilled beef wrapped in a soft tortilla.

tamale Masa harina beaten with lard, and smeared, pastelike, into a real corn husk. After a spicy meat filling is added, the husk is rolled up and then steamed. Don't eat the husk!

tortilla Thin "pancake" of ground dried maize or masa harina either deep fried or steamed. Used for every dish of the Tex-Mex cuisine, it is never out of sight and should arrive with the menu.

tortilla chips Deep fried tortillas cut into triangular shapes. Perfect for scooping up guacamole and refried beans—send back to the cocina if they aren't hot and crisp.

tostado Fried tortilla covered with refried beans, shredded lettuce, chicken or beef, cheese, onions, and guacamole.

GRAINS OF PARADISE

Jalapeño (pronounced "hal-a-PAIN-yo") peppers are the peanuts of Texas. High in iron, and in vitamins A and C, these fiery pods, called "grains of paradise" by Mexicans, are eaten by the hands-ful. A small, fat, dark green pepper, the jalapeño is the classic garnish for nachos. Jalapeños are eaten whole and raw with slabs of barbecue, chopped into salsa cruda, baked in corn bread, and added to ranch-style pinto beans.

If adventuresome, lubricate your lips and enter a jalapeño-eating contest. The current world's record is 108 peppers eaten in one hour.

Don't forget that a jalapeño can burn more than your palate—never rub your eyes after eating one.

Texas Menu No. 3

CHICKEN-FRIED STEAK

Chicken-fried steak should always be made with an inexpensive cut of meat—round steak is as fancy as you should get. The meat is cooked until it is tender enough to cut with a fork, and the crust is crisp and light. The steak is always accompanied by mashed potatoes and a cream gravy made from the meat drippings. The gravy is poured over both the meat and the potatoes and flecked with lots of black pepper. Genuine chicken-fried steak should never be served dolled up on china plates or in a fancy setting.

cornbread

black-eyed peas

fried okra

mashed potatoes with skins left on

silverware rolled up in paper napkin bent out of shape

LIZ SMITH'S CHICKEN-FRIED STEAK AND CREAM GRAVY

iced tea

lots of salt and pepper

lettuce and tomato salad with homemade Thousand Island dressing (mayonnaise and catsup)

chicken-fried steak

rivers of cream gravy

STEAK

2 pounds round steak
Salt and pepper
3 eggs
¼ cup flour
Shortening (Texans use lard but Crisco or liquid vegetable shortening can be used)

GRAVY

1 or 2 tablespoons flour
1 cup milk (whole or skim) or a mixture of milk and water at room temperature (for a richer gravy, use half-and-half)
Salt and pepper

Cut steak into generous slices about ⅛ to ¼ of an inch thick. Sprinkle with salt and lots of black pepper. On a flat surface, using a mallet, hammer, longneck, or Dr. Pepper bottle, beat the steak to tenderize it and make it somewhat thinner.

Break the eggs into a dish and beat them lightly. Lay out flour on a large plate. Melt or pour shortening into a large, deep skillet, using enough so that it is about ½ to ¾ of an inch deep. Heat over medium-high heat until it is quite hot—steak should bubble nicely while cooking.

Dip pieces of steak first in egg, then in flour to coat well; slide steak into the oil and cook for about 8 minutes on one side. Turn steak and cook about 4 minutes on the other side. (If all the steak will not fit in the skillet at one time, cook it in two or three batches, keeping cooked pieces warm.) Remove slices and drain on paper toweling; keep in a warm place while making gravy.

Pour off all but about 2 tablespoons of grease from the skillet and return skillet to heat. Sprinkle flour into the skillet and cook for about 1 minute, stirring with a fork or wooden spoon, loosening brown particles. Add milk, a little at a time, stirring constantly. Continue cooking and stirring until gravy is smooth and quite thick. Add salt and pepper to taste. Pour over chicken-fried steak. Serves 4.

THE ENDLESS THIRST
Breaking the *Dry Spell*

Don Meredith

Texans drink a lot and often. Liquids, both alcoholic and nonalcoholic, are vital. Iced tea knows no season, Dr. Pepper is idolized. Artesia beats out any other bottled water. Of course, the weather has plenty to do with the vast quantities of beverages consumed daily. That Lone Star sun is persistent, and sweating buckets is common all year round. Texans pop salt-tablets often—loss of salt is also considered a good reason to keep drinking margaritas.

The need to drink so much, so frequently legitimizes the Texas good-time spirit. As long as there is something to drink, the party mood never quite stops. The legions of longneck fans are regularly drinking either their own instate-brewed firewater or cerveza from south of the border. A Texan can never leave home (or his air-conditioned Cadillac) without a full "roadie"—the chances of dehydrating before reaching Neiman-Marcus make it a necessity. Home garages feature an icebox filled with liquid refreshments in case someone gets thirsty going from back door to car door, or from party to party.

★
STILL DRY AFTER ALL THESE YEARS

It is not all right to buy and drink alcohol *everywhere* in Texas. Individual counties determine their liquor-consuming fates—some have been dry since Prohibition, others switch back and forth. The rule of thumb in Texas is: the drier the county the more religious its citizenry. It is legal for residents or visitors of a dry county to go to a wet one to buy alcoholic beverages for personal consumption in any amount they desire. The liquor may be taken to a restaurant in a dry community—but no more than 288 fluid ounces, which is roughly equivalent to one quart of liquor or one case of beer. Any greater quantity is against the law.

WHAT TO DRINK: PART I
BEER

Texans love to pop-a-top on a cold one. And if at all possible they pop the top of one of five in-state brewed beers. They are particularly fond of beer in longneck bottles—when the bottle is not being drunk from, it can be used to pound steak for chicken-fried steak or as a persuader in a Gilley's parking lot brawl.

When forced to drink nationally-distributed beers, Coors, Bud, Schlitz, or Falstaff will do. If in New Orleans for the weekend, the switch may be made to Dixie Beer or Jax. European beers are not tolerated.

THE BIG FIVE

LONE STAR. Calls itself Texas's "national beer"; is the number one favorite in the state. Started the longneck craze. Brewed from artesian waters. The San Antonio brewery is a big tourist attraction and Lone Star's popularity continues with T-shirts, hats, and accessories bearing its logo.

PEARL. Runs second to Lone Star. Also brewed from Texas spring water, its canned version may be more popular than the longneck.

SHINER. The underdog longneck, brewed in tiny Shiner, Texas, by the Spoetzl Brewery. Has a cult following and is drunk mostly at UT and in rural grocery stores in German communities around Shiner, Houston, and San Antonio.

TEXAS PRIDE. This canned beer is the one to buy when the 7-Eleven or U-Totem is out of the above. Doesn't quite live up to the state's reputation for biggest and best.

GILLEY'S. Somehow this beer tastes and seems right when you're sweaty from doing the Cotton-Eyed Joe or riding the bull at Gilley's. But never taken seriously anywhere except the dance hall's premises. The can is a great take-home Texas souvenir.

MEXICAN BEERS

TECATE. Has been called the Mexican Coors because of its great popularity. A strong-tasting beer, it must be drunk from its red aluminum can with a wedge of lime perched on the rim, which is later squeezed into beer, making it slightly fizzy-tasting. Salt may be put on the hand and licked between sips.

DOS EQUIS. An elegant-looking longneck from Monterrey, instantly recognizable by the two Xs on label and gold foil cross between a light and dark beer in color, it is also called Dos Eckis.

CARTA BLANCA. Calls itself "the *cerveza exquisita*" but doesn't quite live up to the name. Good with nachos but should not accompany the whole meal.

BOHEMIA. Tastes better in Mexico and the border towns. Doesn't travel as well as the other beers but does have its fans.

SUPERIOR. A light *cerveza*, generally bought by the caseload when at the border. Pretty label.

WHAT TO DRINK: PART II
MARGARITAS

A Texan's favorite mixed drink, the margarita is the Bloody Mary of the Southwest. It is never called Daisy, the Spanish translation of its name, and never called Margie. Especially addictive when accompanied by nachos or tortilla chips and salsa cruda.

A good margarita is neither sugary-sweet nor too sour. It must be served icy-cold, but whether straight up or on the rocks, the salt-rimmed glass is a must. Connoisseurs insist on fresh lime juice from Mexican limes (*limones*), and only Mexican brands of tequila—Cuervo, Sauza, and Herradura (stock up on these during a Border Town Binge). The color of the margarita is also important—it should not be too pale or too Prell-like. A nice greenback shade of green is terrific. Frozen margaritas are not taken seriously by purists, but they can be delicious, and are considered responsible for the presence of a blender in nearly every Texan's home.

WHERE TO FIND THE BEST MARGARITAS IN TEXAS

NINFA'S Any location in Texas but the original Navigation Boulevard restaurant in Houston still the best. Order by the pitcher.

EL RANCHO *303 East First Street, Austin.* Made with real lime juice; a favorite drinking spot for the UT crowd.

EL FENIX Locations in Dallas, Fort Worth, Houston. Great frozen ones.

TEXAS TIN-HORN BARBECUE AND SALOON *1605 South Post Oak Road, Houston.* Pitchers dotted with lime slices.

Mail-order margaritas. AUSTIN BEVERAGE CO. *8311 Research, Austin 78758. 512/836-2390.* Frozen margarita mix in its own gallon bucket, a powdered concentrate to mix with water first, then add tequila. Shipped UPS, $5.95.

THE GENUINE TEXAS MARGARITA RECIPE

2 cups Mexican tequila
2 cups freshly squeezed lime juice
1 cup Triple Sec
1 lime cut into wedges
Salt, coarse grind
Crushed ice

In a large pitcher, combine tequila, lime juice, and Triple Sec; refrigerate till thoroughly chilled. To serve, rub the rim of chilled wineglasses with lime wedges. Invert glasses and dip rims ¼ inch into salt and twirl. Shake off excess. Fill glasses with crushed ice and margaritas. Makes 10 drinks.

WHAT TO DRINK: PART III

OTHER OPTIONS

DR. PEPPER.

Grandpa of soda pops, Dr. Pepper was first concocted in 1885 in Waco, Texas, at a popular hangout called the Old Corner Drug Store, by a beverage chemist named Charles Alderton. Alderton named his creation after Dr. Charles Kenneth Pepper, a Virginia druggist who had rejected Alderton as a possible suitor for his daughter's hand. The drink and the name survived; the romance didn't.

Dr. Pepper's distinctive taste—it contains no cola—has for years led to unfair accusations that it is made from prune juice. A concoction of thirty-three different ingredients, Dr. Pepper's secret formula is said to be more complicated than Bunker Hunt's income tax form.

MESCAL. The

Texas maverick's drink. Made from the agave plant, mescal precedes tequila in the distilling process. Like tequila, it is served with a lime wedge and salt. Bottle must have a *gusano*, the maguey worm, floating at its bottom. Last person to be served from bottle gets the pleasure of eating the worm, considered a gourmet's delight. Mescal has a rougher image than tequila. It can make you mean.

ARTESIA WATER. Texas's first

bottled water, the Perrier of Texas. Water is from Edwards Aquifer in the Hill Country of Central Texas. Amber-colored bottle keeps Texas men from feeling embarrassed about ordering Artesia in a bar.

ICED TEA. Tex-

ans drink iced tea (pronounced "ahs tea") all year long. The best is homemade and left to steep all day in its pitcher on the porch or patio. Slices of lemon are optional but mint leaves, considered sissy, are definitely out.

EATING OUT
HOW TO SPOT THE REAL THING

It's high noon, your stomach is growling, and you've got a hankering for one of the great Texas cuisines. You can't find the Yellow Pages and no *Texas Monthly* restaurant guide is handy. What do you do? Follow these simple guidelines for spotting the correct place serving just what you're hungering for.

THE GENUINE TEXAS BBQ PLACE

- Mesquite wood stacked outside
- Flapping screen door with rusting Mrs. Baird's Bread or Rainbow Girl sign nailed to it
- Brown butcher paper instead of plates, great for soaking up grease from meat
- Evidence of the pit—either inside or outside
- Smell and see the smoke rising; place should look like it's on fire
- Choice of sliced and chopped barbecue
- White bread only. No rolls, French bread, croissants, etc.
- Plastic cutlery, never silverware—even stainless steel
- Toothpicks in an empty Tabasco sauce bottle
- Fly swatter

THE GENUINE TEX-MEX RESTAURANT

- One or two serapes draped on chairs
- Paintings on velvet of bullfighters, sequined sombreros, on the walls
- Hot sauce and fresh tortilla chips brought to the table with the menu
- Dishes named "Combination," "Regular," "Fiesta," or for a city or state in Mexico: "Saltillo," for instance
- Mexican beers on the menu
- Inexpensive prices
- Cactus collection
- Pralines wrapped in waxed paper served at end of the meal
- Shell no-pest strip
- Red plastic roses and red plaster bulls
- Fly swatter

THE GENUINE CHICKEN-FRIED STEAK RESTAURANT

- Police cars and pickup trucks with gun racks parked outside at noontime
- Smell of grease hits you in the parking lot
- Sound of pounding meat is audible on entering
- Cook's hands coated with white flour
- Chicken-fried steak is first selection on the menu, listed as "house specialty"
- Not expensive
- Fly swatter

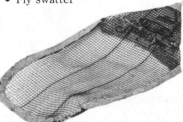

Chapter 10
HOOTIN' & HOLLERIN'

HOWDY Y'ALL

Y'all is a collective term used to address more than one Texan, even if only one Texan is present at the time. If a rancher meets another rancher in the Waller County feed store and says, "Y'all come over to the Big Spread," he's probably referring to all his friend's kinfolk, including Great-aunt Minnie from Splendora. The expression has something to do with the expansiveness of the Texas personality; invitations are always extended to include herds of people, some of whom the host may never have met. It doesn't matter; y'all are invited anyhow.

SHOOTIN' THE BULL
A Texas Lexicon

Even though Texas is a big ol' state, citizens from all corners of it talk more or less the same way. Here are some expressions to use if you want to try to sound like you hail from Bug Tussel, Dime Box, or Dallas. Sprinkle liberally with Spanish and cover with a cow-pattie-thick layer of bull.

a far piece An unspecified but long distance. If you go a far piece in New York you will be in Connecticut or Pennsylvania; if you go a far piece in Texas you'll most likely still be in Texas.

agitated as a June bug In a tizzy.

a good time was had by all Phrase used by Texas newspapers to sum up any social gathering from a barbecue to a wedding shower to a graduation party.

ah surely doooo Texan for yes.

air machine Air conditioner in West Texas.

bald prairie A bare piece of land — of which there is lots in Texas.

bet your boots A sure thing, something guaranteed. "You bet your boots the Aggies will whup the Bears."

bidness Business. Used by everyone from the preacher to the president of the state's biggest company. "Bidness is booming."

big ol' Gargantuan; massive — i.e., Texan. *Big* is not enough to describe exceptionally large things. "He's got him a big ol' spread, 'bout a hunnerd thousan' acres."

Blue Norther A strong cold wind that comes down from the North. Can bring a forty-degree drop in temperature in a few hours.

booger Term of endearment for someone who is a clever little troublemaker.

boy howdy! Not a greeting. An exclamation of surprise or amazement. Heard frequently when naive country cowboys come to the city.

buckaroo (1) Term for small Texas children. (2) A friend; pal.

buffalo chip A dropping of cow manure.

calf scramble A rodeo event. Not a breakfast of steak and scrambled eggs.

Channel No. 5 What the smell emanating from the Houston Ship Channel is called by people who live around it.

chilihead Chili freak. Seen at all chili cookoffs.

chuck wagon The cow country mess wagon. Charles "Chuck" Goodnight invented it.

Colorado Kool-Aid Coors beer.

cow pattie A dropping of cow manure.

cute as a speckled puppy dog Usually describes a young girl.

cutter (1) Clever devil; a wheeler-dealer. Probably derived from the fact that cutting (singling out) a calf from a herd takes a lot of skill. (2) A ranch horse used to control cows.

dadburn it! Nothing to do with arson; used at a time of pique or frustration. "Dadburn it! That cow just knocked me upside the head."

damn tootin'! You bet. Used by down-home types.

the devil's beatin' his wife A climatic condition in Texas when it's raining and the sun is still out.

East River wetbacks A Texan's name for all the people who've moved from New York City to Houston and Dallas; the new alternative to *Yankees*.

get down and come in Welcome. Has nothing to do with dancing to disco music or entering a building. Just a friendly greeting.

get het up To be upset about something; a condition that happens when the Aggies beat the Longhorns.

girl Used to address any female, old or young. Always used endearingly. "Girl! You better get yourself home."

git your body down (or over) here Come on over. Could be an invitation to the Big or Little Spread or some honky tonk devil addressing his angel.

SAY IT RIOT (RIGHT)

To camouflage yourself in Diboll ("Dye-ball") or Refugio ("Re-FURy-oh"), here's a quick lesson on how to sound like a Tejas native.

- Diphthong vowels (*vowel* becomes "vaowl")
- Shorten words by dropping a syllable or a letter (*help* becomes "hep")
- Lengthen words by stretching them as if they were rubber bands (*great* becomes "gr-a-a-a-ayt")
- Drop the *g* from most *ing* words (*hankering* becomes "hanke-rin' ")
- Use short *a* sounds when a long *i* might ("maht") seem to be in order
- Move *oo* sounds up closer to the front of your mouth (*you* and *do* rhyme with *hue* and *few*)
- Change short *e* sounds to short *i* sounds (*pencil* becomes "pincil")
- Keep in mind that in Texas the *r* is pronounced, not swallowed as it is in most Southern accents.
- Perhaps most important of all, always sounds as honest and sincere as the day is long, even though you don't mean a pig's teat of it.

Even if you memorize all these rules, however, you can give yourself away if you slip up on one of the following tricky pronunciations.

all	oil
athalete	athlete
aw riot	all right
ax	ask
bye-oh	bayou
dill	deal
gin-yew-wine	genuine
hail	hell
hate	heat
heighth	height
mere	mirror
rill	real
shore	sure
thang	thing
thoo	through
whup	whip
yew	you

give a holler Keep in touch with a Texan. "Give a holler next time you're in Waco."

goin' steppin' To go out on the town, Texas-style; usually means an evening of dancing and drinking, "They're goin' steppin' at the Pink Boot tonight."

gussy up Dress up; adorn. "That salesgirl was gussied up like she was fixin' to pose for *Vogue* magazine."

Hang up your saddle and stay a spell Texan's greeting to a visitor.

hanker To long for something; e.g., the way a Texan who has moved out of state longs for real good Tex-Mex food.

hog heaven A state of utter happiness. A cowboy is in hog heaven when he scores a sixty-eight in bull riding.

hoof it To move faster; to get a move on. "You'd better hoof it if you don't want to be late."

hoot and holler (1) Verb meaning to act up, carry on; to have a good time. (2) Noun referring to someone who is wild and fun-loving. "That Sharon Alice is a hoot and holler."

hotter than a two-dollar pistol Compliment to a Texas woman. A girl who's really going places. "Sissy Spacek is hotter than a two-dollar pistol out there in Hollywood."

in high cotton Sittin' pretty — like when the well comes in.

it'll make your spurs jangle A situation that turns you on, makes you happy, and shakes you up a bit, too; condition after too many margaritas in the Cadillac Bar in Nuevo Laredo.

It's nice to have to squint your eyes again The sun is out after a long cloudy spell.

Juneteenth June 19; the day that commemorates the emancipation of Texas slaves. Blacks in Texas host lots of parties, barbecues, and rodeos.

kickers (1) Boots. (2) Cowboys or cowgirls, especially ones who drink and dance real good.

kin ah hep yew? Whaddya want? Usually used by storekeepers, everywhere from Neiman's to the local saddle shop.

larrupin' Tasty; delicious. "She whupped up the most larrupin' cobbler I ever ate."

laugh and scratch Have a good time; enjoy oneself. "Every time we go over to Louise Ann's we just laugh and scratch all night long."

longneck A tall bottle of beer with a long, thin neck. Very popular. Texas is one of the few places in the U.S. where beer is still marketed in this kind of bottle.

loose boots A Texan who loves to dance, usually hogs the dance floor — and the ladies or gents.

ma'am Word Texan males use to address any woman over the age of two. Used instead of "what?" "pardon?" or "huh?"

mañana *Tomorrow* in Spanish. Used to express procrastination. "I'll fix the screen door mañana."

THE BIGMOUTHS

Texans pride themselves on having big mouths. Mouthing off about everyone and everything is all-important within the Lone Star state. So it is not a mere accident of birth that the nation's most famous film critic, the leading syndicated gossip columnists, and one of the top television news anchormen were all born Texan. To make sure you don't miss a tidbit, slow down for the lowdown on these powerful wagging tongues, who put and make money where their mouths are.

AILEEN "SUZY" MEHLE. *El Paso.* Column under her pen name appears five times a week in the New York *Daily News* and is nationally syndicated. Whips up frothy items about the Southampton-to-St. Moritz set. Cozy chatter written in a now-who-else-would-tell-you-these-things tone about the divorces, mergers, and dividends of gilt-edged bluebloods in America and Europe and those clamoring to be included in the ranks of the rich. Has an alarmingly charming way of twisting the Hammacher Schlemmer knife into her subjects.

MAXINE MESINGER. *Houston.* Texas's leading in-state gossip columnist. Her "Miss Moonlight" column—filled with comments on oillionaires, heart surgeons, River Oaks socialites, and visiting celebrities—appears daily in the Houston *Chronicle.* Maxine has an amusing penchant for hacking up the English language and has coined words uniquely her own—*swankienda* is her word for a ritzy house in Texas. Has a very down-home, folksy style—"The Cooleys are planning mucho entertainment and natch, fireworks"—but does come up with plenty of juicy tips on what's happening in Hollywood, Las Vegas, and New York. Has her own sprightly radio show, too.

DAN RATHER. *Wharton.* Recognized as one of the most knowledgeable reporters and analysts on the national political scene, news correspondent Rather took over as anchorman and managing editor of "The CBS Evening News" when fellow Texan Walter Cronkite retired. First caught the public's attention in 1961 with his riveting coverage of Hurricane Carla, which struck the coast of Texas. For three days Rather, then news director of Houston's KHOU-TV station, was stranded on Galveston Island in the middle of the ferocious storm. Has won numerous awards and Emmys for his tough, hard-hitting broadcasts. Will always be remembered for standing up and talking back to President Nixon when he was a White House correspondent.

REX REED. *Brownwood.* Nationally syndicated columnist. Also has a monthly column in *Vogue.* His caustic, freshmouth comments and snappy sarcasm caught on like a brushfire with the public. Known for his absorbing interviews and film criticisms, Rex does go on record as being a professional gossip. Many appearances on the "Tonight Show" and "The David Susskind Show" vouch for his reputation for saying exactly what he thinks.

LIZ SMITH. *Fort Worth.* Started her nationally syndicated chatty gossip column in the spring of 1979 after writing gossip items for years as the assistant to Cholly Knickerbocker. Lizzie doesn't rock too many glamour boats, but does come up with good steady Hollywood/New York scoops for local New York NBC news program, "Live at Five." Honorary den mother to all transplanted Texans in New York City.

mariachis Strolling guitar ensemble heard in Tex-Mex restaurants. Always singing "Cuando Caliente el Sol."

maverick (1) An unbranded cow. (2) An independent person. The way a Texan views himself.

meadow muffin (1) A dropping of cow manure. (2) Term of endearment for a woman.

muled up Mad and stubborn at the same time. "I've never seen him so muled up."

no flies on her A good-looking Texas gal; someone like Jaclyn Smith or Phyllis George.

ol' country boy Any male acquaintance; has nothing to do with age or status. "That Halston's a nice ol' country boy."

over yonder Down the street; across town; over international waters. Anywhere farther away than six feet.

peesplasher Indoor toilet.

peckerwood Pejorative term for anyone you don't like.

petroleum ghettos Suburban-type neighborhoods around Houston inhabited by transplanted workers attracted by the petrochemical industry.

pistol Someone pleasantly ornery; a cutter.

pop a cold one Drink a beer. Often used as an invitation to get rowdy. "Y'all come on over and pop a cold one."

porcupine eggs Cockleburs. These stickly little boogers get stubbornly stuck in the manes of horses and the tails of cattle.

prairie strawberries What the cowboys called the red beans they ate day after day on the trail drives.

prickly heat What hot weather in Texas is called; also known as cactus climate.

right neighborly Helpful; kind. Texas-style friendliness. "Lady Bird is right neighborly," Stonewall residents might say.

right thar Specific location. "The outhouse is right thar."

rustle up To round up or gather up someone or something. Often refers to food. "Let's rustle up some tacos and chili for supper." Do not confuse with cattle rustling.

she looks like she's been ridden hard and put up wet Originally said about horses, but has come to mean someone who has been through a lot.

sidekick Pal or buddy. A loyal friend.

slingin' the bull Texas-style gossip.

smushed A condition animals such as polecats and armadillos end up in on Texas roads.

snow birds People who come from the North to winter in South Texas, where it's warm.

sod buster A country plough boy.

sumbitch Son of a bitch. "That there sumbitch stole my girlfriend right out from under my eyes."

tail chasing (1) Hunting for wild game during the season. (2) Hunting for women all year long.

tallywhacker A male organ often seen in the streets of Dallas on OU weekend.

tarred Tired. Has nothing to do with feathering. "I'm sick and tarred of those damn armadillos digging up my azaleas."

Tejas An Indian word meaning "friends" and original name of what is now Texas.

Texian What a person living in Texas prior to 1845 was called. Daughters of the Republic of Texas are proud to have many in their family trees.

tight as a jug A stingy person.

tighten up To get down to some real serious lovin'. "Me and DeWayne are gonna tighten up tonight."

tump Knock over; spill. A combination of *turn* and *dump*. "You better mind that glass of iced tea, you're about to tump it over."

ugly Rude. Has nothing to do with appearance. "That New York operator sure was ugly to me."

weather Any unpleasant meteorological condition such as rain, sleet, snow, or hurricane. "Looks like we're gonna have us some weather."

well, I swan! Exclamation of wonder. Country women use this phrase often when they've just heard some particularly good gossip.

y'all come back, ya hear now Texan's way of inviting you back again; a sign of hospitality; a sure sign your company was liked.

Yankee Anyone born north of the Red River. Used disparagingly. "The biggest mistake of her life was marryin' that damn Yankee."

young 'uns The kids. "We're taking the young 'uns to Six Flags over Texas."